Native Lands

Native Lands

CULTURE AND GENDER IN INDIGENOUS
TERRITORIAL CLAIMS

Shari M. Huhndorf

UNIVERSITY OF CALIFORNIA PRESS

University of California Press
Oakland, California

© 2024 by Shari M. Huhndorf

Library of Congress Cataloging-in-Publication Data

Names: Huhndorf, Shari M. (Shari Michelle), 1965– author.
Title: Native lands : culture and gender in Indigenous territorial claims / Shari M. Huhndorf.
Description: Oakland, California: University of California Press, [2024] | Includes bibliographical references and index.
Identifiers: LCCN 2024004762 (print) | LCCN 2024004763 (ebook) | ISBN 9780520400177 (hardback) | ISBN 9780520400184 (paperback) | ISBN 9780520400191 (ebook)
Subjects: LCSH: Indians of North America—Land tenure. | Land tenure in literature. | Indian arts. | Indian literature. | Indigenous women—Political activity.
Classification: LCC E98.L3 H84 2024 (print) | LCC E98.L3 (ebook) | DDC 346.04/3208997—dc23/eng/20240220
LC record available at https://lccn.loc.gov/2024004762
LC ebook record available at https://lccn.loc.gov/2024004763

33 32 31 30 29 28 27 26 25 24
10 9 8 7 6 5 4 3 2 1

For Rita, Emilio, and Miguel

We are the original owners of this country. Our land was stolen from us by the Euro-American invaders.... My maps are about stolen lands, our very heritage, our cultures, our worldview, our being.... Every map is a political map and tells a story—that we are alive everywhere across this nation.

JAUNE QUICK-TO-SEE SMITH, in Julie Sasse,
"Postmodern Messenger"

CONTENTS

List of Illustrations xi
Acknowledgments xiii
Note on Terminology xvii

Introduction: Native Lands 1

1 · Bodies of Land: Culture and Gender in Indigenous Dispossession 23

2 · "Mapping by Words": Cartography in *Tracks* and *Solar Storms* 59

3 · Scenes from the Fringe: Gendered Violence and the Geographies of Indigenous Feminism 87

4 · Contested Landscapes: Kent Monkman, Zacharias Kunuk, and the Art of Indigenous History 117

Conclusion: Bodies of Land, Redux 147

Notes 157
Works Cited 171
Index 191

ILLUSTRATIONS

1. Nicholas Galanin, *Never Forget*, 2021 *2*
2. Adriaen Collaert, *Allegory of America*, from "The Four Continents," 1580–1600 *25*
3. Jan van der Straet, called Stradanus, *Allegory of America*, 1587–89 *28*
4. John Gadsby Chapman, *Baptism of Pocahontas*, 1840 *36*
5. Four Pueblo Children from Zuni, c. 1880 *46*
6. Frank Cushing, Taylor Ealy, Mary Ealy, and Jennie Hammaker, c. 1880 *46*
7. Kent Monkman, *Miss America*, 2012 *57*
8. Rebecca Belmore, *Fringe*, 2007 *88*
9. Scene from *Vigil*. Rebecca Belmore, *The Named and the Unnamed*, 2002 *105*
10. Scene from *Vigil*. Rebecca Belmore, *The Named and the Unnamed*, 2002 *106*
11. Scene from *Finding Dawn*, directed by Christine Welsh, produced by Svend-Erik Eriksen, National Film Board of Canada, 2006 *111*
12. Scene from *Finding Dawn*, directed by Christine Welsh, produced by Svend-Erik Eriksen, National Film Board of Canada, 2006 *115*
13. Albert Bierstadt, *Mount Corcoran*, c. 1876–77 *125*
14. Kent Monkman, *History Is Painted by the Victors*, 2013 *127*
15. Scene from Zacharias Kunuk, *Maliglutit (Searchers)*, 2016 *138*
16. Scene from Zacharias Kunuk, *Maliglutit (Searchers)*, 2016 *143*
17. Heather Campbell, *Methylmercury*, 2017 *152*

ACKNOWLEDGMENTS

Native Lands owes its existence to friends, family, and colleagues who have sustained me, intellectually and otherwise, over the long period of its development. It is a pleasure to thank them here. The book came into focus during weekly walks with my writing partner Carolyn Chen, who helped me define key concepts and work through difficulties. Her comments on multiple drafts of the manuscript improved the work in every way. Conversations with Cheryl Suzack clarified the book's central questions and stakes. She provided valuable advice on the entire manuscript at a critical stage, and her pathbreaking contributions to Indigenous feminism have always been a guiding influence. I owe special debts to Karen J. Ford for pushing me to be a better thinker and writer over years of sustaining friendship. This book began and ended with conversations with her. My friendship with Dalia Kandiyoti began in graduate school, and it's impossible for me to imagine an intellectual world, or any world at all, without her. Her advice on the manuscript helped me rethink its framework. Sarah Jackson got me through writing and life, including during the pandemic. What she has taught me about courage, commitment, and social justice shaped my thinking here. Lynn Fujiwara's friendship has long been a lifeline. At the beginning of this project, she urged me to think harder about its gendered dimensions, and her advice provided a foundation for all that came after.

Other friends and colleagues generously engaged in critical conversations, read chapters, suggested sources, offered valuable advice, and provided additional kinds of support. I could have no better colleague than Tom Biolsi, who has provided intellectual guidance, superlative professional advice, friendship, and the best cat stories. Life at the University of California, Berkeley, would be altogether different without him. Catherine Ceniza Choy is a model of leadership, scholarly and otherwise, and she has enriched my work in every way. Beatriz Manz is an inspiration, and listening to her remarkable stories over a glass of wine is a pleasure, privilege, and lesson in how to bring together social justice commitments with scholarship. I am grateful for collaborations with Eric Cheyfitz, whose friendship and intellectual rigor have pushed my thinking in new and better directions. Arnold Krupat introduced me to the world of Native literary studies, helped me find a place within it, and remains a model of scholarly excellence. Conversations and collaborations with other scholars, including colleagues and graduate students at UC Berkeley and the University of Oregon, have influenced my work, perhaps in ways that would surprise them. Special thanks to Jean Barman, Jessica Bissett Perea, Hector Callejas, Olivia Chilcote, Amanda Cobb-Greetham, Raúl Coronado, N. Bruce Duthu, Marco Flores, Will Gow, Carla Hesse, Pilar Jefferson, Katie Keliiaa, Salar Mameni, Kendrick Manymules, Peter Nelson, Michael Omi, Jeff Ostler, Jeanne Perreault, Leigh Raiford, Sarah Ray, Carolyn Smith, Jen Rose Smith, David Vázquez, Louise Westling, and Sarah Whitt. Alex Strada and Tali Keren deepened my understanding of the connections between culture and politics and convinced me that art can change the world. Invitations from Jessica Bissett Perea, Eric Cheyfitz, James Cox, Daniel Heath Justice, Arnold Krupat, Scott Richard Lyons, Cyle Metzger, Annette Portillo, Cheryl Suzack, and Louise Westling provided valuable opportunities for feedback at key stages. My brilliant graduate students, past and present, have pushed me to think harder and better as they move our fields in promising new directions.

Other kinds of support have also been important. Funding from the John Simon Guggenheim Memorial Foundation, the University of California, Berkeley, and the University of Oregon provided necessary time for research and writing. At the University of California Press, I am grateful to my editor, Niels Hooper, for his critical attention to the manuscript and for guiding it through the acquisitions process. Two outside readers and a member of the faculty editorial board for the Press, who remain anonymous, provided astute comments that improved the work immensely. Nora Becker masterfully steered the book through production, and Steven Baker provided copyediting that clarified key concepts as well as my prose. Rebecca Belmore, Heather Campbell, Nicholas Galanin, Zacharias Kunuk, Kent Monkman, and Jaune Quick-to-See Smith permitted me to reprint their amazing work. I am also grateful for permissions from the Cumberland County Historical Society, Denver Art Museum, Garth Greenan Gallery, Isuma Productions, Montreal

Museum of Fine Arts, Morris and Helen Belkin Art Gallery, National Film Board of Canada, OZ Art NWA, and Peter Blum Gallery.

Some sections of *Native Lands* have appeared in other publications. A version of chapter 3 appeared in *Signs: Journal of Women in Culture and Society*. Earlier readings of some texts discussed in the book appeared in the volumes *The Oxford Handbook of Indigenous American Literatures* (ed. James H. Cox and Daniel Heath Justice), *The Cambridge Companion to Literature and the Environment* (ed. Louise Westling), and *New Directions in Law and Literature* (ed. Elizabeth Anker and Bernadette Meyler).

My deepest gratitude, as always, belongs to my family. My parents, Roy and Charlene Huhndorf, have modeled integrity and a selfless commitment to community that makes me aspire to do better. Along with my sister, Charlsie Huhndorf-Arend, they have provided unwavering support that enabled me to imagine and pursue a path in the peculiar world of academia. My family in Alaska provides a place to return home and reminds me of the things that matter. This book is dedicated to my beloved children, Rita, Emilio, and Miguel. Over the years I have spent on this project, they have grown into young adults who now teach me about life and the meanings of social justice. My greatest joy comes from them and the promise they represent for a better world.

NOTE ON TERMINOLOGY

Throughout this book, I use "Native," "Indigenous," and (less frequently) "Aboriginal" more or less interchangeably, usually in lieu of the narrower and more contested term "Indian" (which does not include, among other groups, Alaskan or Canadian Inuit). "First Nations" refers specifically to Canadian Indigenous communities (except for Inuit and Métis). All of these terms, of course, are products of colonization used to distinguish Indigenous peoples from Europeans and, more recently, to denote their common historical and political situations, but they fail to register the immense diversity of the Indigenous world. When referring to specific Native societies, I use tribal names.

Introduction

NATIVE LANDS

In spring 2021, the words "Indian Land" appeared in 45-foot-high white letters in the desert near Palm Springs, California. The installation, created by Tlingit and Unangax̂ artist Nicholas Galanin as part of the Desert X biennial exhibition, simulates the iconic Hollywood sign that overlooks downtown Los Angeles, about 100 miles west of Palm Springs. When it was constructed in 1923, the Hollywood sign served as an advertisement for real estate in new, whites-only communities in Los Angeles,[1] thereby defining the land as a commodity for purchase while promoting racial segregation. It was also an act of erasure. By presenting the land as empty and available, the Hollywood sign obscured the long histories of Gabrielino Tongva people in the region along with their territorial understandings and claims. Like the Hollywood sign, Galanin's installation advances understandings of land that bear on questions of possession but in altogether different ways. Galanin created the "Indian Land" sign, as he explains, to "challenge land ownership."[2] Titled *Never Forget*, the installation is an act of memory that calls up the enduring presence of Indigenous people within and beyond the Palm Springs area, even as the words "Indian Land" assert Native territorial claims in the present (fig. 1). As part of the project, Galanin established a GoFundMe page to raise money for the growing Land Back movement, which seeks the return of homelands to Native communities. *Never Forget*, then, is at once an act of cultural representation, a call to action, and a material intervention in Indigenous endeavors to reclaim traditional territories. I begin with Galanin's installation because it exemplifies close ties between Indigenous cultural production and Native land reclamation as they have taken shape over the past fifty years. During this period, I argue in the following pages, Native artists, filmmakers, and writers have expressly used their work to represent

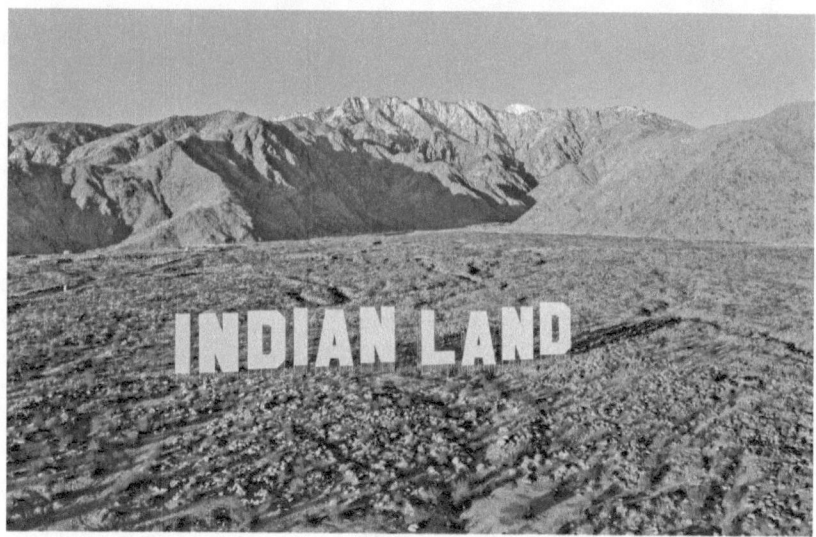

FIGURE 1. Nicholas Galanin, *Never Forget*, 2021. Courtesy of the artist and Peter Blum Gallery, New York.

Indigenous histories and meanings of land in ways that support Indigenous territorial claims. In my reading, Native visual and literary culture of this period constitutes a radical political imaginary that challenges the political authority and territorial possessions of settler nation-states such as the United States and Canada, refutes extractive colonialism on Native lands, and envisions a future that draws together territorial reclamation with social justice, including gender justice, for Native people.

Galanin created *Never Forget* in the context of contemporary Native organizing that has drawn far-reaching public attention to Indigenous territorial claims. The best-known event occurred on the Standing Rock Sioux Reservation in North Dakota in 2016, when the construction of the Dakota Access Pipeline (DAPL) across Native lands prompted the largest Indigenous resistance movement in recent history. As representatives of more than three hundred Native nations gathered on the reservation, social media posts called global attention to the tribes' battle against pipeline construction and prompted many non-Native allies, including Hollywood celebrities, to join the protest. The #NoDAPL movement represents only one of several recent events that have brought unprecedented attention to Indigenous campaigns for territorial rights. In 2020, in another prominent example, opposition to pipeline construction across Wet'suwet'en treaty territory in British

Columbia entailed blockades on community land as well as on rail lines across Canada, making global headlines. Through international movements such as Land Back and women-led Rematriation, as well as local organizing, Native groups seek to reclaim land, protect sacred sites, exercise environmental stewardship over traditional territories, impede resource extraction, and revive land-based cultural practices. The climate crisis heightens the urgency of these endeavors and strengthens public support for them. Widening recognition of Indigenous dispossession has given rise to the practice of land acknowledgments and prompted governmental and even private returns of homelands to Indigenous communities.[3]

Indigenous dispossession and territorial control remain the principal features of ongoing settler colonialism, and struggles over land have always occupied center stage in Native politics in the aftermath of European invasion. But Native activism over the past fifty years departs from predecessor movements in some important respects. Responding to renewed federal assimilation policies and accelerated resource exploitation on Indigenous lands in the mid-twentieth century,[4] Native organizers created political projects centered on collective land rights, political autonomy (or sovereignty) for Indigenous nations, and the revitalization of traditional beliefs and practices suppressed by colonialism (M. Johnson 2016; P. Smith and Warrior 1996). This focus distinguished Native organizing from the civil rights movements of the 1960s and aligned more closely with global campaigns for decolonization. In addition, it sparked renewed interest in treaties as the basis for nation-to-nation relationships and revived the legal use of Aboriginal title, the common-law doctrine that Native land rights arise from longtime use and occupancy of traditional territories. Activist claims have centered not only on legal rights to land but also on the place-based nature of traditional cultural practices and Indigenous identities, or the understanding that community identities themselves depend on access to ancestral lands and waters (M. Johnson 2016, 4, 7–8). Exemplifying this strategy, activist George Manuel famously insisted in a foundational text of the era, coauthored with Michael Posluns, that "our culture is every inch of our land," and he became the first to propose the idea of a "fourth world" of Indigenous peoples united by a "common attachment to the land" (Manuel and Posluns [1974] 2019, 6). Shared relationships with the land and histories of colonization in turn provided the foundation for a new global concept of "Indigenous peoples," which in the 1980s coalesced into an international political movement (Niezen 2003). The new global scale of Indigenous identities and activism, along with the territorial and political rights that stem from the precontact status of Native communities, present fundamental challenges to settler nation-states such as the United States and Canada, calling into question their political authority, territorial possessions, and geographical boundaries. To be sure, Native organizing over the past fifty years has taken multiple and sometimes contradictory forms. But events ranging from the 1969 occupation of Alcatraz Island—where activists wrote "Indian Land," the same term used in Galanin's installation, on the walls of the former federal prison—to present-day reclamation movements are united by their shared emphasis on territorial rights that emerge from distinct Indigenous histories on the land and place-based cultural traditions.

Since the 1960s, Native organizing has yielded unprecedented restorations of Native lands. In 1970, the return of Blue Lake to Taos Pueblo became the first instance of the United States returning land to a Native nation, and the following year, Congress passed the Alaska Native Claims Settlement Act, the largest Indigenous land claims settlement in US history. The Canadian Supreme Court's decision in *Calder v. British Columbia* (1973) marked the first acknowledgment by the Canadian legal system of Aboriginal title and opened the door for a new era of treaty making and land claims in that country. Between 1970 and 1985, Indigenous communities in Canada filed 280 land claims; to date, the Canadian government has signed twenty-five modern treaties with Indigenous communities, some of which include rights to self-government. In 1993, the Nunavut Land Claim Agreement, the largest Native land claims settlement in Canadian history, established a separate territory under Inuit control. These settlements are undeniably complex, sometimes requiring Native communities to make significant concessions for limited territorial rights, leading some critics to charge that settler nation-states recognize Indigenous land rights only to extinguish them.[5] Nevertheless, territorial gains have enabled some Native communities to rebuild social infrastructure, assert sovereignty rights, and revitalize languages and place-based cultural practices in ways that proved impossible in previous eras. Today efforts to reclaim Native lands continue, among other ways, in protests against extractive industry and legal endeavors to enforce treaty rights and restore land stewardship to Indigenous people.[6] To make their claims, Native people invoke legal agreements such as treaties, long histories on the land that underlie Aboriginal title, and the brutality of dispossession, thus leveling both legal and moral charges against settler nation-states. Underscoring the significance of traditions in this era of Native resurgence, they emphasize cultural understandings of land as the center of Indigenous identities. The 2016 Standing Rock movement, for example, not only opposed environmental threats and treaty violations created by the pipeline. Organizers also asserted that extractive industry breaches beliefs, rooted in traditional Indigenous epistemologies, in the sacredness of land. "Defend the Sacred" became a rallying cry of the #NoDAPL movement, and participants designated themselves as "water protectors" to denote proper relations with a natural world viewed as sacred. These entwined strategies for asserting Native territorial rights, writes historian Miranda Johnson, depend on "the construction of a new archive ... about [Native communities'] connection to place, their traditions regarding the use of specific lands and waters, and their memories of treaty negotiations" (2016, 9).[7]

This new archive, I argue in this book, encompasses contemporary Native art, literature, film, and other forms of cultural production. Indigenous culture has long played a key role in representing Native histories and epistemologies in ways that challenge European expansion. But in the post-1960s era, many Indigenous artists and writers have created works that expressly align with the strategies of new Native land-based movements. Some of the works that I analyze—such as Louise Erdrich's *Tracks* (1988), Linda Hogan's *Solar Storms* (1994), and Zacharias Kunuk's *Maliglutit (Searchers)* (2016)—thematize specific histories surrounding major land claims settlements in this period. Others challenge broader patterns of settler expansion and the mythologies that surround them. Such works, like the activist strategies described by Johnson, depict longtime Native presence on the land and the violence of settler expansion, thereby leveling a critique of dispossession that lends moral weight to Indigenous claims. Cultural works address the gaps and erasures in dominant narratives by representing the brutal effects of European expansion and Native peoples' experiences of settler colonialism as grievous loss. They also endeavor to restore community knowledge and social practices suppressed by settler policies. Whereas dispossession is premised on Native erasure, culture itself becomes a site of encounter where viewers engage with ongoing Indigenous presence and relationships to land, including those shaped by traditions. As Native cultural production constitutes a means of self-representation that complements campaigns for political autonomy, the imaginative dimensions of culture enable these works to reconceive Indigenous-settler relations in the past as well as the future. Native writers and artists conceptualize possibilities for social and territorial justice premised on Indigenous epistemologies, including cultural beliefs concerning land. At the same time, the works I analyze here probe the limits of activist movements, particularly as they take shape around gender, and conceptualize a political project that positions gender justice as integral to territorial rights. In the following chapters, I focus on the ways that artists and writers engage colonial representations, especially those forms—such as the Hollywood sign referenced in Galanin's *Never Forget*—associated conventionally with dispossession and the subjugation of Indigenous peoples. By calling up a long history of colonial representations that have advanced settler power, Native artists and writers endeavor to displace conventional ways of seeing and remake colonial images for their own purposes. But as their work exemplifies the role of culture in territorial transformations, it raises intriguing questions about the potential of dominant cultural forms and genres to advance Indigenous political claims.

CULTURE AND COLONIALISM

Throughout the colonized world, culture has always played an influential role in European expansion. "The main battle in imperialism is over land, of course," wrote Edward Said in his classic study *Culture and Imperialism*, "but when it came to who owned the land, who had the right to settle and work on it, who kept it going, who won it back, and who now plans its future—these issues were reflected, contested, and even for a time decided in narrative" (1993, xiii).[8] From the origins of the novel in the eighteenth century and throughout the age of imperialism, literary narratives provided a means by which Europeans came to "know" nether regions of the world and ultimately to conquer them. In stories that Europeans told about the imperial encounter, colonized people appeared as inferior races, as people without history or culture who passively accepted European rule. Such representations proved critical in the expansionist project. Imperialism and colonialism, Said explained, are not "simple act[s] of accumulation and acquisition." Rather, "both are supported and perhaps impelled by impressive ideological formations that include notions that certain territories and people *require* and beseech domination" (1993, 9; emphasis in original). But, in imperial contexts, culture has played other roles as well. Said analyzed how the novel has constituted a form of resistance to European expansion by providing a means for colonized people to reshape understandings of imperial encounters, define their histories and identities on their own terms, and imagine narratives of emancipation. Thus, in Said's analysis, culture is a "battleground" where "various political and ideological causes engage one another" in contests for territorial control (1993, xiii).

Although Said took no account of Indigenous peoples in his work, the argument that imperial power relations are secured by ideological as well as physical force holds true in Native colonial contexts. Imperial discourse, Said contended, has hinged on the idea that "'they' were not like 'us,' and for that reason deserved to be ruled" (Said 1993, xi). To countenance the warfare, mass slaughter, and removals that freed Native land for occupation, settlers depicted Native people as the "savage" antithesis of European "civilization" or erased them altogether, thereby eclipsing their territorial claims.[9] Indeed, the idea that Native peoples were inherently inferior—that they were a "dying race" reliant on the "guidance of a superior civilization," in legal scholar N. Bruce Duthu's words—provided the primary rationale for dispossession (Duthu 2009, 82–83). In settler states such as the United States and Canada, stories about encounters with Native savagery have provided the core of national origin stories, shaping literary canons and popular culture alike. In these narratives, settlers found assurance of their superiority and thus their rights to the land. In Indigenous contexts, however, dispossession has hinged not only on who inhabits the land and the meanings of Native bodies (e.g., the savagism-civilization binary that has long been a focus of scholarly attention) but also on ideological shifts in the meanings and uses of land itself. As scholars have more recently argued, the appropriation of Native territories was enabled by the European transformation of land into property, an object to be owned, exchanged, and exploited for profit. This transformation, too, took shape in part in the realm of culture.

This idea of land as property finds roots in the emergence of capitalism in early modern Europe, when it superseded contending beliefs in a transition that Max Weber famously characterized as the "disenchantment of the world." In *The Production of Space*, Henri Lefebvre argues that space, including land, is created through social processes and power relations that shift over time. Every society "produces a space, its own space," and under capitalism, the property principle becomes dominant (Lefebvre 1991, 31, 252–53). Capitalism subordinates land to the "unifying but abstract principle of property," antithetical to the sacred and lived experience (Lefebvre 1991, 252; see also Herman 2008). Rendered as transparent, homogenous, and demystified object, devoid of animacy and spiritual presence, land becomes a commodity for exchange and exploitation. These capitalist transformations of land, contends Robert Nichols, underwrite the dispossession of Indigenous people in settler colonial contexts. Dispossession "transforms nonproprietary relations into proprietary ones while, at the same time, systematically transferring control and title of this (newly formed) property. It is thus not (only) about the *transfer* of property but the *transformation into* property." In this and other ways, Indigenous dispossession and capitalism are "historically coupled" (Nichols 2020, 30–31, 97; see also Harris 2004). Exploring this process in the American colonies, legal scholar K. Sue Park recounts how seventeenth-century colonists "turned land into an object that could be alienated like chattel, and into an equivalent of money" (Park 2016, 1014). This transformation departed dramatically from precolonial English property law and contrasted with Native practices, which might entail usage rights but not exclusive individual ownership, enclosure, or sale (Park 2016, 1010, 1023–29; Banner 2005, 81; O'Brien 2003). Imposing this new conception of property fueled European economic development and territorial expansion by making Native land available for purchase, thus enabling the formation of colonial nation-states (see, for example, Bhandar 2018, 355). Throughout the Americas, state formation, settlers' desire for land, and capitalists' pursuit of wealth depended on territorial acquisition and together drove the relentless dispossession of Indigenous communities.[10]

Culture facilitated the conception of land as empty space and its transformation into property, though this fact often remains overlooked in Indigenous contexts. The idea that culture "makes place," that "places are real-and-imagined assemblages constituted via language" and other forms of representation, has become commonplace within and beyond the discipline of geography (Hubbard, Kitchin, and Valentine 2004, 7). Cultural representations disseminate, promote, and ultimately reify the spatial configurations associated with particular regimes of social power. In early modern Europe, writes geographer Neil Bromley, changing understandings of land found expression in cartography as the pictorial map gave way to maps and surveys drawn to scale. This new visual regime reduced land to a grid, an inert object disembedded from social relations and thus "desocialized and depoliticized." In this way, maps and surveys, in Bromley's words, became the "handmaiden[s] of property" because of their "active role in the inauguration of a revolutionary enframing of land." This process of "imagining a space as a purely abstract and empty site that has meaning only in terms of the logic of private property" was also "organized forgetting." It promoted settler expansion because "a native space—dense with meanings, stories, and tenurial relations—could thus be conceptually remapped as vacant land" (Bromley 2003, 126–29). Artistic representations contributed to this transformation, blurring the boundaries between the work of painters and writers and that of cartographers and surveyors, who were often called "artists" in this period (Greer 2018, 276). In painting, developments in Euclidean geometry enabled the visual technique of linear perspective that created a sense of realism, the illusion of looking at land itself rather than at its representation. This facilitated a sense of mastery that geographer Denis Cosgrove labels the "visual appropriation of space" and that was "closely bound up with the practical appropriation of space" in emergent capitalism and European expansion (Cosgrove 1985, 45–46).[11] As technique, linear perspective became the foundation of land surveys, maps, navigation and cultural forms alike, underscoring connections between cultural practices and material instruments of dispossession. Such renderings of land as abstract space, emptied of social meanings and reduced to a grid, worked in tandem with representations of Native people as "savages" in the Lockean sense—a race incapable of proper (proprietorial) land use and thus doomed to disappear in modernity—to facilitate dispossession (Bromley 2003).

Although the association between racialization and dispossession has received more attention, European expansion and settler projects of nation-building have relied equally on gender—as myth and metaphor as well as material practice—to facilitate the appropriation of Indigenous territories. Expansionist discourse drew connections between Native women's bodies and land that in turn animated stories that colonists told about their imperial voyages. "Explorers and travelers," writes historian Pamela Scully, "rendered the Americas through a gendered and sexualized reading that saw the land as a woman, often as a passive indigenous woman, therefore open to the embrace and penetration of Europe" (Scully 2005, 4, 13; see also Hulme 1985, 18; and Blunt and Rose 1994, 10). By portraying conquest as a sexual relationship and constructing land as sexualized space, such representations drew on the logic of patriarchy to naturalize the subordination and dispossession of Native people. This logic in turn obscured colonial violence by recasting conquest as (sexual) consent. The era of European expansion and the subsequent period of nation-building on Indigenous territories were characterized by such sexualized imaginings, as national mythologies relied on the figure of the acquiescent Native woman to depict settlers as legitimate heirs to the land. In this later era, colonialism proceeded, in circular fashion, through the reordering of gender. Reform policies, such as those regarding education and land tenure, undermined community identities by supplanting traditional kinship networks with the patriarchal nuclear family as part of a broader scheme to free Indigenous land for colonial settlement. Indeed, the transformation of land into property itself depended on the removal of women from positions of power in order to privatize communally held Native territories (Lawrence 2004, 47; Bhandar 2018). Images played a part in these material practices by depicting gendered reform policies as racial uplift, thereby advancing an expansionist project that hinges on the imposition of Western gender hierarchies. Today connections between dispossession and gendered violence manifest, among other ways, in the heightened vulnerability of Native women in areas of resource extraction, in part because of the "man camps" that support extractive industry (see, for example, National Inquiry into Missing and Murdered Indigenous Women and Girls 2019, 593; Knott 2018; and Amnesty International 2022).

Just as culture has advanced Indigenous dispossession, it is also a powerful tool for redefining Indigenous bodies, histories, and territories, with material consequences for land claims. Indeed, the era of Native land reclamation that commenced in the late 1960s has generated a renewed Indigenous critique of dispossession that finds expression, among other outlets, in cultural representations. As the following chapters demonstrate, this critique entails exposing the brutality of settler expansion and the policies designed to annihilate the beliefs, practices, languages, gender roles, and kinship structures at the center of Native societies. As this critique calls into question the legitimacy of settler political power and territorial claims, it unravels the racial logic that positions settlers as superior and the ideology of progress that underwrites expansion. Beyond their role as contestatory knowledge, cultural works also revive Indigenous territorial beliefs that counter the abstract principle of property and the notion of land as empty space, often by depicting what Leslie Marmon Silko describes in a classic essay as storied landscapes. "Our stories cannot be separated from their geographic locations, from actual physical places on the land," she writes; "there is a story connected with every place, every object in the landscape," and these stories endow the land with spiritual meanings (Silko 1996, 58). Indigenous meanings of land encompass long histories of use and occupancy that underlie Indigenous territorial claims along with spiritual understandings, such as those concerning the sacredness of land, that undermine rationalizations of resource exploitation and the status of land as property. This emphasis on traditional beliefs characterizes contemporary Indigenous land politics more broadly. "The theory and practice of Indigenous anticolonialism, including Indigenous anticapitalism," argues Glen Coulthard, "is best understood as a struggle primarily inspired by and oriented around *the question of land*—a struggle not only *for* land in the material sense, but also deeply *informed* by what the land *as system of reciprocal relations and obligations* can teach us about living our lives in relation to one another and the natural world in nondominating and nonexploitative terms" (2014, 13; emphasis in original).[12] These critiques, as Coulthard suggests, address not only *who* should hold rights to the land but also which human relationships to the land are appropriate, thus calling into question the notion of possession itself. Culture, in these contexts, plays a vital role in extending Native beliefs that challenge colonial ideologies and provide a foundation for social justice projects. If culture "makes place" to enable dispossession, Indigenous art, film, and writing endeavor to remake place to support Indigenous territorial claims.

Throughout this book, I am especially (though not exclusively) interested in the role of visual culture in colonial contests over the meanings and uses of land. Visuality has played a key role in the commodification of land and the subordination of Native bodies, both of which further dispossession. As vision became, in one critic's words, the "master sense of the modern era" (Jay 1988, 3), it positioned the seeing subject as the source of knowledge and the world as knowable object, its rational mechanisms made comprehensible through observation. Acts of looking thus became acts of power that advanced empirical science and capitalist logic so as to underpin various forms of social authority (Foster 1988, x). In the territorial transformations that accompanied the transitions to capitalism and colonialism, visual representation reduced land to physical surfaces, emptying it of history along with sacred and experiential meanings to promote its use as property. At the same time, the dynamics of the gaze objectified racialized people and assigned them to subordinate social places, with particular implications for Native women.[13] Indeed, race—in its conventional definition, the idea that bodies are legible and physical characteristics correspond to underlying traits—is itself premised on visual logic. Some of these dynamics are specific to Indigenous contexts. As the nineteenth-century invention of visual technologies coincided with the consolidation of settler nation-states in the Americas, Native people quickly joined the ranks of the most widely represented people in the world, their images circulated in photographs, ethnographic displays, world's fairs, films, and national monuments in ways that supported the colonial project. These images relied on progressivist racial logic that defines

Indigenous peoples as inferior and confines them safely to the historical past. The "visual fixation," explains Johannes Fabian, "depend[s] on distance, spatial and temporal," or the "denial of coevalness," defining Native people in terms of difference and situating them outside the time and space of modernity (Fabian 1983, 121). The hypervisibility of such images underlies an abiding social invisibility, making it impossible to see Native people as part of the contemporary world. Rendered placeless and timeless, Native peoples have been stripped of a contemporary political presence and, hence, claims to land.

Paradoxically, however, visual images are in some ways suited to Indigenous political purposes. Arguably, the openness of the visual signifier, more than verbal narrative, better enables images to carry contrary meanings that disrupt as well as reproduce discourses of power. Moreover, images hold the power to counter social invisibility by demanding attention to contemporary Native peoples and issues, while the association between visual technologies and modernity can undermine the progressivist racial logic that situates Native peoples in the historical past. *Native Lands* takes shape in part as an extended analysis of the ways that Indigenous artists and writers negotiate the visual, exploring its limits and possibilities for asserting Indigenous territorial claims. This focus distinguishes my project from the small but important body of work that considers how Native literature represents Indigenous geographies (K. Johnson 2007; Brooks 2008; Goeman 2013),[14] as well as from valuable scholarship that has focused on "visual sovereignty," or the ways that visual self-representation by Native people aligns with the political project of sovereignty with less emphasis on the politics of land (see, especially, Raheja 2013 and Rickard 2011).[15] At times for Native artists and writers, grappling with visuality entails rejecting it altogether, as when authors rework narrative cartographic traditions to subvert the meanings of land that inhere in visual maps (the subject of chapter 2). In other instances, Native artists adapt the same visual genres that have historically been associated with dispossession to disrupt colonial ways of seeing and the authority of dominant representations. By revising the conventions of landscape painting, Western film, nude photography and other genres (as discussed in chapters 3 and 4), these artists create works that reverse the colonial gaze, provide alternative histories of encounter, and redefine the meanings of Native bodies and territories. But even as Native artists and writers challenge histories of colonial representation and revise visual genres for their own purposes, they inevitably confront the enduring influence of colonial discourses that threaten to mute subversive meanings. Culture, in my analysis, is a site where the meanings of bodies and territories are created and contested, and where colonial and Indigenous understandings collide, with material consequences for ongoing disputes over land and social power.

THE POLITICS OF CONTEMPORARY NATIVE CULTURE

Beyond supplementing the "new archive" that supports contemporary Native territorial claims, the cultural works analyzed in this book probe the limits and contradictions of these political movements, including those that take shape around gender. It often remains overlooked that the dispossession of Indigenous communities has hinged on the social marginalization of Indigenous women, the replacement of traditional kinship networks with patriarchal social structures, and sexual violence. These are not incidental effects of dispossession. Instead, as Indigenous feminists have argued, European expansion and settler power have cohered in and through colonial gender relations (the subject of chapter 1). Indigenous communities and political movements, Sherry Pictou explains, have internalized patriarchal ideologies so that "Indigenous women and gender-diverse persons struggling for gender and social justice find themselves having to navigate through the ways patriarchal colonialism is manifested by the state, as well as within their own communities and related political organizations" (Pictou 2020, 373). Exemplifying how patriarchy has reshaped Indigenous communities and activism, the movements that emerged in the aftermath of the 1960s have generally privileged the knowledge and leadership of men, enacting, in one critic's words, "male-dominated tribal politics under the guise of 'tribal sovereignty'" (Jaimes Guerrero 2003, 67; see also M. Johnson 2016, 10; and Lawrence 2004). During this era, Native women have responded by creating organizations that address gender oppression (see chapter 3). Just as the shared experience of dispossession has given rise to collective Indigenous endeavors to reclaim land, and indeed the very notion of a shared Indigenous identity itself, colonial transformations of the social places of Indigenous women have underwritten collective efforts to achieve gender justice. Nevertheless, despite the work of Native women activists and scholars, the gendered dimensions of dispossession and their enduring consequences remain neglected as an urgent concern associated with the status of Indigenous people in settler nation-states. Indigenous women's endeavors to address gender injustice have sometimes been met with hostility not only from the dominant society but also from inside Native communities. Indigenous feminism, explains Cheryl Suzack, "has elicited a backlash that challenges its motives, integrity, and decolonising objectives through overt and implicit resistance that calls into question the 'authenticity' of its social and political project" (Suzack 2015, 262). Even today, Indigenous studies scholars "frequently compartmentaliz[e] gender, sexuality, and feminism," Joanne Barker observes, "bracketing them off from analysis of 'more serious political' issues such as governance, treaty and territorial rights" (Barker 2017b, 10–11). For these reasons, settler colonialism "needs to be redefined," Pictou insists, "in a way that will demand the eradication of gender violence and seek gender justice in strategies for decolonization" (2020, 373).

Culture, I argue, plays a crucial but neglected role in redefining settler colonialism and reconceptualizing Indigenous political projects to encompass gender justice. In the period under scrutiny here, Indigenous women have turned to literature, art, and other cultural forms to bring to light their lived experiences of ongoing colonialism, exposing fundamental connections between dispossession and gendered violence that extend to the present. As these works counter the silencing and erasure of Indigenous women in histories of European expansion and ensuing settler social formations, culture itself becomes a site of community memory that answers the neglect of Native knowledge and experiences in settler colonial scholarship (De Vos and Willman 2021). These works demonstrate not merely that gendered violence is a consequence of colonial assaults on land, culture, and political power, but also that dispossession in fact *materializes through* the subjugation of Native women. As this critique challenges settler territorial possession, it directs attention to structural issues that underlie the marginalization of women and gender-diverse people along with their vulnerability to violence in the present. Beyond its role as anticolonial critique, Native culture constitutes a form of knowledge production that thwarts the erasures and distortions in colonial representations. Such production entails depicting, among other things, Indigenous women's complicated social roles, including those of community and spiritual leadership, and gendered ways of knowing and land-based practices. Finally, by building on the experiences and perspectives of Indigenous women and gender-diverse people, the imaginative dimensions of culture enable these works to envision new political endeavors that draw together sovereignty, territorial claims, and gender justice. Because of the geographical ubiquity of violence against Native women—the fact that it transects boundaries of Indigenous communities and colonial nation-states—these artists' and writers' works limn the distinctive contours of a transnational Indigenous feminist project while also facilitating a feminist rethinking of Native land politics that insists on the urgency of gender. In so doing, these cultural works demonstrate the impossibility of addressing "more serious" issues of governance and treaty and territorial rights apart from issues of gender. They insist, in other words, that Indigenous campaigns for political and territorial rights must entail gender justice.

Native culture at once contributes to and potentially reimagines activist endeavors, but it is also a site where the tensions and contradictions of contemporary Indigenous politics come to bear. These include the role of Native traditions in the current era of land reclamations. As George Manuel, in his influential *The Fourth World* (1974), developed the concept of a shared Indigenous identity that has transformed Native politics, he defined the "common [Indigenous] attachment to land" as both historical and cultural. In addition to the experience of European colonialism, he argued, Native people worldwide share values that distinguish them from other social groups and bear directly on territorial conflicts. "The struggle of the past four centuries," as he characterized it, is between "two ideas of land": the European idea that land "can be speculated, bought, sold, mortgaged, claimed by one state, surrendered or counter-claimed by another" versus the "fourth world" idea that land is the source of culture, "our Mother Earth," and that the "animals who grow on that land are our spiritual brothers" (Manuel and Posluns [1974] 2019, 5–6). In the post-1960s era, this idea has generated a renewed Indigenous critique of dispossession premised on traditional cultural beliefs that carries implications for material action. If the notion of land as object underlies dispossession and resource exploitation, an understanding of land as sacred, as Vine Deloria Jr. and Daniel Wildcat explain, entails "a radical shift in awareness and behavior" because nature appears not "as full of resources but [as full] of relatives" (V. Deloria and Wildcat 2001, 94). Yet, even as the idea of a shared Indigenous culture centered on land presents a powerful challenge to ongoing dispossession and extractive colonialism, it risks reiterating the colonial paradigms that it seeks to contest. Whereas the experience of colonialism does in fact draw Native people together across geographical boundaries, culture distinguishes them from one another. Setting aside the specific beliefs and practices of Native communities in the interest of a common Indigenous identity resonates with colonial depictions of Native people as a single, homogenous entity defined in contrast to

Europeans. Native alliances have always contended with the challenges posed by cultural differences and conflicting interests among communities. But in this era, the new idea of a common Indigenous culture glosses over those differences to advance the shared political project of land reclamation. The Native art, literature, and film of this period, as the following chapters demonstrate, often represent traditional territorial understandings to foreground Indigenous epistemologies suppressed by colonialism and advance Native territorial claims. At times these works center on traditions of individual communities, but at other times, they are premised on vague, overly generalized notions of Indigenous culture, a problem especially in some prominent Native literary texts of the period.[16]

Representing Native people as a unified entity defined by nonproprietary relationships to land creates other problems as well. Historically, colonial discourse surrounding land use, emerging from the ideas of John Locke, has defined Indigenous communities as premodern precisely because of the absence of property, thus turning traditional territorial relationships into a rationale for dispossession (see, for example, Bhandar 2018, 5, 29). As the ideological opposition between the property regime and traditional Indigenous relations to land risks reiterating this expansionist logic in our own era, the notion of an Indigenous identity situated outside capitalist dynamics potentially reprises other colonial practices. Colonial subjects, I have argued elsewhere, have long identified with an idealized Native aligned with nature as a means to forge their own symbolic ties to the land while also concealing their implication in the violence of dispossession. Positioned outside the time and space of modernity, this imagined figure of the Native thus bolsters rather than challenges the colonial order (see Huhndorf 2001). Within the sphere of capitalism, contends Iyko Day, the "idealized figure" of the Native facilitates the pursuit of "romantic anticapitalism," a means by which racial whiteness distorts its role in capitalist relations, counters the alienation and social degeneration of capitalist modernity, and ultimately regenerates itself (Day 2015, 117). Placing Native people outside the dynamics of capitalism thus constitutes a double-edged political strategy. Although it poses a powerful critique of ongoing dispossession and resource exploitation, it risks reinscription, so that it appears to reiterate the same colonial logics and dynamics that it seeks to dismantle.

But perhaps most crucially, situating Indigeneity outside the capitalist social order belies the contradictory terrain on which Native social realities unfold. On one hand, as Eric Cheyfitz argues, "the communal cultures of

Native Americans, where land was the antithesis of property: literally 'mother earth,' a part of the extended kinship structures of Native communities," still persist "in the theory and practice of Indigenous communities across the Americas" (Cheyfitz 2019, 13). On the other hand, colonial dynamics have transformed the Native world in ways that constrain possibilities for Native territorial rights. Many Native communities seek the return of traditional territories as property because this provides the only means to secure control over the land. Moreover, in the latter half of the twentieth century, as ever more resources have been discovered on Native lands, Native communities have been increasingly pressed into resource extraction as the condition for economic self-sufficiency and political sovereignty.

In the United States, connections between sovereignty and resource exploitation came to the fore in the 1934 Indian Reorganization Act, which returned some measure of self-government to Native communities while imposing a governance structure that facilitated extractive industry on tribal lands (see, for example, LaDuke and Churchill 1985, 109–10). In the period under scrutiny in this book, these connections are perhaps most apparent in my own Native community in Alaska. In 1971, the Alaska Native Claims Settlement Act, the largest Indigenous land claims settlement in US history, made oil extraction in Prudhoe Bay the condition for settling Alaska Native peoples' territorial claims and providing Native communities with the resources necessary to meet pressing social needs.[17] More recently, the prospect of a natural gas pipeline across Wet'suwet'en territory in 2020 divided the community between those who protested the pipeline in order to protect territorial rights and those who saw possibilities for badly needed jobs and economic development. Because settler nations have deliberately impoverished Native communities, these situations present impossible choices, pitting cultural and territorial preservation against economic imperatives that include feeding, educating, and providing health care and job opportunities to Native community members.[18] Such instances exemplify the vexed connections between sovereignty and land use in the contemporary Native world, and they call on us not to dismiss all instances of participation in the property regime and resource extraction as colonial collusion but rather to consider how Native people reckon with competing community needs under intolerable constraints created by settler governments. Today, land remains the center of Native community histories and identities as well as the place where sovereignty is enacted, but ongoing settler colonialism often means that some limited measure of sovereignty comes at the cost of territorial rights and traditional relationships to the land.

The often-contradictory relationships among territorial rights, economic self-sufficiency, and sovereignty sometimes find a place in Native cultural production, as when the characters in Erdrich's novel *Tracks* become complicit in colonial practices, including resource exploitation, as the condition for retaining their land. At other times, cultural works of this era emphasize cultural ideals while glossing over the hard choices that constitute Native realities. The fact that culture at once partakes in and stands apart from material social dynamics thus leads to conflicting outcomes. Distance from the social world enables culture to address the losses and erasures brought by colonialism while imagining other futures—the first step in accomplishing real-world change. At other times, though, culture risks disregarding the hard dilemmas created by colonial policies, including those that pit traditional Indigenous beliefs, such as those surrounding land, against the material conditions necessary for Indigenous community survival.

. . .

The following chapters analyze the intersections of culture, gender, and Indigenous territorial politics in works that paint a picture of land struggles as an unbroken history from the earliest European voyages to the "New World" to the present. My analyses revolve around the following questions: What role has culture played in deciding the meanings and uses of land in the context of Indigenous territorial disputes? How do contemporary Native artists, filmmakers, and writers represent Indigenous histories and meanings of land, rework colonial geographies, and in other ways advance Indigenous territorial claims? Finally, how do cultural works represent the gendered dimensions of dispossession as well as Indigenous understandings of women's knowledge and social roles, and what are the implications for contemporary Native politics? To engage these questions, I focus on a range of visual and, to a lesser extent, literary works by contemporary Native artists and writers in the United States and Canada. Reflecting the transnational dimensions of Indigenous politics in the period examined in this book, this approach foregrounds Indigenous histories and issues—specifically those surrounding land, gender, and their interconnections—that transcend colonial national boundaries.[19] It also aligns with the activist project of denaturalizing settler geographies and the settler nation-state, thereby opening the possibility for new territorial and political formations.

Chapter 1 lays the foundation for the book by establishing intrinsic connections among culture, gender, and dispossession during three pivotal periods of European expansion: the early years of exploration and discovery, the era of settler nation-building on Indigenous lands, and subsequent endeavors to eliminate Native communities through assimilation. It begins by analyzing changing iconographies of the Indigenous woman's body in such prominent images as *Allegory of America* (c. 1587–89) by Johannes Stradanus and *Baptism of Pocahontas* (1840) by John Gadsby Chapman. In these incarnations, the figure of the Native woman's body serves as colonial allegory, its meanings bound up with questions about who holds legitimate claims to the land and the social places of Native people in the emerging colonial order. If gendered myths and metaphors naturalized European claims to Native lands and masked the violence of expansion, settler nation-building also depended on the material reordering of gender. The remainder of the chapter explores how nineteenth-century assimilation policies further eroded Native territories by supplanting Native kinship networks with the patriarchal nuclear family and socially marginalizing Native women. Cultural representations proved instrumental in these projects too, as when government photography cast the imposition of domesticity as integral to the "civilizing mission." As these histories illuminate the centrality of gender in European expansion and settler colonialism, they set the stage for an analysis of contemporary Indigenous culture as it endeavors to alter meanings of Native lands, bodies, and the colonial encounter in ways that have material bearing in territorial disputes.

The subsequent chapters analyze Native cultural works created during key periods of the post-1960s era, beginning in the 1980s, when prominent Native women writers began to create narratives about women's experiences of violence under settler colonialism, assert their own territorial understandings, and recover Native women's knowledge and influential social roles (the subject of chapter 2); then moving to the early 2000s, when Native women artists' protests against contemporary gendered violence brought to light its roots in historical dispossession and prompted the emergence of social movements such as #MMIWG (Missing and Murdered Indigenous Women and Girls) that unite gender justice with land reclamation (chapter 3); and to the 2010s, a period of national reckoning in Canada when Native artists revised gendered visual narratives of the West to challenge settler mythologies and support their own projects of nation-building and territorial claims (chapter 4).

As these works exemplify political strategies of post-1960s Indigenous land activism, they underscore the intrinsic gendered dimensions of ongoing settler colonialism while envisioning political projects that join together gender justice with Native territorial rights.

In the period examined in this book, Louise Erdrich and Linda Hogan count among the first high-profile Native novelists to create stories centered on Native women. Chapter 2 analyzes Erdrich's *Tracks* (1988) and Hogan's *Solar Storms* (1994), each of which engages actual historical land conflicts along with those that waged in the post-1960s era. *Tracks* tells a story about the ruinous aftermath of the 1887 General Allotment Act in an Anishinaabe community, the crucial context for the White Earth Land Settlement Act of 1985, whereas *Solar Storms* relates the devastation that ensued in Cree and Inuit territories in the 1970s as a result of the James Bay hydroelectric project in Canada, tracing this devastation to the historical ravages of the fur trade. As these novels recount the destruction that befell Native communities through dispossession, they focus especially on the brutal consequences for women, exposing gendered violence as integral to European expansion. At the same time, they counter colonial representations of silent, acquiescent Indigenous women that have rationalized expansion by depicting Native women's perspectives and vital social roles. As part of their gendered critique of dispossession, both novels thematize colonial maps to scrutinize colonial transformations of land as they call up Native narrative cartographic traditions that have historically established Indigenous claims in legal territorial disputes. The stories set colonial and Indigenous cartographic traditions against one another to limn conflicting understandings of land that pit traditional tribal life against capitalist development, so that the novels themselves constitute Indigenous cartographies. In the only chapter of *Native Lands* that does not focus on visual representations, this discussion nevertheless shows how Native writers negotiate the dynamics of the visual, in this case by working within a long tradition that geographer Margaret Wickens Pearce (1988) labels "mapping by words." By bringing to light Indigenous territorial understandings along with the savagery of dispossession and its connection to gendered violence, *Tracks* and *Solar Storms* undo the logic that equates European expansion with progress while lending weight to Native territorial claims in the period when the authors wrote these novels.

After chapter 2's examination of historical connections between dispossession and gendered violence, chapter 3 draws out the ways that histories of dispossession underlie violence against Indigenous women in the present. In the United States and Canada, Indigenous women are far more likely to experience sexual violence than any other group, a problem that Amnesty International describes as a "legacy of history." This chapter examines three visual works created in response to the 2002 arrest of Robert Pickton, the most notorious serial murderer in Canadian history. The disproportionate number of Aboriginal women among his victims drew public attention to Native women's vulnerability and set the stage for current political movements that address missing and murdered Indigenous women and girls. In the performance *Vigil* (2002) and the photograph *Fringe* (2007), Rebecca Belmore counters dominant understandings of the murders as the aberrant work of a psychopath by embedding them in structural violence that emerges from Indigenous dispossession. Christine Welsh's documentary film *Finding Dawn* (2006) similarly connects the Pickton murders to ongoing territorial conflicts as it endeavors to alter understandings of the women as "unworthy victims." Exemplifying the neglected role of culture as anticolonial feminist practice, these artists illuminate the gendered dynamics of settler colonialism as they make visible Indigenous women's presence in rural and urban geographies, thereby reclaiming these spaces as Indigenous places of home. At the same time, by challenging the colonial meanings of Indigenous women's bodies discussed in chapter 1 and endeavoring to turn sexualized women's bodies into figures of protest, they grapple with the limits and possibilities of visual genres for an Indigenous feminist project centered on territorial rights.

Chapter 4 examines how Native artists revise genres historically associated with dispossession to undermine settler mythologies and advance their own projects of nation-building and territorial claims. As geographical space, the West is the locus of mythologies that rationalize expansion and fashion settler national identities, the ideological work of conventional Western narratives. This chapter focuses on two Indigenous remakes of iconic visual narratives of the West: Kent Monkman's painting *History Is Painted by the Victors* (2013), a revision of Albert Bierstadt's celebrated nineteenth-century landscape *Mount Corcoran* (1876–77), and Zacharias Kunuk's film *Maliglutit (Searchers)* (2016), a remake of John Ford's acclaimed Western film *The Searchers* (1956). Monkman is known for reworking nineteenth-century landscape paintings, which he has described as "billboard[s] for the expansion of the West." In *History Is Painted by the Victors*, he populates Bierstadt's empty landscape to make visible Native histories on the land and the violent territorial conflicts obscured in conventional paintings. He also "queers" the landscape, calling attention to sexuality as a site of colonial violence as well as a means for reconceiving the past and future of contested lands. Like Monkman's painting, Kunuk's film *Maliglutit (Searchers)* subverts settler mythologies of expansion, in this case by revising Ford's film about the US West to relate an alternative history of the Arctic, a parallel "frontier" that embodies Canadian national identity. As part of its project of critique, *Maliglutit* calls up a suppressed colonial history of violence against Inuit women, exposing the social ruptures and violence brought by settler expansion in the Arctic. At the same time, the film foregrounds Inuit presence and the Inuit gaze, offering a vision of social restoration premised on traditional Inuit values in the aftermath of the historic 1993 Nunavut Land Claim Agreement. In the context of a national reckoning in Canada caused by ongoing Native territorial claims and high-profile inquiries into the nation's treatment of Indigenous peoples, these acts of reinscription depict the West as contested space, offer alternative Western narratives that challenge settler mythologies and territorial possession, and engage in Native projects of nation-building and land claims premised on gender equity.

The conclusion considers the ways that Native women artists engage Indigenous land activism in the Arctic regions, an important but neglected area in Native American and Indigenous studies. Here I examine two works: *Native American Land Reclamation Project* (2000), a multimedia installation by Erica Lord that responds to a 1998 US Supreme Court decision limiting sovereignty and land rights for Alaska Native communities; and the painting *Methylmercury* (2017) by Heather Campbell, which protests the entwined crises created by the Muskrat Falls hydroelectric dam and disappearances of Native women in Labrador. As these works subvert colonial representations of gendered bodies and lands to displace conventional ways of seeing, they use image making to envision political projects that encompass gender justice along with territorial claims within and beyond the Arctic. They thus provide an apt conclusion to this book.

ONE

Bodies of Land

CULTURE AND GENDER IN INDIGENOUS DISPOSSESSION

From the earliest days of imperial expansion, Europe's arrival in the "New World" inevitably prompted questions about how to represent these unfamiliar geographies and their Indigenous inhabitants. For nearly three hundred years, the task of representing America fell to the allegorical figure of the Indigenous woman. The forms that America took changed over time, as did its geographical referent. In its earliest incarnations, in the aftermath of Columbus's journeys, America signified the entire Western Hemisphere, but by the years preceding the American Revolution, the image stood for the restive British colonies that would become the United States. In these various incarnations, one thing remained constant: the figure of America as Native woman drew on Europe's established hierarchical ordering of gender as a framework for representing imperial relations and dispossessing Indigenous peoples. I begin *Native Lands* by examining how, throughout the periods of European expansion and settler nation-building on Indigenous territories, iconographies of the Native woman's body served as colonial allegories, their meanings bound up with questions about who holds legitimate claims to the land and the social places of Indigenous people in the emerging colonial order. If, in these periods, gendered myths and metaphors rationalized European territorial control, the subsequent consolidation of settler power depended on the material subjugation of Indigenous women. The second part of the chapter considers how nineteenth-century reform policies in the United States and Canada imposed a form of social organization that centered on the patriarchal nuclear family and undermined Indigenous kinship structures, most of which were matriarchal—a process that unfolded in part through culture. As these histories demonstrate intrinsic connections among culture, Indigenous dispossession, and patriarchy, they set the stage for the analysis of contemporary Indigenous culture and activism that follows, specifically the ways that artists and writers endeavor to alter understandings of the colonial encounter, Native bodies, and Native lands to conceive of a political project that unites gender justice with territorial claims.

In early modern Europe, the image of America as Indigenous woman first appeared as part of an emerging secular symbolism of global geography. America joined the tripartite world of Europe, Asia, and Africa to compose the "four continents," each one personified by a woman surrounded by representative attributes of her respective region, in a cultural paradigm that endured for centuries. The notion of land as female was overdetermined by the influence of Latin grammar, classical mythology, and a patriarchal system that associated women with nature in order to subject both to possession and control (see Higham 1991, 47–48; see also Ortner 1974, Kolodny 1975, Westling 1996, and Rose 1993). Although each region took female form, the four continents stood in hierarchical relation to one another. Europe commonly appeared as an aristocrat or noblewoman, elegantly dressed and surrounded by implements of the arts, sciences, religion, commerce, and classical architecture. These signifiers of Enlightenment registered her superiority to the remaining three continents. Usually ranked as second to Europe, Asia typically flaunted silks, pearls, and other treasures, but connotations of despotism and indolence betokened a society in decline in contrast with an ascendant Europe (Morrell 2014).

Images influenced by early explorers' accounts depicted Africa and America, by contrast, as part of the natural world of exotic plants and animals, their state of undress registering their uncivilized difference from Europe (see, for example, Morrell 2014 and Le Corbeiller 1961). These "uncertain continents," in Anne McClintock's terms, appeared in European lore as "libidinously eroticized," as a "porno-tropics for the European imagination—a fantastic magic lantern of the mind onto which Europe projected its forbidden sexual desires and fears" (McClintock 1995, 22). In an iconography that conflated women's bodies with land, sexualization contributed to the imperial fantasy that Africa and America were readily available for conquest, as if the land herself desired European possession. Such images influenced popular European understandings of distant regions of the globe and promoted expansion. During the age of exploration, atlases often included images of the four continents, advancing the idea that Europe was destined to rule the world.[1] Giovanni Battista Tiepolo's ceiling fresco

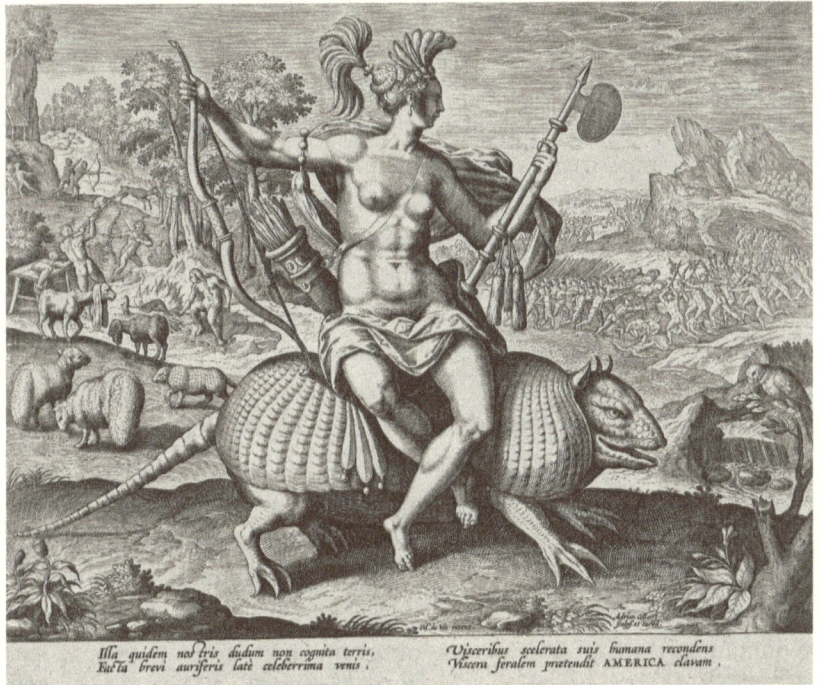

*Illa quidem nostris dudum non cognita terris,
Facta brevi auriferis late celeberrima venis.*   *Visceribus scelerata suis humana recondens
Viscera feralem praetendit AMERICA clavam.*

FIGURE 2. Adriaen Collaert, after Maerten de Vos, *Allegory of America*, from "The Four Continents," 1580–1600. Courtesy of The Metropolitan Museum of Art, New York.

Allegory of the Planets and Continents (1752), perhaps the most celebrated artistic rendering of the four continents, overtly ties Europe's superiority to the promise of global dominance. Here Europe appears adjacent to heaven, visible only after the viewer ascends stairs that first reveal views of America, Africa, and Asia, which offer their treasures to her.

Among the four continents, only America appeared, in one art critic's words, as a "fierce savage," distinguished not by gender (each continent, after all, took the form of a woman) but rather by her brutality (Le Corbeiller 1961, 210).[2] A prominent late-sixteenth-century engraving created by Adriaen Collaert after Maerten de Vos, for example, features America as a young, nearly nude Native woman adorned in a feather headdress and seated on an armadillo who embodies colonial hopes and anxieties, fantasies of boundless wealth along with fears of Native violence (fig. 2). In Vos's image, America brandishes a spear in one hand and a bow and arrow in the other, while scenes of cannibalism and warfare play out in the background.

Her penchant for cannibalism marks her as brutally violent and, in a European world shaped by Christianity, even diabolical, so that in this schema Indigenous peoples ranked low on the scale of humanity, if indeed they could be considered as humans at all. (In subsequent eras, the notion of Native savagery would crystallize in racial categories that defined Native people as biologically inferior, a ready justification for conquest.) Although violence is the dominant theme, America's jewels and other adornments register the promise of wealth. Vos's figure of America is also remarkable for her sexualization, a trait that signifies her availability and, because she represents the hemisphere, the availability of the "New World" for possession.[3]

As the conquest unfolded, the figure of the Native woman whose body represents land would change over time to serve shifting expansionist imperatives. This chapter analyzes how gendered images of Native people helped to consolidate colonial power at three pivotal historical moments: the early years of European exploration and discovery, the period of settler nation-building on Indigenous lands, and subsequent campaigns to eliminate Native communities through assimilation. In the first half of the chapter, I focus on two eminent artworks—Johannes Stradanus's *Allegory of America* (1587–89) and John Gadsby Chapman's *Baptism of Pocahontas* (1840)—to examine how cultural images of sexualized, submissive Native women naturalized European appropriation of Indigenous lands and later promoted colonial nation-building while obscuring the violence of dispossession. As these prominent works demonstrate the role of image-making in advancing the colonial mission, they illuminate how associations between Native women's bodies and land established during the early modern era assumed changing political meanings throughout the centuries of conquest. Gender proved instrumental in dispossession not only as colonial logic advanced through myth and metaphor but also as a material practice of social reform. In the assimilation era that commenced in the nineteenth century, the subject of this chapter's latter half, colonial notions of Native women's bodies, promoted through the history of image making recounted here, rationalized policies that instilled patriarchal social structures as a means to extinguish Indigenous claims to land. In these histories, cultural representations joined with material practices to marginalize Indigenous women in ways that endure to the present, shaping the terrain on which contemporary Native cultural production and political movements take place.

PICTURING THE NEW WORLD:
STRADANUS'S *ALLEGORY OF AMERICA*

When Johannes Stradanus created *Allegory of America* toward the end of the sixteenth century, he drew on the representational tradition of the four continents to personify America as a sexualized Native woman. But, whereas conventional iconography depicted each of the four continents as female, Stradanus's image cast imperial discovery as an encounter between genders to portend the inevitable subordination of these new lands to Europe. Inspired by Amerigo Vespucci's accounts of his voyages between 1497 and 1504 to the place he labeled "Mundus Novus," or the "New World," the image appeared as the first engraved plate in *Nova Reperta*, an influential print series that chronicled scientific and geographical (imperial) discoveries during the Renaissance (fig. 3). In contemporary scholarship, *Allegory of America* has come to exemplify the gendering of the imperial venture, or the ways that colonial discourse summoned the logic of patriarchy to decipher Europe's nascent relationships with previously unknown peoples and territories (see McClintock 1995, 24; Montrose 1991; and Markey 2012). Stradanus's image calls up oppositions between male and female, culture and nature in European discourse, so that the established hierarchical ordering of gender naturalizes European dominance over the New World. Here a feminized America appears as part of nature, surrounded by flora and fauna, her physical form mirroring the organic shapes around her. In a classic essay, Sherry B. Ortner argues that the "cultural thinking that assumes the inferiority of women" emerges from an "underlying logic" that associates women with "something that every culture devalues, something that every culture defines as being of a lower order of existence"—that is, nature. "Women are being identified or symbolically associated with nature," she explains, "as opposed to men, who are identified with culture," defined as the "superior" order of human consciousness and a means by which to bring nature under control (Ortner 1974, 67–68, 72–73). Exemplifying this logic, Vespucci appears, in contrast with America, as clothed (cultured), holding an astrolabe (a signifier of European technology) and a crucifix (religion), with the ships he commands (order and progress) in the background. His utterance "America" rouses the woman, who appears to have been sleeping in her hammock, in an act of naming and claiming that iterates that America's history came into being only with the arrival of Europeans. Thus, in Anne McClintock's words, did imperial expansion find "both its shaping figure and its political sanction

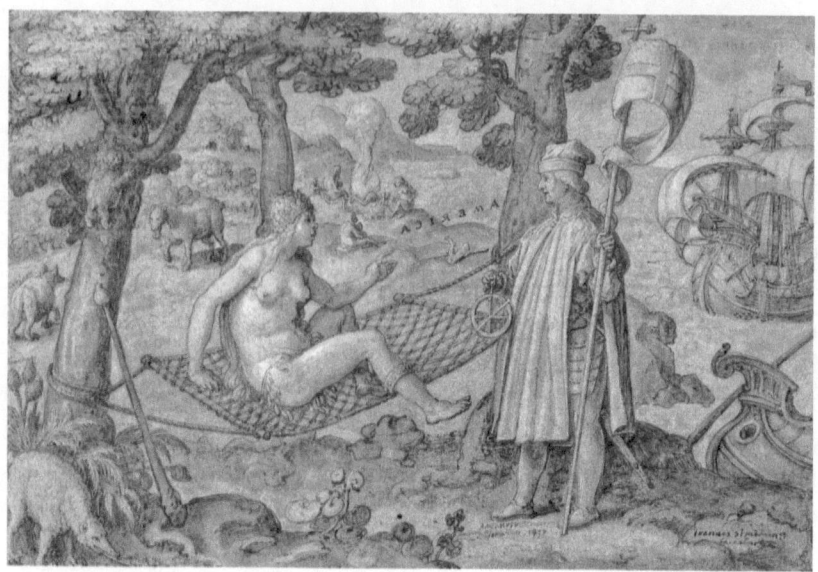

FIGURE 3. Jan van der Straet, called Stradanus, *Allegory of America*, 1587–89. Courtesy of The Metropolitan Museum of Art, New York.

in the prior subordination of women as a category of nature" (1995, 24). Beyond contrasting feminine nature with masculine culture, *Allegory of America* casts the meeting between Vespucci and America as erotic encounter. The nude America, critics have argued, rises to meet Vespucci in a gesture that appears to express her own desire—and, by extension, the desire of the New World—to be possessed (see Montrose 1991, Markey 2012, and de Certeau 1988). In images such as *Allegory of America*, viewers found confirmation of the natural superiority of Europe along with the inevitability of its dominance over the world.

If *Allegory of America* exemplifies the patriarchal logic of imperial discourse, so too does it illuminate the role of gender in broader Enlightenment-era transformations of land that enabled Indigenous dispossession. In accounting for women's subordination under patriarchy, Ortner takes for granted that nature is "something that every culture defines as being of a lower order of existence," but in fact the devaluation of nature is a historically and culturally specific phenomenon that commenced in early modern Europe. *Allegory of America* registers this transformation. Vespucci holds an astrolabe, one of the instruments—along with surveyor's tools and cartographic technologies—that enabled the abstraction of land through quantification and measurement. The spatial revolution that commenced in the Enlightenment, writes historian Allan Greer, transformed medieval understandings of land to enable "a more territorial approach to political authority" that "inspir[ed] global exploration and the pursuit of overseas empire" (2018, 276–77, 283). In Stradanus's image the pursuit of empire manifests in the figure of the explorer and the galleons behind him. The subjugation of land, though, took shape not only through the reduction of space to an abstract, homogenous grid but also through gendering. Just as the association of women with nature helped to establish patriarchy, as Ortner argues, the association of nature with women diminished land to an object of exchange and exploitation. Explaining the rise of property relations in Europe, geographer Gillian Rose writes that the "discursive transcoding between Woman and Nature" and their mutual association with reproduction made both entities available for the pleasure of and appropriation by men, a process in which visual representations played a crucial role. Images reduced both women and gendered lands to "a commodity, passive and prostrate, able only to welcome the gaze of the owner of the canvas," thus giving the masculine spectator "material and visual power over property, whether that be land or the image of a woman" (Rose 1993, 88–89, 96–97). But in imperial contexts, as *Allegory of America* shows, the gendering of land takes distinct forms. Images of feminized America—unlike, say, those of the verdant English countryside that Rose analyzes—appear as threatening, libidinous, and sinister. A scene of cannibalism unfolds in the background, signifying depravity. Gendering is an act of subordination in itself, but in Stradanus's image and elsewhere, the threat created by America urgently demands other forms of containment and control, a promise brought by the (masculine) imperial figure of Vespucci along with the ordering devices of the astrolabe and cross. Such representations of America's menace invert the actual dynamics of conquest: it is *she*, rather than the imperial figure of Vespucci, who poses a danger of brutal engulfment that must be subdued, even violently.

These cultural images brought material changes for feminized land as well as its Native inhabitants. The experiences of Native people remain neglected in colonial studies in part because representations such as *Allegory of America* constitute acts of erasure. In these images, Native people appear not as actual occupants of the territory but as allegorical figures representing qualities of the land (hypersexuality, violence) that beseech control. Nevertheless, the qualities of these allegorical figures would be ascribed to Indigenous communities as well. Most obviously, cannibalism became a dominant trope of

Native "savagery" that cast Indigenous people, rather than European invaders, as violent aggressors. Similarly, the collapsing of human figures into the gendered landscape characterized colonial depictions of the continent's Indigenous inhabitants. In *Allegory of America*, the figure of America is visually contiguous with the land: her torso appears as a segment of the tree trunk behind her, and her body mirrors the forms of the natural world. By contrast, Vespucci stands apart from the natural world, distinguished from it by the use of light, the fact that he is clothed, and the angularity of his body. The notion of the Native as part of the natural world became a ubiquitous colonial trope with clear implications for territorial rights: because Native people are part of the land to be brought under control, they cannot have claims to it. Whereas in Europe images of feminized landscape ordered gender and class relations under capitalism, the gendering of land in imperial contexts naturalized the subordination of Native lands and people alike, with particular implications for Native women.

The ramifications of European conquest for Native women become clear not in what *Allegory of America* depicts but in what it obscures. Stradanus drew this scene more than eighty years after Vespucci's voyages as a retrospective reflection on the moment of imperial encounter. Equally, the image projects a future that places the continents surely and inevitably under European control. This certitude belies the fact that Vespucci wrote his account in a moment of profound uncertainty, when the outcome of imperial encounter remained unknown. The scene depicted in *Allegory of America*, contends Renaissance scholar Louis Montrose, likely alludes to an event recounted in Vespucci's renowned 1504 letter about his third voyage (1991, 4). The passage describes not a scene of submission but rather one of staunch resistance—crucially, resistance led by Native women: "As we jumped on shore, the men of the land sent many of their women to speak with us. . . . We saw a woman come from the hill, carrying a great stick in her hand. When she came to where our Christian [one of Vespucci's men] stood, she raised it, and gave him such a blow that he was felled to the ground. The other women immediately took him by the feet, and dragged him towards the hill. The men rushed down to the beach, and shot at us with their bows and arrows" (Vespucci [1502–4] 2011, n.p.). Here Vespucci presents a world where Native women speak on behalf of their people and lead efforts to repel European invaders. Taking this account as a starting point, we might reinterpret *Allegory of America* not as a scene of submission but instead as an image that at once invokes and obscures the threat to European domination posed by

Native women. In Stradanus's depiction, the woman rises as if to meet Vespucci, an act that is usually interpreted as sexual acquiescence but might instead indicate menace (after all, she has a weapon by her side). The scene of cannibalism in the background—at the center of the frame, underscoring its importance—amplifies this threat, insinuating that Vespucci and his mariners might meet the same fate. But other elements of the scene serve to contain this threat. The woman gestures toward Vespucci and opens her mouth as if to speak (just as the Native women speak in Vespucci's account), but the image registers only his utterance "America," an act of naming that silences the woman and claims her—and, by extension, the land and people she represents—as his possession. The fact of her nudity seems to signify assent to possession while registering (as does the cannibalism scene) her inherent inferiority and thus the need to dominate her. We might understand *Allegory of America*, in other words, as an expression of anxiety about the agency of Native people (especially women), a containment of women's resistance as recounted in Vespucci's letter, and an assertion of European dominance over and against this resistance.

What are the stakes in taking Vespucci's story as the starting point for reinterpreting *Allegory of America*? Most obviously, his tale of Native women-led resistance exposes patriarchy as neither natural nor universal and potentially challenges the various hierarchies it underpins. In early modern Europe, writes Montrose, representations of an "Amazonian anticulture precisely invert[ed] European norms of political authority," so that "a conceptual space for reversal and negation was constructed within the world picture of a patriarchal society" (1991, 26). By extension, this "reversal and negation" of patriarchy calls into question the subjugation of Native people and territories premised on the prior hierarchical ordering of gender. Vespucci's account of Native women attacking his crew casts further doubt on the legitimacy of the expansionist project by depicting strenuous resistance and contradicting the persistent idea that Native people passively submitted to European invaders, as *Allegory of America* suggests. Perhaps most important, tying Vespucci's story to Stradanus's image takes the image out of the realm of pure allegory and into the realm of material social processes. Allegory abstracts the colonial encounter, effacing the experiences of Native people and the practices of conquest. The fact that *Allegory of America* recasts an actual historical event in order to suppress Native women's resistance directs our attention to the dynamics of conquest, the role of culture within them, and the consequences for Native people.

The gendered dynamics of conquest exemplified by *Allegory of America* would reshape the social places of Native women in the centuries that followed. By silencing and naming the woman "America," *Allegory of America* anticipates the broader silencing of Native women in dominant representations in which they appear, if at all, as mute, negligible figures. (These silent figures, as we shall see, recur in the work of contemporary Native women writers and artists as subjects of critique, a means of making legible the historical silencing and marginalization of Indigenous women.) In addition, such images inaugurated a tradition of representation that depicted Indigenous women as acquiescent figures and sexualized collaborators in conquest, thus obscuring women's complicated historical roles (including leadership). Notwithstanding his own account of Native women's resistance to the invaders, Vespucci himself promoted the idea that Native women were "lascivious beyond measure," possessed by "inordinate desires," very "libidinous," and showing an "excessive desire for [Europeans'] company" (Vespucci [1502–4] 2011, n.p.). The figure of the sexualized, acquiescent Native woman stands in contrast to that of Native chiefs and warriors, gendered male in settler memory but not always historical fact, who resisted conquest and became subjects of an ambivalent popular fascination with "savagery." So ubiquitous are these notions that in our own era few see meanings other than submission in images of Native women, including *Allegory of America*. The sexualization of Native women also spurred material acts of violence against them that commenced with Columbus's voyages and continue to the present (the subject of chapters 2 and 3).[4]

By sexualizing Indigenous bodies and lands, *Allegory of America* registers the significance of gender in advancing the ideologies and material practices of dispossession. But images of Native women would play different roles as colonial imperatives changed over time. Vespucci wrote his account and Stradanus created *Allegory of America* in the early decades of expansion, when Europe staked its first imperial claims across the globe. During this era, acquiring land, quelling Native resistance, and naturalizing European territorial possession constituted the primary goals of the imperial project. In the centuries that followed, settler colonialism would require nation-building on Indigenous lands and contending with the "Indian problem," the persistent obstacles that Native people posed to the consolidation of settler power. In these tasks, too, images of Native women would play a critical role. But in this era, such images would take new forms as they served emerging endeavors of "indigenizing" settlers, formulating national identities distinct from Europe, and securing settler territorial and political dominance.

INDIGENIZING THE NATION: JOHN GADSBY CHAPMAN'S *BAPTISM OF POCAHONTAS*

In the US Capitol Rotunda in Washington, DC, art tells a story about the nation's history and identity, as well as about the place of Native people within them. Plans began for the design of the US Capitol in 1793 in the aftermath of the American Revolution, when the nascent nation set about the intertwined tasks of defining an identity apart from Europe and expanding its territorial base, primarily through military campaigns against Indigenous nations.[5] The Capitol became (and remains) important as both symbol and seat of governance, a means of representing the origins and principles that define the United States as a nation. Construction on the Capitol Rotunda commenced in earnest in 1818, after the end of the War of 1812 when the British set fire to much of Washington, DC, and burned the Capitol building, which was then under construction. The building was designed to resemble the Pantheon, one of the most celebrated monuments of ancient Rome. In these early years of the republic, neoclassical architecture located US origins in the democracies of ancient Greece and Rome, thus appropriating a long history that created a sense of permanence for the fledgling nation. The art in the Rotunda tells another, more recent story of origins in which Native people play key roles. The Rotunda features eight historical paintings mounted between 1819 and 1855. Four depict scenes from the revolutionary period, including the 1776 presentation of the Declaration of Independence to Congress and George Washington's 1783 resignation of his army commission, the act that established civilian control of the US military. The remaining four paintings show scenes of exploration and discovery such as Columbus's 1492 landing and De Soto's 1541 arrival at the Mississippi River. Here and throughout American culture, stories of expansion provide the foundation of national identity. But defining expansion as an integral part of US identity raises the thorny question of the inevitable violence of dispossession. The paintings in the Capitol Building exemplify the role that Indigeneity would play in the stories that the new republic told about itself and how these stories would reconcile the ongoing violence of expansion with proclaimed national ideals.

In the years leading up to the American Revolution, the figure of America in the four-continents iconography underwent a significant change. Whereas throughout the era of exploration, she had signified the Western Hemisphere, in the latter half of the eighteenth century she came to represent more narrowly the British colonies in North America (Fleming 1965, 66). This new America typically had long, dark hair, a feathered headdress, and a bow and arrow or tomahawk, and sometimes appeared with tobacco leaves (a quintessentially American crop) or the colonial American flag (Fleming 1965, 73–74). She looked dramatically tamer than the Caribbean-influenced imaginings of Stradanus and other artists of the earlier centuries of European exploration. Gone, for instance, were allusions to cannibalism. But, in this new incarnation, she still rationalized America's subordination to Europe, symbolizing a place rather than a polity with competing claims to sovereignty (Higham 1991, 13). Whereas throughout the age of exploration, she had signified the availability of land for European possession, by the mid-eighteenth century her role was to justify ongoing British control of the rebellious American colonies. In this context, she often appeared as a daughter to Britain and sometimes hid behind the British throne, as if Britain were her protector and benefactor. Predictably, this figure of America lost relevance as the colonies sought independence. The campaign for independence confronted significant opposition among some Native nations that had forged agreements and relationships with Britain, and this fact, too, made an Indigenous woman an uneasy symbol for the new republic. Consequently, after the American Revolution, the newly independent colonies sought more masculine and racially white personifications of the nascent nation, including those of George Washington and Uncle Sam (Higham 1991, 30).

Although in the postindependence era she no longer represented America as geographical entity, the figure of the Indigenous woman continued to symbolize relationships between Native peoples and settlers in ways that facilitated the changing colonial project. In the years after independence, the challenges of expanding its territorial reach and solidifying its political power inevitably brought the United States into conflict with Native communities. Settler society, in Patrick Wolfe's often-cited words, "required the practical elimination of the natives in order to establish itself on their territory" (Wolfe 2006, 389). In the United States, the project of elimination took multiple forms, including large-scale military campaigns waged for more than a century after independence, Indian removals, and later, assimilation policies to eliminate the obstacles Native communities posed to settler power. In what Wolfe labels "a zero-sum contest over land" (2001, 868), the interests of the two sides were irreconcilable. Yet the imperative of elimination and the violence it entails contradict the liberal ideals of freedom, democracy, and justice that grant political authority to settler nation-states. At stake in its treatment of Native people was the national image and even the legitimacy of the new republic, as a later debate in the House Committee on Indian Affairs clarified: "All [responsibility for Indians] rests in the hands of the government; their action will be scrutinized at home and abroad, and we will be held to a strict and rigid accountability to the world for our conduct" (cited in Olund 2002a, 143). Such contradictions were symbolically resolved in the realm of culture. Allegory, writes literary scholar Jean Seznec, "is often sheer imposture, used to reconcile the irreconcilable, ... lending decency to the manifestly indecent" (Seznec 1953, 274). In the nineteenth-century United States, this political work of reconciling the irreconcilable fell to the allegorical figure of the Indigenous woman.

In the US Capitol Building, John Gadsby Chapman's *Baptism of Pocahontas* (1840) exemplifies how stories about Indigenous women addressed settler imperatives of the era. Tales about Pocahontas, especially her (likely apocryphal) rescue of John Smith, had long played a preeminent role in settler mythologies (see Green 1975 and Tilton 1995). But Chapman's painting focuses on a part of Pocahontas's life that had theretofore received less attention: her baptism in 1613 or 1614 in an Anglican church at Jamestown, when she became, it is widely believed, the first Native convert in the English colonies (fig. 4). Through this subject, the image addresses the effects of settler institutions on Native people and, by extension, collective anxieties about Native conquest. In Chapman's painting, the baptism of Pocahontas is a scene of Native redemption. This meaning emerges from a series of contrasts between settlers and Native people, and between those Native people who align themselves with settlers and those who do not. The settlers in the painting—the officiating minister, guards, witnesses to the ceremony, and Pocahontas's future husband, John Rolfe—are literally elevated above the Native figures and shrouded in bright light; most are clad in light-colored—or, in the case of the minister, bright white—clothing. Here lightness carries racial as well as religious (moral) connotations; along with the elevated placement of the figures in the scene, it registers settler superiority. On the other side of the canvas, Pocahontas's kinfolk appear cast in darkness in scant or traditional clothing (signifiers of "savagery"). Between the two groups, Pocahontas kneels with head bowed before the officiating minister, dressed in white as light falls on her from above. Like America in Stradanus's image, she is a silent, submissive figure. Her position at the top level of a stepped dais, elevated above her kinfolk, signals that her embrace of the colonizing culture represents uplift. In contrast to Stradanus's *Allegory of*

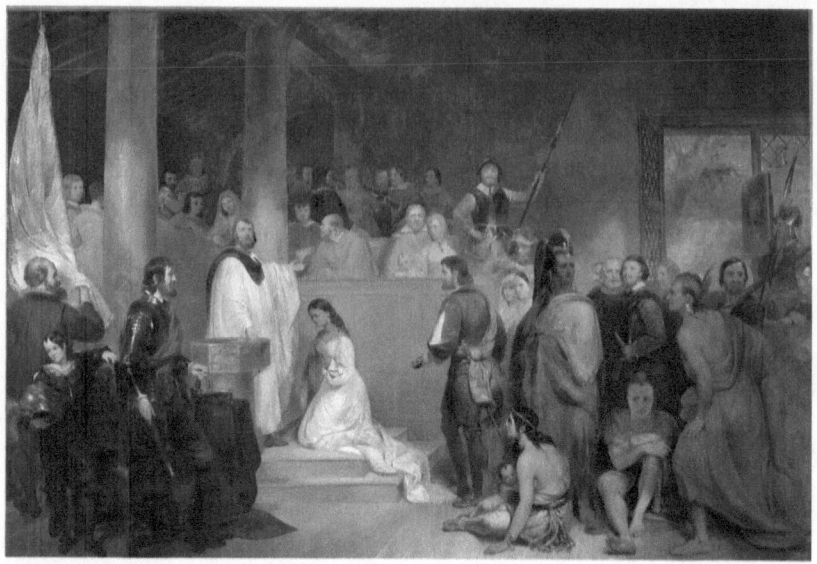

FIGURE 4. John Gadsby Chapman, *Baptism of Pocahontas*, 1840. Courtesy of the Architect of the Capitol, Washington, DC.

America, the scene includes no specific reference to land, so that it obscures territorial conflicts that raged during Pocahontas's lifetime as well as in the period when Chapman painted. Instead, the painting advances the notion that settler colonialism benefits, and even redeems, Native people.

Like *Allegory of America*, *Baptism of Pocahontas* invokes and obfuscates the nature of ongoing Native resistance to settler expansion. The painting calls up that resistance primarily through the menacing figure of Opechankanaugh, uncle of Pocahontas and leader of the Great Uprising of 1622, who turns ominously away from the ceremony. Historically, the establishment of Jamestown, the site of Pocahontas's baptism, was a brutal affair. The Great Uprising was part of the Anglo-Powhatan Wars, which commenced in 1610 when the settlers attacked a Native settlement, burning houses, destroying cornfields, and slaying men, women, and children. Warfare continued, though intermittently, for more than thirty-five years as settlers worked to expand their territorial control. In 1613, they captured Pocahontas, daughter of Powhatan, leader of the powerful Powhatan Confederacy of Algonquian-speaking nations. The baptism took place during her captivity. Her marriage to John Rolfe, which transpired soon after, might have been arranged to secure a peace settlement. The negotiated peace, however, was short-lived. In the Great Uprising of 1622, the Powhatan

Confederacy sought to expel the colonists in a military struggle that lasted for well over two decades.

The *Baptism of Pocahontas* calls up this conflict by featuring Opechankanaugh but reframes the stakes. The contest depicted in the painting does not center on land as it did historically, and because the scene separates Pocahontas from her kinfolk, it does not center on race (even though race provided a key justification for subordinating Native people during the period when Chapman created the painting). Rather, it takes shape as a clash between good and evil, or civilization and savagery—by then the dominant cultural paradigm for the colonial relationship. In this way the painting aligns the interests of "good Indians" (represented by Pocahontas) with those of the settlers, dismissing Native resistance as savage rejection of superior white society. This meaning reflected not only on the Anglo-Powhatan Wars, the historical context of Pocahontas's baptism, but also on settler expansion during Chapman's own era. Chapman received his commission in 1837, at the height of the removal era, when government officials and militias rounded up Cherokee, Choctaw, Creek, Seminole, and Chickasaw people from their homelands in the southeastern United States and forced them on a death march to Indian Territory (present-day Oklahoma). Thousands of Native peoples—probably around a quarter of those who faced removal—perished along what became known as the Trail of Tears. Confronting this controversy, viewers found assurance in Chapman's painting that the colonial project was not only inevitable (because of the superiority of Anglo society) but also ultimately benefited Native peoples themselves.

Beyond recasting conquest as benevolence, the image draws on gender as a framework for addressing other nineteenth-century political dilemmas. In Chapman's painting, Pocahontas's future husband, John Rolfe, stands behind her, registering her incorporation into Anglo society through marriage as well as baptism. In one sense, the marriage narrative symbolically reconciles the opposing interests of settlers and Native people. Still today, despite the history of settler violence surrounding the events depicted in the scene, the official description of the painting indicates that Pocahontas's baptism and marriage to John Rolfe "helped to establish peaceful relations between the colonists and the Tidewater tribes" (Architect of the Capitol n.d.). Too, this ostensible reconciliation maintains Anglo dominance because in this union Native people are represented by a woman so that the painting, like *Allegory of America*, invokes Europe's hierarchical ordering of gender in order to naturalize Native subordination. Within colonial discourse, such stories about Indigenous women who had sexual relationships with colonial agents had a long history with clear implications for territorial rights. In the context of colonial nation-building throughout the Atlantic world, argues historian Pamela Scully, such stories provided a "foundation myth" for settler states. The myth, she explains, centers on a "a young woman tied to the land through her natal heritage ... and reproductive capacity. A male foreigner arrives needing legitimacy to justify his conquest and so marries the local woman and brings forth a child whose presence, if only symbolically, affirms the fathers' right to the soil" (Scully 2005, 5). If *Allegory of America* genders the land as female to naturalize expansion, in these stories, conversely, Native women's bodies represent land, so that sexual possession bestows territorial rights.

Finally, during the time period when Chapman created the painting, the marriage narrative called up nineteenth-century racial discourse that positioned Indigeneity (unlike Blackness) as assimilable to whiteness and miscegenation as a potential solution to the "Indian Problem." Taking Native women as marriage partners, some assimilationists proposed, provided a means to dilute Native blood and ultimately eliminate Native territorial claims (Wolfe 2001, 885). Crucially, sexual partnerships in this schema conferred rights not only to land but also to Indigenous identity itself, thus distinguishing the new nation from its European origins at the time when US national identity was being forged. Stories about these sexual unions also symbolically absolve the new nation of conquest. Even today, the myth of the "Indian princess grandmother," as Vine Deloria Jr. describes it, represents at once a "blood tie with the frontier" integral to American identity and "an attempt to avoid facing the guilt [settlers] bear for the treatment of the Indian" (V. Deloria [1969] 1988, 4).

The differences between Stradanus's *Allegory of America* and Chapman's *Baptism of Pocahontas* mark a momentous transition in the status of Native communities from foreign to domestic, from separate sovereigns to subordinates incorporated into the settler nation-state. This new status required a new method of elimination other than warfare and removals, one anticipated by Chapman's baptism scene. By the late nineteenth century, in the decades that followed Chapman's commission, assimilation had become the centerpiece of government policy in the United States and Canada. In both countries, the goal of assimilation was, simply put, to absorb individual Native people into settler society so as to eradicate Native communities as a whole. "Our object," as Deputy Minister for Indian Affairs Duncan Campbell Scott stated as the assimilation campaign developed, "is to continue [the assimilation process] until there is not a single Indian in Canada that has not been absorbed into the body politic, and there is no Indian question" (Truth and Reconciliation Commission 2015b, 54). The elimination of Native people, policymakers hoped, would in turn eliminate their claims to the land.

In the assimilation era, connections between Native women's bodies and Native lands changed yet again. Whereas in previous phases of conquest gendered colonial representations naturalized European expansion and facilitated colonial nation-building, nineteenth-century assimilation policies dispossessed Native communities through the material subjugation of Native women. To be sure, the social marginalization of Native women was not new to this period: from the earliest days of conquest, cultural representations of Native women as silent, submissive, and sexualized figures found a corollary in European practices of dealing only with Native men in trade and political negotiations, thus upending traditional social roles in many Native communities. Assimilation, by contrast, aimed systematically to reorganize Native social structures to align with European gender hierarchies as a means to subordinate Native societies and extinguish their hold on the land. Such political projects drew in part on the sexualization of Native women advanced through cultural representations. Historian Jean Barman has demonstrated that, in nineteenth-century British Columbia, for example, "aboriginal women became sexualized as prostitutes" to curtail their agency and transform Native societies as a whole (1997–98, 243). These efforts took shape in part as a spatial project, as colonial officials condemned the "big houses" inhabited by extended families for ostensibly encouraging illicit behavior and advocated instead for the creation of single-family homes, where women became increasingly vulnerable to violence. The production of domestic space contributed not only to the containment of Indigenous women but also to the assimilation of entire Indigenous societies by undermining traditional kinship systems and cultural practices. The "campaign to tame the wild represented by Aboriginal sexuality," explains Barman, "had two principal goals. The first was to return Aboriginal women home. The second was to desexualize Aboriginal everyday life, in effect to cleanse it so that the home to which women returned would emulate its colonial counterpart" (1997–98, 258, 251). The effects were dramatic, as the transformation of the home privileged the patriarchal nuclear family over traditional kinship networks that afforded power and protection to women. Sexualization, confinement to domestic space, and social and economic disempowerment render Native women disproportionately vulnerable to violence to this day (the subject of chapter 3).⁶

In nineteenth-century assimilation policies, the replacement of traditional kinship structures with the patriarchal nuclear family played a fundamental, though often overlooked,⁷ role in social reform. "The redefinition of women's work [as domestic labor] and Native American assimilation were part of the same phenomenon," contends Jane E. Simonsen (2006, 12). Indeed, the assimilationist project, writes geographer Eric Olund, found its "highest expression in the cult of domesticity," so that "access to *universal* legal rights depended upon conforming to the *particular* gender roles and property relations deemed civilised in nineteenth-century white middle-class American society" (2002b, 164). The most transformative assimilation policies include the boarding (or residential) school policy, the 1887 General Allotment Act in the United States, and the 1876 Indian Act in Canada. Within Native American and Indigenous studies, these policies are the subject of extensive scholarly literature. I recount them here to emphasize their entwined spatial and gendered dimensions, which have been less widely considered, so as to bring to light the frequently overlooked entanglements of gender, dispossession, and property formation during the assimilation era. In this era of social reform, culture continued to play a crucial role.

"KILL THE INDIAN, SAVE THE MAN": EDUCATION AND THE GENDERED LOGIC OF DISPOSSESSION

In spring 2021, a Canadian anthropologist made a grim discovery at Kamloops Indian Residential School in British Columbia. Using ground-penetrating radar, she found evidence of more than two hundred unmarked graves on school grounds. As Indigenous communities grieved, searches at other schools soon led to additional discoveries of more than a thousand unmarked gravesites. As this book goes to press, that number has increased dramatically as investigators continue to look for the remains of Indigenous children at other residential schools throughout Canada. In the United States, these searches are just beginning. In both countries, boarding school survivors have long told of missing children, facts well known (though not publicized) by officials. As early as 1907, a report by an Indian Affairs chief medical officer, Peter Bryce, indicated that up to one-quarter of all children who attended residential schools died there, and at one school the death rate was 69 percent. Although tuberculosis was the major cause, Bryce laid blame for the deaths on the appalling conditions at the schools. But officials kept few records of deaths and often destroyed those that did exist,[8] so that they received little attention beyond Indigenous communities. In Canada, that practice changed with the 2008 launch of the Truth and Reconciliation Commission. Survivors testified to abuse, sexual assault, neglect, malnutrition, and suicides at the schools, along with their grief over family separation and the loss of cultures and languages (Truth and Reconciliation Commission 2015a). Their stories resonate with those told by Native people in the United States, but here the government has so far taken only preliminary measures to uncover this history.[9] In both countries, confronting the history of Native boarding school education is part of a national racial reckoning. As survivors attest to violence experienced by Native children and families in the schools, they belie notions of settler benevolence, a key meaning of Chapman's *Baptism of Pocahontas*, and call into question the actual reasons for assimilation policies. This point, at least, is becoming clear. The "deep meaning" of Indian education, as historian David Wallace Adams explained in a foundational work, was the transfer of Native territory into settler hands: "The Protestant ideology, the civilization-savagism paradigm, and the White hunger for Indian land were all mutually reinforcing and hopelessly intertwined as factors influencing the educational campaign to assimilate the Indian. . . . As the Indian is pushed off the canvas of American life, the land remains for the taking" (1988, 21, 23; see also Adams 1995).[10]

In the late nineteenth century, the centerpiece of assimilation was mandatory education in government-funded schools (called off-reservation boarding schools in the United States and residential schools in Canada), far from Native students' homes.[11] In 1879, Carlisle Indian Industrial School opened as the first federally sponsored boarding school established under the new policy in the United States, and it became the model for dozens of other schools that opened in the following years as boarding school education became mandatory for all Native children between the ages of five and 18 (though in practice the policy was unevenly enforced).[12] Carlisle founder Richard Henry Pratt's infamous motto—"kill the Indian, save the man"—disclosed the grim purpose of the schools: to eradicate Native differences and absorb Native peoples into so-called civilized society. Children were taken forcibly from their homes, and many did not return to their communities for years on end, if at all. Support for mandatory boarding schools and for assimilation policies more broadly began to falter in the 1920s, but Native student enrollment in boarding schools continued to increase for most of the century and peaked in the early 1970s. During that era, the rise of Native activism, combined with a shift in federal Indian policy toward emphasizing self-determination, began to lower the number of Native children in boarding schools. In particular, the 1978 Indian Child Welfare Act gave Native parents the legal right to deny their children's placement in boarding school. Consequently, most remaining schools closed in the 1980s and early 1990s.[13] In Canada, the establishment of Indian residential schools followed a parallel history, as a government policy of "aggressive assimilation" fostered development of a nationwide network of schools after 1880. Even before the implementation of formal assimilation policies, residential school education had been part of government and church practice for a half century, with the first school opening in 1831. It became compulsory for all Aboriginal children in 1920, when public support for boarding schools in the United States began to falter, and the program continued through the middle of the twentieth century, with the last residential school closing in 1996.[14] Between 1831, when the Mohawk Institute opened in Ontario, and 1996, when the last school closed, an estimated 150,000 Aboriginal children in Canada attended residential schools.

In the nineteenth-century United States, argues historian David Wallace Adams, three dominant strands of thought gave rise to colonial reform efforts in boarding schools: Protestantism, capitalism, and republicanism. Reflecting these ideals, the schools' program consisted of missionization, basic education, and domestic and industrial training. In this context, Protestant ideals dovetailed with those of nascent capitalism in the emphasis on individualism and the sanctity of private property, values that contradicted the communal orientation of traditional Native life (Adams 1988, 4). Whereas tribal communities typically frowned on acquisitiveness and redistributed wealth through such practices as giveaways, boarding schools trained Native students to value material wealth and private property. In fact, instilling greed was a primary goal of education. It is a "misfortune," declared members of the prominent reform society Friends of the Indian, to make a child "so absolutely unselfish that he wants to give away everything." Instead, they contended, bringing Native peoples "out of savagery" entailed making them "intelligently selfish" and desirous of "trousers with a pocket in them, and with *a pocket that aches to be filled with dollars*" (Barrows 1897, 11; emphasis in original).[15] In reality, though, boarding school education trained Native students for a lowlier social position than these aspirations suggest. During the school year, children spent half the day in manual labor training, and many students spent summers in "outing" programs in which they performed domestic and agricultural labor for families in the community (see, for example, Keliiaa 2019 and Whalen 2016).

In the boarding schools, argues K. Tsianina Lomawaima, efforts to transform Native societies took shape on "the battleground of the body" through gender reform (1993, 231), though this fact remains neglected even in current conversations. Educators aimed to undermine traditional kinship structures, which typically afforded Native women significant social influence, and replace them with the patriarchal nuclear family. This imposition represented a significant departure from Native women's traditional social roles. Historically, women's roles have varied dramatically across the thousands of Indigenous societies in the Americas, so that no generalization holds true across Native America. Moreover, reliable sources on women's roles are difficult to find. While colonial practices, including the creation of boarding schools, aimed to interrupt Native peoples' social memory, European men drastically underrepresented Native women in early written sources about Indigenous communities and often misconstrued their roles in the sources that do exist (Scully 2005; Braund 1990; LeMaster 2014; Barman 1997–98). A few examples, though, convey a sense of the kinds of social influence Native women have traditionally exercised.[16] Although there is evidence of gendered oppression in some precontact Native societies (LaRocque 1996), many, if not most, were matrilineal, with women playing substantial roles in kinship structures and community leadership. Among the Haudenosaunee, only clan mothers selected tribal leaders and could depose them at will. In Cherokee societies, women wielded substantial spiritual and political influence and played an equal role in society (see, for example, Perdue 1998). Creek women held power to declare and end war and also decided the fate of captives (see Braund 1990). In many Native communities, women played social and spiritual roles that were as powerful as those of men and often included responsibilities to distribute food, negotiate trade, and make decisions about land. Women fought in wars and hunted animals. Nor were gender roles typically rigid or inflexible. Even where gender determined the division of labor, as Rebecca Tsosie demonstrates in her research on Indigenous women's leadership, Native societies often permitted individuals to adopt social roles other than those conventionally assigned to their perceived gender (2011, 32). In addition, in many societies Native women, unlike their European counterparts, exercised a high degree of sexual autonomy (Barman 2011).

Under the new system of social organization taught by the boarding schools, by contrast, Native men became heads of household, while Native women learned "new identities, new skills and practices, new norms of appearance, and new physical mannerisms" consistent with nineteenth-century domestic ideals (Lomawaima 1993, 231; see also Adams 1995, 173–81). In 1901, Estelle Reel, the first woman appointed as superintendent of Indian schools in the United States, penned the voluminous *Course of Study for the Indian Schools of the United States*, a standard curriculum that conveyed the fundamental significance of gender and domesticity in colonial education and assimilationist endeavors more broadly. The *Course of Study* covers nearly three dozen topics, from basic academic subjects such as arithmetic and reading to industrial and academic training, often with detailed instructions on goals and methods of subject mastery in students' training (precisely when, how, and for what purpose students should learn, for example, to till or irrigate the soil, master a French seam, or bake bread). Its clear emphasis is "systematic industrial training" to transform each child into a "willing worker," reflecting the extent to which a primary aim of boarding school education was to make Native labor available for the capitalist economy (Reel 1901, 5–6; Whitt 2020).[17] The *Course of Study* assigned educational goals along gender lines. While it privileged agriculture as the foundation of boys' education, the *Course of Study* included instruction on other suitable forms of manual labor such as blacksmithing, carpentry, and shoemaking. Girls' duties and occupations centered on the home. "The ideal training for girls is that which will instill a love for home and make good, neat housekeepers," Reel instructed (1901, 149). To these menial tasks she attached lofty values. She described sewing, for example, as a means to encourage "thought, care, precision, neatness, self-reliance, individuality, refinement of taste, and a higher appreciation of time and its opportunities"—in short, a means to "the building of character through the hand" (233). In truth, though, by relegating Native women to domestic labor, boarding schools consigned them to a place of social and economic marginality. Indeed, vocational training in boarding schools, in Lomawaima's words, was "training in dispossession under the guise of domesticity, developing a habitus shaped by messages about subservience and one's proper place" (Lomawaima 1993, 231).

Photographs counted among the means of propagandizing the boarding school experiment by recasting colonial reform as racial uplift (see Mauro 2011). Many schools hired their own photographers, and Pratt himself commissioned photographs from Carlisle and other institutions as a means to secure government funding by illustrating their ostensible success. The Bureau of Indian Affairs used photographs to document the schools' activities, often exhibiting the images—and even Native students themselves in simulated classroom settings—in such forums as world's fairs (Trennert 1987).[18] Widely circulated, such images, often arranged in before-and-after pairs, relied on the status of the photograph as "document" to promote the boarding school policy as a successful means of social reform. The "before" photographs were taken upon the children's arrival at school, and the "after" photographs were taken some months later. Typically, changes in clothing, hairstyle, spatial location (often from "wild" outdoor settings to "domesticated" indoor spaces), and position (from sitting or squatting to standing upright) demonstrated the ostensible improvements brought by Western education. As in Chapman's *Baptism of Pocahontas*, lighting was significant as well, registering a transition from dark to light that implied both moral and racial uplift (in some "after" images, even the children's skin appears lighter). In many images, Native boys appeared in military uniforms and patriotic postures surrounded by US flags (see, for example, Margolis 2004, 92). Such photographs were positioned as evidence of the success of the civilizing mission and the pacification of Native children so as to generate financial resources for the schools. In this way, these cultural images not only conveyed colonial ideologies but also bolstered material support for projects of social reform.

In many before-and-after sequences, the social transformations wrought by boarding school education took shape around gender. Changes in attire, occupation, and demeanor depicted by the photographs entailed conformity to nineteenth-century gender ideals. Photography, writes Gillian Rose, "is the visual medium most active in gendering women by picturing their bodies in certain ways and in certain places" (2003, 8). Many boarding school photographs showed girls involved in household labor such as cooking or laundering, underscoring the significance of domesticity in the civilizing mission. The before-and-after sequence reproduced here exemplifies the ways that, in the schools, the civilizing process took shape through the reordering of gender (fig. 5). The highly staged studio photographs depict four Zuni Pueblo children—Tsai au-tit-sa (renamed Mary Ealy), Jan-i-uh-tit sa (Jennie Hammaker), Teai-e-se-u-lu-ti-wa (Frank Cushing), and Tra-wa-ea-tsa-lun-kia (Taylor Ealy)[19]—upon their arrival at Carlisle Indian School, circa 1880, and then again one year later. In the "before" image, the girls are standing with the boys seated in front of them, insinuating that the dominance of women

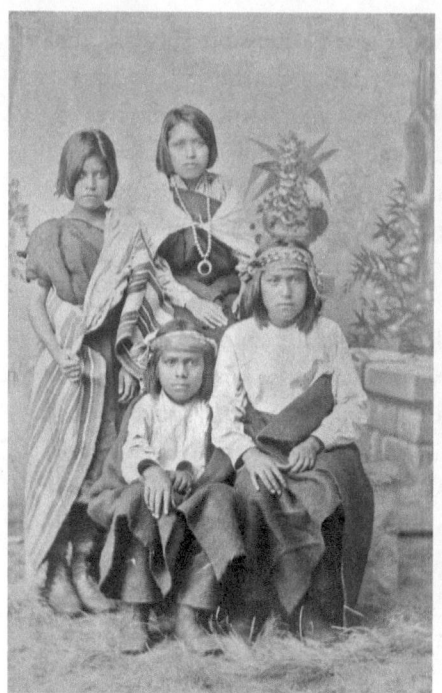 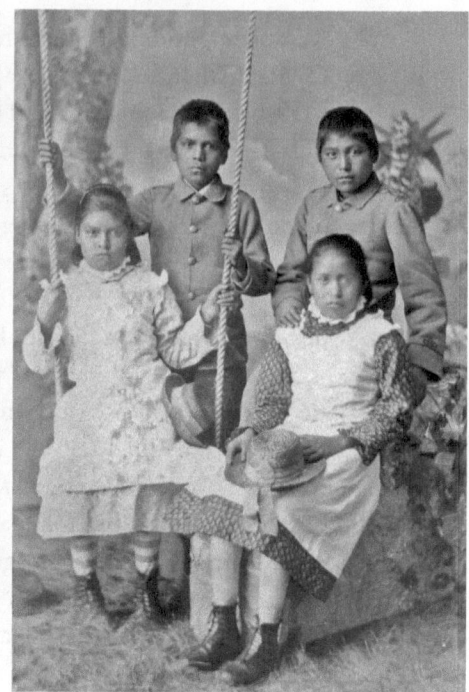

FIGURE 5 (Left). Four Pueblo Children from Zuni, c. 1880. Courtesy of Archives and Special Collections, Dickinson College, Carlisle, Pennsylvania.

FIGURE 6 (Right). Frank Cushing, Taylor Ealy, Mary Ealy, and Jennie Hammaker, c. 1880. Courtesy of Cumberland County Historical Society, Carlisle, Pennsylvania.

was itself cause for reform. The "after" photograph, by contrast, features the children conforming to practices of male dominance. Here the girls appear sitting in properly subservient positions with the boys standing protectively over them. The boys' hair is now cut short and they wear military-style uniforms, while the girls appear with long hair and modest dresses. In contrast with Chapman's *Baptism of Pocahontas*, in which the Native men appear as threatening, here the boys' military-style clothing denotes political containment. The whiteness of the girls' clothing carries not only racial but also sexual connotations by indicating purity. The physical space, too, has been transformed to appear as domestic and a place of leisure, belying the schools' emphasis on manual labor. By advancing the notion that Native people were, or were at least quickly becoming, part of the colonial nation-state, the photographs obscured ongoing territorial (including military) conflicts that continued to rage throughout the boarding school era. In so doing, they masked the ultimate goal of assimilation: the acquisition of Native land.

The effects of boarding school education have been dramatic and enduring. Physical abuse and sexual assault in the schools, long a theme of Native cultural production, became a major subject of testimony in the Truth and Reconciliation Commission beginning in 2008. The legacy of this violence still plagues Native families and communities. The imposition of gender hierarchies transformed the social places of Native women, who confront social precarity and suffer disproportionately high levels of sexual violence (see chapter 3). Many Native families trace the loss of their traditional languages and cultural practices to time spent in the schools. Such losses also carry political significance by undercutting cultural differences that provide a key rationale for political autonomy. An additional purpose of boarding school education was to condition Native peoples to accept land loss. In the assimilation-era United States, land loss took place in large measure through the General Allotment Act, the land reform policy enacted in conjunction with mandatory boarding school education (see Adams 1988, 18).

TRANSFORMING NATIVE LANDS THROUGH THE GENERAL ALLOTMENT ACT

In 1877, as the assimilation era commenced in the United States and Canada, anthropologist Lewis Henry Morgan published *Ancient Society*, a book that would reshape understandings of social differences in popular and scholarly circles alike. Human societies, Morgan postulated, advance through stages of progress from savagery to barbarism before ultimately breaking through to civilization (exemplified, of course, by Europe). As societies scale the ladder of progress, they pass through stages of development defined by such attributes as modes of subsistence, family and social organization, linguistic practices, spiritual beliefs, and relationships to land. Societies in the stage of savagery, Morgan argued, are hunters and gatherers; agriculture subsequently emerges in the stage of barbarism and becomes more advanced in civilization. Morgan identified monogamy, patriarchy, private property, and monotheism as other attributes of advanced societies. The transition from matriarchy to patriarchy as embodied in the nuclear family, contended Morgan, reiterating arguments of other influential social scientists of his era, was a particularly important aspect of progress that facilitated the emergence of private property and met the consequent need to determine paternity for purposes of inheritance (see Allen 1999, 1093). Drawing on Morgan's arguments,

Friedrich Engels's *The Origin of the Family, Private Property, and the State* (1884) underscored connections between patriarchy and the transition to capitalism, contending that as men amassed wealth, the patriarchal family ensured the legitimacy of the children who would inherit their father's possessions. Such was the ideological context that informed assimilation policies. The notion that universal stages of progress accounted for human difference was at the center of these policies and rationalized, among other things, reformers' insistence on imposing the patriarchal nuclear family, private property, and agriculture on Indigenous societies, as well as prohibitions on traditional practices. By lauding such changes as "progress," assimilationists obfuscated the ways that such policies advanced Indigenous dispossession.

Nowhere are connections between patriarchy and private property clearer than in the General Allotment Act, or Dawes Act, a cornerstone of the campaign for assimilation in the United States. Passed by Congress in 1887, the act divided collectively held reservations into parcels of property that were then allotted to individual tribal members, who were typically granted US citizenship.[20] (Imposed citizenship, too, counts among assimilation measures because it undercut tribal autonomy and belonging; significantly, the assimilation era culminated with the 1924 Indian Citizenship Act, which extended US citizenship to all Native peoples born in the United States, whether or not they desired this status.)[21] The General Allotment Act, as Theodore Roosevelt famously described it, was "a mighty pulverizing engine to break up the tribal mass" (Roosevelt 1901, n.p.). By allotting tracts of land to tribal members, reformers hoped to instill in Native peoples an appreciation for private property, encourage individualism and self-interest, sever tribal community bonds, and ultimately integrate Native peoples into the dominant society. "At its core," writes historian Frederick Hoxie, the General Allotment Act "was an assertion that the gap between the two races [Indian and white] would be overcome and that Indians would be incorporated into American society. They would farm, participate in government, and adopt 'higher' standards of behavior. The statute assumed that landownership, citizenship, and education would alter traditional cultures, bringing them into 'civilization'" (2001, 77). Assimilation hinged on transforming communally held lands into private property, thus imposing the colonial idea that land is an object to be bought, sold, and cultivated for profit. The division of land into parcels was anathema in traditional belief systems. A Nez Perce chief reacted to allotment by saying, "They asked us to divide the land, to divide our mother upon whose bosom we had been born, upon whose lap we had been reared"; in this way, he equated the act of dividing land to homicide (as reported by US senator Henry Teller during congressional debate on the Dawes Act, cited in Olund 2002a, 142).[22] Beyond converting reservations into individually owned tracts of property, the Dawes Act extended US power over Native lands. In the words of historian Emily Greenwald, it "sought to reorder Indian space and extend U.S. territorial authority [by replacing] ... experiential space with mathematically measured space," thus "transform[ing] Indian territory into U.S. territory" (Greenwald 2002, 7).

From the outset, the "problem" of Native occupation of the land had been at the center of allotment. "Wild Indians," wrote Interior Secretary Carl Schurz, "hold immense tracts of country which, possessed by them, are of no advantage to anybody, while, as is said, thousands upon thousands of white people stand ready to cultivate them and to make them contribute to the national wealth" (Schurz [1881] 1973, 46). In fact, the legislation precipitated massive land loss for Native communities. After allotting parcels of land to individual tribal members, the government declared unallotted lands as "surplus" and opened them to white settlement. While this process immediately diminished reservation lands, other factors led to further losses in the decades that followed. Unlike collectively held reservation lands, allotments were subject to taxation; Native allottees often found the taxes impossibly high, causing many to lose their lands to tax forfeiture.[23] Fraudulent sales added to these problems,[24] and to make matters even worse, the desperate poverty on many reservations drove others to sell their lands to obtain vital necessities such as food. "Starvation makes fools of anyone," writes Louise Erdrich in her historical novel *Tracks*, a fictional rendering of the ruinous aftermath of the Dawes Act, so that some "sold their allotment land for one hundred poundweight of flour" (Erdrich 1988, 8). When the act was passed in 1887, tribes held 138 million acres in reservation land, but by 1934, when the Indian Reorganization Act ended allotment, reservation lands had been reduced to 48 million acres. Because of the policy, in other words, two-thirds of reservation land passed out of Native hands.

Like the boarding school policy, the General Allotment Act placed gender at the center of colonial reform. "Social transformation was coextensive with spatial transformation," explains geographer Eric Olund, and in this case, social transformation entailed dismantling traditional kinship structures and replacing them with the patriarchal nuclear family (Olund 2002a, 133). Consistent with Morgan's concept of social progress, reformers understood private property, the nuclear family, and agriculture as interrelated dimensions of assimilation, and the General Allotment Act forced Native people to establish individual family farms on privately held tracts of land. (In practice, though, farming often proved impossible because allotments were located on nonarable lands and families lacked the requisite tools for agriculture.) Reformers also pressed Indigenous people to form nuclear families under male heads of household and engage in Christian marriage. Under the original legislation, married women were ineligible for allotments, and although this provision changed,[25] reformers distributed larger plots of land and assigned title to male heads of household, an allocation that secured men's social and economic power while disproportionately dispossessing Native women. Under allotment, women also lost social standing through relegation to domestic labor; while they tended to home and children, men performed wage labor or agricultural work (Simonsen 2006, 12). This new division of labor diverged from women's traditional roles in many tribes as caretakers of their land who controlled vital food supplies, thus further undercutting women's social influence. Missionaries encouraged the construction of frame houses (Greenwald 2002, 53), so that women were confined to newly created domestic space, a location that created social marginalization, vulnerability to violence, and means of controlling women's mobility and sexuality. In all of these ways, the legislation, in geographer Eric Olund's words, twinned "property and family... to produce the patriarchal domestic space idealised by white middle-class reformers of the nineteenth century, the spatial configuration that was seen as the necessary underpinning of American civilisation" (Olund 2002b, 153–54). Thus, as allotment dramatically transformed the space of the reservation from communally held territory into individual tracts of property, it upended social organization based on extended kinship networks to make the nuclear family central. The effects for Native women were devastating.

As a means of assimilation, the General Allotment Act failed. However, the act was only nominally about assimilation. "The real aim of this bill," wrote US senator Henry Teller, a critic of the policy, "is to get at the Indian lands and open them up to settlement. The provisions for the apparent benefit of the Indian are but the pretext to get at his lands and occupy them" (cited in Bobroff 2001, 1607–8). As a means to dispossess Native people and extend US government control over Native land, the act proved far more effective. Officially, allotment caused the loss of 90 million acres, or two-thirds of reservation land, but these numbers are misleading. Many Native people (especially those designated as "full bloods") who retained title to their lands were deemed "incompetent" and lost control of (though not always title to) their lands to government agents, who frequently leased these lands to outside interests. Allotment left the remaining land base of reservations in a checkerboard pattern, with noncontinuous Native-held parcels. In addition to shifting reservation demographics so that on many reservations the majority population was now non-Native, checkerboarding contributed to a loss of tribal legal control over reservation land, a fact that today contributes to the increased vulnerability of Native women to domestic and sexual abuse (see chapter 3). Allotment constituted an assault on tribal sovereignty in other ways as well, by negating tribes' authority to determine their own membership and instituting blood quantum as a means of determining tribal citizenship, a test that many legitimate tribal members failed because they could not meet the dubious criteria set by officials. In these ways, allotment worked in tandem with boarding school education: both policies ruptured community ties, encouraged accumulation of private property, mandated the transition to an agricultural economy, imposed domestic ideals, and aimed to convince Native peoples that they would inevitably lose their lands to more "civilized" people (see Adams 1988, 18–19). All the while, reformers insisted that allotment was fundamentally benevolent, a means of "civilizing" the "savage." Casting reform as progress, in Olund's words, "enabled a certain claim to innocence on the part of American society" by transforming the "cant of conquest" into the "'gift' of civilization," thus "eras[ing] colonialism from American political discourse" (Olund 2002a, 129).[26]

GENDER, IDENTITY, AND LAND UNDER THE INDIAN ACT

In its dealings with Native nations, Canada followed a path parallel to that of the United States by undermining the political autonomy, cultural practices, and ultimately territorial claims of Indigenous communities. But, whereas the United States waged war with Native nations through most of the nineteenth century and commenced formal assimilation policies only as the century drew to a close, Canadian assaults on Indigenous communities relied primarily on assimilation from the beginning with initial policies implemented decades before similar endeavors in the United States.[27] In 1857, the Gradual Civilization Act—legislation that presaged the Dawes Act—allowed for the enfranchisement of educated Indigenous men fluent in English or French; upon enfranchisement, these men lost their legal rights as Native people and were classified as British subjects.[28] The act aimed to diminish the Native population along with the land base of reserves by allocating to enfranchised Native men up to 50 acres of reserve land as private property. Such early measures were voluntary, but after Canada gained independence from Britain in 1867, assimilation became mandatory. Beginning in the 1870s, the federal government included education in treaty negotiations with First Nations, and the expansion of residential schools after 1880 dramatically increased the numbers of Indigenous children in such institutions. Beyond education, the most influential Canadian policies centered on identity and band membership. The government's assertion of its power to determine who would, or would not, count as a community member itself constituted an attack on Native autonomy. Moreover, colonial regulation of band membership provided a means to diminish the overall population and control access to land—the ultimate goals of assimilation.

As in the United States, the dispossession and disempowerment of Native communities in Canada took shape through gender reform.[29] The 1857 Gradual Civilization Act offered the possibility of enfranchisement and property rights only to men, and if men made that choice, their wives and descendants automatically lost Native status as well. Colonial legislation, in other words, redefined the status of Native women and children so that it depended on marriage to or descent from a Native man (Lawrence 2004, 50). Between 1869 and 1951, the Canadian government instituted a series of additional assimilation policies that undermined traditional gender roles and social organization so as to center the patriarchal nuclear family in Indigenous communities. The 1869 Gradual Enfranchisement Act stipulated that Native women who married non-Native men would lose Native status and rights to band membership. By creating the concepts of status and nonstatus Indians and adding blood quantum as the criterion for Native identity, the act not only asserted the government's power to determine who counted as Native but also shifted the criterion to race, a category antithetical to traditional ways of determining identity and belonging. By definition, blood quantum criteria decrease the numbers of people who count as Indigenous and hold claims to land, leading some Native studies scholars to describe blood quantum requirements as a form of genocide (see, for example, M. Jaimes 1992 and Garroutte 2003). The Gradual Enfranchisement Act also disrupted traditional kinship systems by imposing patrilineage, so that children's identity was determined by paternity, even though traditionally most Indigenous communities were matrilineal. Under the Gradual Enfranchisement Act, women and children became subject to the will of the male head of household, thus elevating male authority and diminishing women's social status. The act further limited women's social influence by requiring European styles of governance in the form of elected band councils and excluding women from voting or running for office.[30] (Indigenous women were prevented from participating in tribal government until 1951.) As this measure disrupted traditional means of governance, it further marginalized Indigenous women who had previously played crucial—and, in some contexts, determinative—roles in community decisions.

At the center of Canadian assimilation policies was the 1876 Indian Act, which remains the most significant and enduring legislation affecting Indigenous communities. Imposed unilaterally by the federal government on Aboriginal communities, it set criteria for band governance, land use, membership, education, and other crucial matters while also severely curtailing the nation-to-nation relationship between Britain and Aboriginal communities established before Canadian Confederation and diminishing the new government's recognition of Aboriginal title to Indigenous territories. The Indian Act superseded the General Enfranchisement Act, extending some of its terms, including those mandating governance through European-style band councils, and it established the agent system, whereby a government-appointed agent managed the reserve and held the power even to overturn band council decisions. Aboriginal people were restricted from leaving reserves without the Indian agent's permission. The legislation broadened Canadian control over Indigenous communities and territories through the regulation of Aboriginal identities. It recognized only "status Indians," a category that generally required membership in an Aboriginal band with an established reserve or a treaty with the federal government, as well as adherence to certain lifestyles, the definitions of which changed over time. Adopting particular occupations, such as farming, educational achievement, and military service, for example, forced Aboriginal peoples to lose their Native status and become Canadian citizens, regardless of their wishes. Beyond granting the federal government the sole authority to determine Aboriginal identity, the Indian Act undercut Aboriginal self-determination in other ways as well by forbidding traditional cultural practices, depriving bands of the capacity for self-government, and denying Aboriginal peoples the right to vote in federal and provincial elections. The Indian Act remains in force in Canada, though with some significant amendments.

Like its counterparts in US policy, the Indian Act joined together gender hierarchies, territorial appropriation, and colonial control as it disproportionately marginalized and dispossessed Aboriginal women. The act, observes Brenna Bhandar, was grounded in Victorian cultural beliefs that associated private property ownership with civilization, privileged men as property owners, and defined women's identities and status through their relationships to husbands and fathers (Bhandar 2018, 159). Native women who married non-Native men automatically lost status and band membership. This did not hold true for Native men; moreover, their non-Native wives, whatever their race, gained Native status through marriage. In addition, because the legal category of status Indian adhered only through male lineage, children of Aboriginal women who married outside the band were ineligible for band membership or Native status. Such changes in status carried far-reaching consequences. Disenfranchised Aboriginal peoples are generally forbidden to live on reserves, so that women who lost status under the Indian Act were forced to leave their communities, prevented from inheriting land, excluded from cultural activities, and denied band annuity payments, thus contributing to deculturation and poverty. Other factors contributed to women's economic precarity. Married women were disallowed from inheriting their husband's property until 1884; even then, they were eligible to receive only up to one-third of his possessions with the endorsement of the Indian agent. The Indian Act continued to prevent women from voting in band council elections, serving in tribal governance, or participating in decisions about the surrender of reserve lands. Finally, whereas Native women had previously held the right to divorce and remarry at will, the Indian Act restricted women's sexual autonomy and rights to divorce and withheld band annuity payments from those women who did not conform to patriarchal mores. The "loss of status was only one of many statutes that lowered the power of Native women in their societies relative to men," explains Bonita Lawrence in an article on gender discrimination in the Indian Act; "because of the many ways in which Native women were rendered marginal in their communities, it was extremely difficult for them to challenge the tremendous disempowerment that loss of status represented" (Lawrence 2003, 8).

The Indian Act also transformed Aboriginal land tenure. One of its original provisions restricted the land base of Native groups to reserves (an area far smaller than traditional territories), and in the 1920s, a period of heightened organizing for Aboriginal land claims, an amendment prohibited communities from hiring legal counsel and fighting for their rights in the courts. Indian agents, who held complete power over community affairs, further contributed to the loss of reserve lands by facilitating sales to outside entities. Meanwhile, government regulation of Aboriginal identity dispossessed countless Native peoples. Between 1876 and 1985, an estimated 25,000 Native peoples (mostly women and their children) lost status under the Indian Act (Lawrence 2003, 9), but because their descendants lost status as well, the effect on the Native population was far greater than this number suggests. Indeed, by 1985, the year of significant amendments to the Indian Act, there were more than twice as many nonstatus than status Native and Métis people. "Legislation ensconced in the Indian Act," writes Lawrence, "had rendered two-thirds of all Native people in Canada landless" (2003, 6). Just as gender determined who had access to Native lands under the Indian Act, the marginalization of Native women facilitated the dispossession of Indigenous communities as a whole. Because matrilineal clans in many societies held control over the collective land base, destroying traditional kinship structures and removing women from positions of power facilitated the privatization, and ultimately loss, of Indigenous territories (Lawrence 2004, 47). Because of the centrality of the subordination of Indigenous women in colonization, argues Bonita Lawrence, "the violation of Native women's rights through the loss of Indian status . . . [must be understood] not as the problems faced by individuals, but as a *collective* sovereignty issue" (Lawrence 2004, 46).

In the mid- and late twentieth century, a series of amendments to the Indian Act returned some powers of self-determination to Aboriginal bands and revised colonial proscriptions of Native identity. Reforms enacted in 1951 and 1962, driven in part by the military service of Aboriginal people during World War II, granted some limited powers for self-government, eliminated bans on traditional cultural practices, and accorded Aboriginal peoples the right to vote in federal and provincial elections. The most sweeping changes, however, occurred in 1985 in the form of Bill C-31, which expanded band control of membership, eliminated the sexually discriminatory provisions of the Indian Act, including those that caused women to lose membership status, and opened the possibility of reinstatement for those women who had previously been disenfranchised and their descendants.

Yet the process of reinstatement has proved a hard road, in part because many bands have opposed the process and some women have suffered violence as a result of their individual or collective efforts to regain status. Ironically, observes Lawrence, many communities "insist on clinging to definitions of Indianness created by the federal government," sometimes because of blatant sexism and sometimes *"as an expression of their sovereignty"* (Lawrence 2003, 12–13, 15; emphasis in original). The "masculinist narratives of self-government and Indigenous rights," Sherry Pictou asserts, manifested when Indigenous male leaders opposed Indigenous women's campaigns to eliminate gender discrimination under the Indian Act, characterizing these efforts as betrayals of Native struggles for self-determination (Pictou 2020, 379; see also Kuokkanen 2019). These fraught divisions illustrate how gender inequity shapes the terrain of Native politics in part by pitting interests of Indigenous women against the exercise of Indigenous sovereignty. Although the Indian Act was ultimately amended to eliminate the gender-discriminatory provisions, the effects of those provisions on Native women continue to this day. Native women experience high levels of poverty, an outcome, in part, of the disproportionate dispossession of women under the Indian Act, their removal from positions of social influence, and their relegation to the domestic sphere under assimilation policies more broadly. In Canada, because of loss of housing or Native status, poverty, and unemployment, women constitute the majority of migrants from reserves to cities. Together, these factors create a condition of social precarity that renders Indigenous women more vulnerable to violence as a direct consequence of colonial policies (the subject of chapter 3).

. . .

Between 2012 and 2016, Cree artist Kent Monkman created a series of monumental paintings based on an unlikely source: Tiepolo's 1752 ceiling fresco *Allegory of the Planets and Continents*. As described at the beginning of this chapter, Tiepolo's masterwork is perhaps the most renowned rendering of the four-continents iconography, a celebration of Europe's superiority and inevitable global dominance. In his series *The Four Continents*, Monkman turns this imperial iconography against itself to condemn rather than laud European expansion. In contrast to the vision of empire as progress in Tiepolo's fresco, Monkman's paintings portray the wreckage and ruin brought by imperialism. "Tiepolo's depiction of Europe is based on the myth of Zeus capturing and raping Europa," explains Monkman, "so I saw these four continents as these metaphors for that kind of raping and pillaging and being exploited" (cited in Sandals 2013, 7). In Monkman's rendering, "Miss Europe" appears as a landscape of brutality and death, with icons of civilization (the Parthenon, the *Mona Lisa*) overshadowed by corpses, spectacles of destruction, and racist emblems that have promoted mass murder. Scenes of

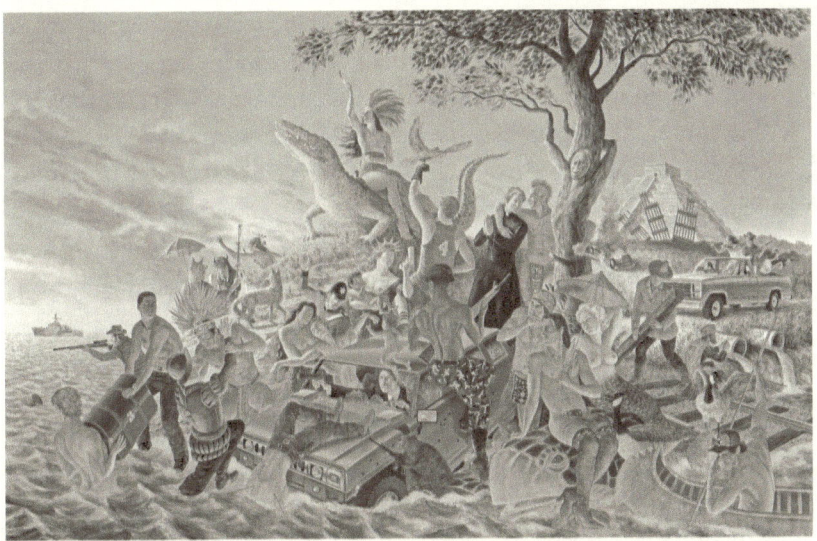

FIGURE 7. Kent Monkman (1965–), *Miss America*, 2012. Acrylic on canvas, 214 × 336 cm. The Montreal Museum of Fine Arts, gift of Jacques and Céline Lamarre. Photo courtesy of the artist.

plunder, destruction, and death similarly dominate "Miss America" with an emphasis on Native conquest (fig. 7). Drawing together the past and present of ongoing colonialism, the painting shows conquistadors and police officers assaulting Native people, colonists looting treasure, and armed gunmen terrorizing those around them. At the same time as these violent scenes subvert the idea of European imperialism as progress, they also unravel the gendered logic that historically rationalized expansion. Whereas conventional four-continents iconography represented each continent as a woman, Monkman's series features his gender-fluid alter ego Miss Chief Eagle Testickle (discussed in chapter 4) in the role of the allegorical figures of America, Europe, Africa, and Asia. This two-spirit figure denaturalizes the hierarchical gender binaries that authorized imperial domination along with the acquisition of Indigenous lands. As America, Miss Chief is no passive figure who invites possession. Instead, she is commanding and lordly, seated atop an enormous alligator on a hill as she surveys the chaotic scene of destruction that unfolds beneath her. If Tiepolo's *Allegory of the Planets and Continents* lauds European imperialism as progress deemed inevitable, Monkman's *The Four Continents* indicts expansion as needless ruin.

Monkman's series *The Four Continents* captures in many ways the projects of contemporary Native culture analyzed throughout this book. The

BODIES OF LAND • 57

Indigenous artists and writers discussed in the following chapters create alternative histories that foreground the violence, including gendered violence, of dispossession so as to challenge colonial ways of seeing, at times by revising canonical images that have supported Indigenous dispossession. Such forms of anticolonial critique do not focus only on past events. Contemporary Native culture makes legible a continuing Native presence on the land in the context of ongoing territorial conflicts. In *The Four Continents*, "Miss America" identifies the continent, with words scrawled in graffiti, as "stolen land" and depicts Native struggles against present-day colonial agents. On both his website and in the published volume of *The Four Continents*, Monkman underscores the relevance of his critique of European expansion for present-day territorial conflicts by including essays that document the long history of Indigenous dispossession, its contemporary effects on Native communities, and Indigenous cultural beliefs that counter colonial ideas about land (see Goulet 2017 and Atleo 2017). Like other Native artists and writers, Monkman thus uses his paintings to engage present-day conflicts and advance a project of territorial reclamation that centers gender justice. In this work, culture itself becomes a battleground over the meaning of history, over the nature of Native bodies and territories, and ultimately, over who holds rights to the land.

TWO

"Mapping by Words"

CARTOGRAPHY IN *TRACKS* AND *SOLAR STORMS*

In a pivotal scene near the end of *Tracks*, Louise Erdrich's 1988 novel about dispossession on an Anishinaabe[1] reservation in the early twentieth century, a clash over land invokes conflicting conceptions of space central to Indigenous colonial contexts. In the scene, the reservation priest, Father Damien, visits the Pillager, Kashpaw, and Nanapush families, bearing grim news that they will likely soon lose their lands because of property taxes imposed by the federal government. Throughout Native America, such colonial appropriations of territory have hinged on the reconceptualization and reorganization of space that in *Tracks* find expression in a map brought by the priest: "Damien unfolded and smoothed the map flat upon the table.... [W]e examined the lines and circles of the homesteads paid up.... They were colored green. The lands that were gone out of the tribe ... were painted a pale and rotten pink. Those in question, a sharper yellow. At the center of a bright square was Matchimanito [Pillager family land], a small blue triangle I could cover with my hand" (172–73). The map represents the reservation as abstract, geometrical space devoid of history and reduced to exchange value—in other words, what Henri Lefebvre describes as the homogenous space of capital, rendered through the "subordination [of land] to the unifying but abstract principle of property," antithetical to the sacred and to "lived experience" (Lefebvre 1991, 252). This conception of space rationalizes settler colonial dispossession and capitalist exploitation, forces that coalesced at the turn of the twentieth century, the time frame of *Tracks*, when federal policies fueled the further expansion of market capitalism by dispossessing Native peoples and making their resources available for the US economy. At the novel's end, the government seizes Pillager land because of unpaid taxes, then lumber companies raze Matchimanito of its rich timber resources.[2]

But this scene in *Tracks* also calls up a different sense of land when Fleur Pillager, the central figure of Native resistance in the novel, expresses "contempt for the map, for those who drew it, for the money required, even for the priest. She said the paper had no bearing or sense, as no one would be reckless enough to try collecting for land where Pillagers were buried" (174). In *Tracks*, because the Pillagers represent the community's past and its traditional spiritual center, their burial grounds are sacred places imbued with collective tribal histories. In my reading, a principal project of *Tracks* is to represent such social dimensions of land that gain political meanings in colonial territorial disputes, the "tracks" of Indigenous occupation that undo the abstraction of capitalist space and underlie Native claims to territory within and outside the novel. Attention to these conflicting conceptions of land thus illuminates the project of *Tracks*—and, I argue, a key project of Native culture more broadly in the post-1960s era—as reterritorialization, the subversion of colonial conceptions of land and assertion of Indigenous territorial claims. Whereas chapter 1 explores the gendered myths, metaphors, and material practices that advanced Indigenous dispossession, this chapter brings to light Native culture's critical engagement with the myriad spatial dimensions of colonization, the material enactments of power on Indigenous land and bodies that fall outside colonial discourses and official histories. The novels analyzed here rewrite dominant histories of expansion with a focus on Native women's experiences of settler colonialism, thus bringing to light the obscured history of gendered violence that has been integral to expansion. As this critique undermines notions of European superiority and the inevitability of settler territorial control furthered by colonial representations, these works underscore the necessity of gender justice in Native territorial claims in the present.

In the map scene, *Tracks* summons historical uses of cartography as an instrument of colonial dispossession, a means of asserting property rights over and against the claims of Indigenous occupants of the land. "As much as guns and warships," geographer J. B. Harley explains, "maps have been the weapons of imperialism": from the earliest days of European expansion, "surveyors marched alongside soldiers, initially mapping for reconnaissance, then for general information, and eventually as a tool of pacification, civilization, and exploitation in the defined colonies" (2002, 57). Such uses of maps emerged from ideological shifts in early modern Europe, the period that marked the entwined beginnings of capitalism and global imperialism. The privileging of the visual and use of mathematical principles to represent geographical space enabled land to be measured and quantified, thus facilitating property claims, taxation, and resource exploitation integral to the dispossession of Indigenous peoples and the development of capitalism. Such cartographies obscured Native presence on the land. Euclidean space is empty space, devoid of social histories, and European toponymies further erased Native relationships with and, hence, claims to territories (Harley 1992, 2002). In these ways, European maps of the colonial period, in Harley's words, constituted "statements of territorial appropriation" that "helped to invent America in the European consciousness," as well as "devices by which a Native American presence could be silenced" (1992, 522, 531). As graphic renderings of Europe's global conquests and a means of "reifying power, reinforcing the status quo, and freezing social interaction within charted lines," maps remain, Harley concludes, "preeminently a language of power, not of protest" (2002, 79).

Yet, contra Harley, Native communities have used maps to assert their own territorial claims throughout the centuries of European expansion. Such maps have often escaped scholarly attention in part because many differ in form from conventional European maps. Although Indigenous maps sometimes take visual forms or have graphic dimensions, they have traditionally taken shape through narrative in a process that Indigenous geographer Margaret Wickens Pearce (1988) labels "mapping by words":

> We have historically constructed an absence of native mapping ... by examining the artifacts which, by definition, were designed to erase native landscapes and render Indians invisible.... To locate native mapping, then, we must look beyond the printed maps of colonial narratives and into the realm of daily mapping activities ... to enlarge the discussion to representations that may not be graphic.... Maps are representations that facilitate a spatial understanding, and mapping is the process of creating and interpreting these representations. (158–59)

As is the case in *Tracks,* Native spatial understandings traditionally encompass the cultural, historical, and social dimensions of territory that arguably lend themselves to expression in narrative (rather than exclusively visual) forms. Looking beyond visual maps and redefining cartography, as Pearce urges, as "representations that facilitate a spatial understanding" enables us to consider literature as a form of Native cartography,[3] as a means of representing Native understandings of land that support Indigenous territorial claims. To parse the ways in which conventional European cartography has promoted expansionist worldviews and relations of power, Harley advocates for a "literature of maps" that would use tools of literary criticism to analyze "cartographic discourse," questions of ideology, the social construction of meaning, authorship, and circulation (Harley 2002, 53). Here I advocate for a "cartography of literature" that would analyze connections between cultural representations and land conflicts in settler colonial contexts, including how Indigenous narratives represent territorial understandings that critically engage the spatial discourses of colonialism and capitalism.

In fact, such a concept of Native literature draws on long-standing Indigenous narrative traditions centered on land claims. Historically, Native protests against dispossession have merged visual and narrative forms to represent community histories on the land, the legal basis of the common law doctrine of Aboriginal title (see Cohen 1960, 274, 278). Since the 1960s, as noted in the introduction, Native communities have relied increasingly on Aboriginal title to provide legal grounds for territorial claims. Representing histories of territorial occupation has for centuries been a key purpose of Indigenous cartographies. In precontact Mesoamerica, writes art historian Barbara Mundy, communities "established their singularity and encouraged the solidarity of their members by invoking a common history" through maps that "expressed their sense of self in relation to the space they occupied" (Mundy 1996, 106). As the conquest unfolded, Indigenous peoples adapted these maps of shared histories and spatial relations to assert legal claims against European dispossession. Throughout the region, literary critic Gordon Brotherston explains, traditional literary accounts called *teoaxoxtli*, with roots in the pre-Columbia era, included maps to establish histories and boundaries of Native occupation of the land. As "political statements to defend land and home," these texts served as legal instruments throughout the twentieth century to establish Native land title (1992, 90, 83). Some Indigenous cartographies emerged as a direct response to European invasion. Beginning in the Columbian era, according to Harley, Native people developed "alternative cartographies" as a "conscious strategy of resistance" to European territorial control by providing a "record of past ownership" and "a challenge to appropriation by the colonists." Like the documents that Mundy and Brotherston describe, these "spatial histories," as Harley labels them, are generically ambiguous, drawing together visual and narrative elements, and this is one reason they have escaped cartographers' attention as maps (Harley 1992, 527–29). By representing places in terms of histories on the land, these cartographies assert an Indigenous presence that contradicts myths of "empty space" that rationalize dispossession as they also underpin Native territorial claims.

Conversely, representing history with a focus on place brings to light local events that unsettle universalist narratives, including those that justify European expansion. Conventional history, contends Paul Carter, "refer[s] neither to the place, nor the people" but construes temporal events as "evidence of a universal historical process" (Carter 2010, xvi–xvii). Taking as an example European arrival in and exploration of Australia, Carter demonstrates that narrating events as if they "unfold according to a logic of their own" creates fundamental similarities among European narratives of so-called discovery across time and place. "This kind of history," he continues, "which reduces space to a stage, that pays attention to events unfolding in time alone, might be called imperial history.... The primary object is not to understand or to interpret: it is to legitimate. This is why this history is associated with imperialism" (Carter 2010, xvi). In this passage, the theatrical metaphor of a stage is significant not only because it registers the scripted nature of imperial history but also because it brings visuality into play: the "primary logic" of imperial history is "visibility," Carter writes, the "satellite eye" that "looks down a telescope," seeing only those events that conform to the narrative of historical progress, rendering Aboriginal people invisible in the process (xv, xx). As a singular, universalist narrative, devoid of geographical or experiential particularities, imperial history "is the temporal counterpart of a Euclidean space" (xix). Carter advocates instead for "spatial histories," which he defines (as does Harley, using the same term) as accounts of historical events in particular places along with the ways that human activity itself brings places into being, a constitutive process that is necessarily cultural: "Such spatial history—history that discovers and explores the lacuna left by imperial history—begins and ends in language" (Carter 2010, xxiii). Because spatial histories are partial and particular, they open the possibility of multiple, contending histories, and they call attention to the enactments of power on material places—in colonial contexts, violence on the land (no longer reduced to a stage) and on Native bodies, including gendered bodies (no longer rendered invisible).

The Native literary texts discussed in this chapter, in my reading, constitute "spatial histories"—in other words, alternative histories and cartographies—that subvert colonial mythologies of dispossession to advance Native territorial claims.[4] I analyze two novels, Erdrich's *Tracks* (1988) and Linda Hogan's *Solar Storms* (1994), each of which thematizes both historical land conflicts and those fought out in the post-1960s era. *Tracks* tells a story about the ruinous aftermath of the 1887 General Allotment Act in an Anishinaabe community, the crucial context for the White Earth Land Settlement Act of 1985; and *Solar Storms* relates the devastation that ensued in Canadian Cree and Inuit territories in the 1970s as a result of the James Bay Hydroelectric Project, tracing this devastation to the historical ravages of the fur trade. As these novels recount the destruction that befell Native communities through dispossession, they focus especially on the brutal consequences for women, exposing gendered violence as integral to European expansion and refuting the colonial logic that equates expansion with progress.

These alternative histories are also alternative cartographies. Both novels feature colonial maps in order to scrutinize transformations of land integral to settler expansion as they call up Native narrative cartographic traditions that have historically established Indigenous claims in legal territorial disputes. The stories set colonial and Indigenous cartographic traditions against each other to limn conflicting understandings of land that pit traditional tribal life against capitalist development, so that the novels themselves constitute Indigenous cartographies. These Native understandings overturn the notion of land as object available for appropriation along with depictions of terra nullius that have rationalized dispossession. The focus on cartography shows these Native writers reckoning with the visual—in this case by using narrative to repudiate the logic of visual maps and relate stories of Native territorial occupations that constitute a process of "mapping by words." As these novels recount Native histories on the land, they use the imaginative dimensions of fiction to create an anticipatory geography. If "maps anticipated empire," in Harley's words, so that lands were "claimed on paper before they were effectively occupied" (Harley 2002, 57), these novels make visible Native occupations to recast contested lands as Indigenous territory. Whereas the colonial representations discussed in chapter 1 depict Indigenous women as acquiescing to European expansion, in *Tracks* and *Solar Storms* they appear instead as leaders of Native endeavors to defend their lands, so that the narratives draw together territorial claims with the restoration of Native women to vital social roles.

"WHO OWNS THE LAND?": LOUISE ERDRICH'S *TRACKS*

In "Who Owns the Land?," an essay published just weeks before the 1988 release of *Tracks,* Louise Erdrich and her coauthor chronicle ongoing land disputes on the White Earth Anishinaabe Reservation and their roots in colonial policies of dispossession (Erdrich and Dorris 1988). These disputes stem from the landmark Minnesota Supreme Court decision in *State v. Zay Zah* (1977), which threw into question the legality of land transfers on the White Earth Anishinaabe Reservation in the decades following the General Allotment Act. Allotment divided collectively held reservation lands into individually owned parcels with the aim of transforming Native peoples into private property owners. Assimilation policies were created to eliminate collective tribal identities and the barriers Native communities presented to the political and geographical unity of the United States. Within a few decades after its passage in 1887, the General Allotment Act caused the loss of two-thirds of Indian land. On the White Earth reservation, however, the effects were even worse. As a result of the policy, only about 7 percent of the 830,000 acres originally set aside for the reservation[5] remained in Anishinaabe possession at the time of the 1977 *Zay Zah* decision (Meyer 1994, 229). Most of the losses had stemmed from illegal tax forfeitures and fraudulent sales in the aftermath of allotment, when federal and local governments colluded with lumber companies to dispossess the Anishinaabe and strip the reservation of its rich timber resources, actions that one historian characterizes as "the corporate terrorism of the pine cartel" (Youngbear-Tibbetts 1991, 97). By calling into question the legal grounds for these land losses, the *Zay Zah* decision reopened the issue of land title in legal conflicts that intensified during the 1980s when Erdrich penned *Tracks*.[6] In "Who Owns the Land?" Erdrich writes that the origin of these land disputes "is buried in history and local politics," a "nightmare [that] began with the General Allotment Act" and encompassed "swindling" on the part of a lumber baron. Events of those years turned into "a land-grab orgy so outrageous that to this day local people ... speak of it with a sense of bewildered shame." Despite the economic and social ruin that consequently overtook the tribe, in their "collective memory," says Erdrich, "the land [is] theirs" (Erdrich and Dorris 1988, 54, 34–35).

The first historical novel among Erdrich's writings, *Tracks* fictionalizes the ruinous aftermath of the General Allotment Act and takes up the question of "who owns the land" by bringing to light buried historical injustices at the root of contemporary conflicts.[7] *Tracks* is the first part of a story told in a tetralogy of novels—the others are *The Beet Queen*, *Love Medicine*, and *The Bingo Palace*—that together tell the stories of an Anishinaabe community through the twentieth century as they endure assimilation policies in the wake of military conquest. Each novel in the tetralogy centers on a single element, and in *Tracks* that element is earth, underscoring the significance of land in the story that unfolds throughout the series. The novel invokes the community's long history on and treaty rights to the land (1), along with land-based practices (hunting, fishing, gathering) and the spiritual beliefs that inhere in the place. For these reasons, land loss has sweeping economic and social consequences that plague characters throughout the tetralogy who struggle to reconstruct their community and regain their territory. *Tracks* begins in 1912, twenty-five years after the passage of the General Allotment Act (discussed in chapter 1), when allottees gained full title to land previously held in trust and so were now subject to property taxes. These changes caused massive land losses even beyond those that resulted from the allotment process itself.[8] The social significance of land becomes clear in the story as the community falls into disarray because of its loss, driven by poverty and starvation to acts that fracture the tribe and weaken its traditions. As it lays bare the expansionist interests at the heart of assimilation policies, *Tracks* reveals the injustice and devastations of land loss to counter the notion of assimilation as progress, the premise of Carter's "imperial histories." At the same time, these Indigenous histories on the land contradict colonial representations of "empty space," replacing them instead with the sacred, experiential, and historical dimensions of land integral to Native territorial claims.

The story begins when an epidemic shatters the community. "We started dying before the snow," relates Nanapush, one of the novel's two narrators, "and like the snow, we continued to fall." In *Tracks*, the ravages of disease are part of a broader pattern of destruction that includes removal, land loss, and government control. "For those who survived the spotted sickness from the south," Nanapush continues, "our long fight west to Nadouissioux land where we signed the treaty, and then a wind from the east, bringing exile in a storm of government papers, what descended from the north in 1912 seemed impossible" (Erdrich 1988, 1). The year 1912 marks the arrival of a new epidemic as well as the imposition of property taxes on allotments. Together, these forces devastate the community and bring about further catastrophes that likewise center on land. As the epidemic wanes, the community falls into disarray. Widespread deaths weaken the ties that bind the tribe together—"our tribe unraveled like a course rope," Nanapush laments, "frayed at either end as the old and new among us were taken" (2). Crushing poverty worsens community divisions and drives tribal members to desperate choices, such as selling allotments for food, while newly imposed taxes cause even more losses. "The land will be sold and measured," Nanapush predicts in the opening chapter, "every year there are more who come looking for profit, who draw lines across the land with their strings and yellow flags" (8–9). So it is, and *Tracks* traces the anguished process that pits tribal members against one another and ultimately culminates in the near dissolution of the community as more and more land slips away. Land loss also precipitates social changes integral to capitalism, including the imposition of wage labor and the transformation of subsistence practices into commercial activities that, in turn, further erode traditional social structures and practices. But throughout the novel, Erdrich tempers this narrative of loss with one of survival by recounting the struggles of the "holdouts"—the characters, such as Nanapush and Fleur, who endeavor to retain land and community traditions. This story about persistence and survival also carries through the tetralogy and ultimately becomes as important as the one about loss.

Two characters, Nanapush and Pauline, tell the story in alternating chapters that pit the viewpoint of a "holdout" against that of an assimilationist. Through their perspectives, the novel contrasts traditional Native worldviews, including those related to land, against those of settler colonialism while drawing out their implications for the community's future. Nanapush is named for the trickster figure in Anishinaabe tradition; as such, he represents cultural continuity as well as qualities specifically connected with the trickster, including creation, healing, and subversion.[9] The assimilationist Pauline, by contrast, is associated with loss and death. Whereas Nanapush is a central figure in the tribe's history and traditions, Pauline's family is marginal, and her ties to the community grow ever more tenuous as the story progresses and she increasingly identifies with the colonizing society. "I wanted to be like my mother, who showed her half-white.... That was because even as a child I saw that to hang back was to perish. I saw through the eyes of the world outside of us. I would not speak our language" (14). At the story's end, she becomes a nun, joins the convent, and is renamed Leopolda.[10]

Throughout the novel, Pauline serves as the voice for settler colonial discourses about assimilation. The idea that "to hang back was to perish" emerged from the idea of progress, the crucial context for the General Allotment Act. But, in truth, assimilation was fundamentally tied to dispossession, as the land loss caused by allotment attests. In one sense, *Tracks* takes shape as an extended refutation of assimilation by inverting the savagism-civilization dichotomy at the center of the idea of progress. Through the conflicting stories of Nanapush and Pauline, *Tracks* draws out the ruinous effects of assimilation and instead valorizes tribal traditions. As colonial policies cause the community to "unravel like a course rope," Nanapush endeavors to bring it back together. Invoking the mode of oral tradition and its integrative function, the immediate purpose of his narrative is to reconcile his "granddaughter" Lulu with her mother, Fleur.[11] Nanapush is also a literal healer: at the novel's beginning, he saves Fleur after her immediate family had succumbed to the epidemic; later he performs a ceremony to cure her mental affliction after her second child dies, and he miraculously heals Lulu's feet after severe frostbite prompts the doctor to urge amputation. He undertakes a journey the reverse of that traveled by Pauline to the convent, fleeing the Jesuit school and rejecting Christianity: "I had a Jesuit education in the halls of Saint John before I ran back to the woods and forgot all of my prayers" (33). His story, too, becomes an instrument of cartography as he recounts the collective histories that draw the community together. Underscoring the connection between cultural traditions and endeavors to retain land, Nanapush is a resistance figure in political terms as well. "I am a holdout," he says, describing his longtime battle against dispossession, which culminates in depredations by the lumber company, "I spoke aloud the words of the government treaty [that surrendered tribal homelands], and refused to sign the settlement papers that would take away our woods and lake" (33, 2).

Pauline, by contrast, exemplifies the destructiveness of the settler colonial project.[12] Her quest to assimilate leads her away from the reservation, first to the "white town" of Argus and ultimately to the convent. Whereas the novel associates Nanapush's traditionalism with survival, Pauline's growing Christian devotion associates her with death. She assumes the task of caring for the dead and dying that is usually reserved for widows, taking pleasure in this occupation that others shun: "I handled the dead until the cold feel of their skin was a comfort, until I no longer bothered to bathe once I left the cabin but touched others with the same hands, passed death on" (Erdrich 1988, 69). She bears responsibility for several deaths in the novel, including that of Fleur's second child, and even attempts to kill her own baby during childbirth. At the story's end, in a heavily symbolic act that extends the novel's critique of Christianity, Pauline strangles her ex-lover Napoleon with her rosary beads when she imagines him to be the spirit of the lake of Anishinaabe tradition, a figure she associates with Satan. Blame for the murder falls on Fleur, and in this and other ways, Pauline works to divide the tribe even as Nanapush seeks to draw it back together. When in the final pages of *Tracks* she becomes a nun, she vows never again to set foot on the reservation. Assigned to teach in a mission school, she becomes complicit in the cultural death that assimilation policies were intended to accomplish.

By drawing out the catastrophic effects of allotment and associating assimilation with death, *Tracks* refutes the rationales for dispossession and exposes instead the expansionist interests at the heart of turn-of-the-century assimilation policies. "Land is the only thing that lasts life to life," reflects Nanapush; "[o]ur trouble came from ... never noticing how the land was snatched from under us at every step" (33, 4). From the novel's beginning, it is the lumber companies' quest for profits that impels land loss, a project buttressed by government assimilation policies. Collusion among church, capital, and the state becomes clear when the conflicts sowed by Pauline advance the land loss. When, for example, she uses love medicine to entice Eli to sexually betray Fleur, the ensuing trouble, in Nanapush's telling, "spread ... to our politics, just like that," by uniting families who favor the lumber company's purchase agreement and pitting them against the "hold-outs" (109–11). In the novel's final scenes, Fleur loses her land as much through community betrayal as through government policy. When the surveyor's crew arrives at Matchimanito, Pauline lauds its task as "the work of Christ's hand" and predicts:

> The land will be sold and divided. Fleur's cabin will tumble into the ground and be covered by leaves. The place will be haunted I suppose, but no one will have ears sharp enough to hear the Pillagers' low voices, or the vision clear to see their still shadows. The trembling old fools with their conjuring tricks will die off and the young, like Lulu and Nector, return from the government schools blinded and deafened. (204–5)

Here, Pauline repeats colonial narratives of inevitable Native demise. But throughout the novel, Pauline proves an unreliable narrator, and Erdrich's tetralogy, which is as much a story of survival as one of colonial destruction, repudiates her prediction. By telling a story about continuity despite the destructiveness brought by assimilation policies, *Tracks* undercuts the idea that Native people would inevitably disappear and their lands would fall into settlers' hands, a key rationale for dispossession.

In *Tracks*, the contest between tradition and assimilation culminates in a scene on Lake Matchimanito. Coveted by the lumber company because of its rich timber resources, Matchimanito is Pillager land, the place where their spirits roam the woods and the home of Misshepeshu, the gold-eyed spirit of the lake and a source of the Pillagers' spiritual power. The lake is, in other words, the locus of conflicting territorial understandings and claims in the novel. Unsurprisingly, then, this scene takes shape as a clash between

Anishinaabe and Christian beliefs. It rewrites the Biblical story in which Christ walks on water, one of the miracles that establishes his divinity. But whereas the Biblical story confirms Christ's power, the lake scene repudiates it. Likening herself to Christ, Pauline undertakes to convert her fellow tribal members when she paddles a leaky rowboat to the middle of the lake during a storm, attracting a crowd of stunned observers on the shore. Although she survives the perilous waves, the spectacle she creates elicits bewilderment and scorn rather than awe. Where Pauline fails, Fleur succeeds. The lake is the site where Fleur's spiritual power manifests, as when she remains submerged underwater for long periods of time, presumably to commune with Misshepeshu. Fleur's ability to walk under the water exposes Pauline's spiritual weakness when she cannot walk on top of it, and the events on the lake compel Pauline to admit that "Christ was weak, I saw now, a tame newcomer in the country... [where] God had no foothold or sway" (192).

Fleur's spiritual abilities manifest in other ways as well. Perhaps even more than Nanapush, Fleur is a "holdout," a member of the powerful Pillager family "who knew the secret ways to cure or kill" (2). At the novel's beginning, Fleur's family members have just perished in the epidemic. But, even in death, the Pillagers inspire respect and sometimes fear among the novel's characters as their spirits roam the woods surrounding Matchimanito near Fleur's home. Among other things, the Pillager spirits represent the enduring power of Anishinaabe traditional knowledge, and their presence marks the woods as sacred space, a place inhabited by Native histories on the land and the site where spiritual power is enacted. Too, the spirits disrupt the rationalism of capital, its reduction of the world to its material dimensions, along with the progressive temporality of colonialism that understands the past as distinct from the present. Fleur shares the Pillagers' abilities. "Power travels in bloodlines," in the words of the novel, "handed out before birth" (31), and throughout the story Fleur's power manifests, among other ways, in her luck with cards and in matters of love and death, including the fates that befall her enemies. Fleur's singular focus is to keep her land, so her enemies are usually those "who come looking for profit" from Anishinaabe lands, those who guided the mappers, and the surveyors "who draw lines across the land with their string and yellow flags" (9). Fleur's spiritual power and her commitment to retaining land are bound up together. When she expresses "contempt" for a map of the reservation divided into parcels paid and unpaid and insists that "the paper had no bearing or sense, as no one would be reckless enough to try collecting for land where Pillagers were buried" (174), she registers an understanding of the historical and spiritual meanings of land antithetical to the idea that it is an object to be bought, sold, and exploited for profit.

If Fleur represents Anishinaabe history and traditions in *Tracks*, her story exemplifies the effects—especially the gendered effects—of settler colonialism on Native communities. She loses her family in the epidemic and then suffers from hunger because settlers have destroyed animal populations and the epidemic leaves fewer survivors to find food. To pay taxes on Pillager land, now converted into a parcel of property, she leaves the community to find wage labor. As Christianity and colonial education transform the community, Fleur, as the holder of traditional knowledge, becomes subject to misunderstanding and derision. "She messed with evil ... dressed like a man," says Pauline, the novel's assimilationist narrator, and "studied ways we shouldn't talk about" so that she "made us frightened." For these reasons, continues Pauline, "some thought that Fleur Pillager should be driven from the reservation" (12). Fleur's story, in other words, captures the destruction and defeat brought by settler colonialism, the shattering losses of community members, land, and beliefs, losses that splinter the tribe. Her story also captures the gendered dimensions of those transformations. When Pauline says that Fleur "dressed like a man" and describes her as "haywire, out of control," (12) she expresses settler colonial expectations of Native women. Throughout the novel, and indeed through the tetralogy as a whole, she is a marginalized figure, living much of the time alone at Matchimanito, the subject of gossip and speculation. The mysteries surrounding Fleur are at the center of *Tracks*. Although she is arguably the most important character in the novel, Fleur remains voiceless, her story told by Nanapush and Pauline. Nanapush frequently admits the gaps in his narration, the parts of Fleur's story that he (and we) cannot know, and Pauline willfully misconstrues what she observes, such as when she blames her for Pauline's own violent acts. In the several Erdrich novels in which she appears, even those with multiple narrators, Fleur never tells her own story. The text thus constructs a protagonist who is the source of power and authority yet remains incapable of speaking. In this way, Erdrich's novel makes legible the silences and erasures of Indigenous women in colonial contexts along with the social dynamics that marginalize them.

Tracks' scrutiny of the colonial reordering of gender and its connection to dispossession culminates in a pivotal scene early in the novel when Fleur is raped. In this scene, Fleur moves temporarily away from the reservation to the "white town" of Argus, where she works in a slaughterhouse to earn money to pay newly imposed property taxes on her family's land. In this respect, her story iterates histories of Indigenous dislocation and removals to urban centers, including the consequent vulnerability of Native women to violence (see chapter 3). The town's geography discloses the connections among capital, church, and the state in Indigenous dispossession, as well as the understanding of land on which it is premised. The church steeple, visible from afar, draws Fleur to the town, its streets laid out on a grid on either side of the railroad depot, streets where stores compete for trade and churches compete for souls. The local priest directs her to the slaughterhouse to find work, and there she supplements her wages by joining a nightly (white) men's poker game. The men regard Fleur in ways that exemplify the devaluing of women, especially Native women in colonial contexts: they "only saw her in the flesh," disbelieving that "a woman could be smart enough to play cards" (Erdrich 1988, 18, 21). But Fleur thwarts these expectations and, astonishingly, wins exactly one dollar at the end of each night, a puzzle that prompts the men to up the ante. When Fleur wins big, the men retaliate by gang raping her and driving her back to the reservation. *Tracks* casts the rape scene as part of the colonial dispossession and violence scrutinized by the novel. When the men rape Fleur, they are retaliating because she both defies patriarchal expectations of women and endeavors to win money to retain her land. In the story, the rape is an act of ruthless violence that is at once an outcome of colonial policies designed to appropriate Native lands (allotment, taxation, deliberate impoverishment) and an act of dispossession in itself (because the men brutalize Fleur for earning money for property taxes). The rape scene, in other words, depicts gendered violence as the outcome of settler colonial practices of dispossession as well as the very paradigm of those practices. At the same time, the scene (set in the early 1900s) reflects on removals of Native women to urban spaces because of economic desperation, a problem that escalated through the twentieth century, and the ways that these women have disproportionately fallen victim to violence (see chapter 3). In figuring the "white town" as a space of ruthless violence exemplified by the rape of a Native woman, the novel, in this scene too, overturns the distinction between savagery and civilization that rationalizes assimilation.[13]

The rape scene both exposes the gendered brutality of dispossession and challenges the gendered logic of settler colonialism. Here the novel calls up a history of colonial representations to invert their meanings. Not only do the rapists see Fleur only "in the flesh," thus reiterating the persistent sexualization of Native women, but she also wears a green dress likened to "a skin of lakeweed," a description that recalls the conflation of Indigenous women with the natural world (22). As the men wait for Fleur to finish work so the card game can begin, she leans over a vat of boiling heads, turning the skulls with a wooden paddle. Although these are animal heads (she works in a slaughterhouse), the image recalls that of the women cannibals in Stradanus's *Allegory of America* (discussed in chapter 1), who also attend to steaming flesh as a mark of their savagery. The scene, in other words, summons a visual iconography that sexualizes Native women, links them with subordinated nature, and thus registers their inherent inferiority and availability for possession. But *Tracks* invokes this iconography to interrupt its conventional meanings. Fleur does not surrender to the men but instead flees from and then fights the rapists while crying out for help. In this instance the novel calls attention to the voice of this mute figure without recounting her words (this is Pauline's narration), thus underscoring the dynamic of silencing that threads through the story.

Nor does the novel reduce the rape to allegory ("rape of the land"). By rendering the event in painful detail, the novel ties the rape to material situations of Native women under settler colonialism. Further, in the context of settler colonial discourse that conflates the ostensible availability of Native women's bodies with the availability of land, the scene recursively calls into question this rationale for Indigenous dispossession. If Fleur's character repudiates settler colonial discourses about Native women, so too does the natural world defy its objectification and reduction to a grid, the mathematization of space that is the work of surveyors in the novel. In the aftermath of the rape, a tornado devastates much of the town of Argus, leaving two of the rapists dead and another gravely disabled. The language in the scene is agential: the low-hanging clouds "became a delicate proving thumb," shaking the slaughterhouse "as if a huge hand was pinched at the rafters," until "a shrill scream" gathered and "at last spoke plain" (27). This passage emphasizes not only agency but also voice, so that the scene gestures to other conceptions of women, land, and their interconnections that are suppressed by the settler colonial processes recounted throughout the novel.

The rape scene anticipates the culmination of the struggle for Matchimanito at the novel's conclusion. Beyond its spiritual meanings, Matchimanito is the spatial and thematic center of the novel: the entire story revolves around the lake, and in each chapter, its characters journey to and from Fleur's cabin; the land, as we have already seen, is imbued with the collective histories and traditional spiritual beliefs of the community, and it is sought by both the lumber company and a developer who envisions it as a resort property. Matchimanito, in other words, is the site where Indigenous meanings of land come into conflict with the forces of capital and the settler colonial nation-state. As Pillager spirits patrol the boundaries of the place, the gold-eyed spirit Misshepeshu, many believe, causes the drowning deaths of those who cross Fleur, especially surveyors and government agents with designs on the land. "Pillager land was not ordinary land to buy and sell" (175), Nanapush insists, and *Tracks* bears out his contention by representing Matchimanito as a place of spiritual presence and power. Nevertheless, Matchimanito is lost in the end. When lumber company workers arrive to expel Fleur from Pillager land, she confronts an unknown fate with nowhere to call home and, out of desperation, sends her daughter Lulu to boarding school. But, even in this moment of desolation, she is far from helpless. In a parallel to the tornado's destruction of Argus, Fleur causes the trees to collapse on the lumber workers, pinning men and their carts under the weight of huge oaks. It would be possible to interpret the loss of Matchimanito as somber corroboration of Pauline's prediction that "the land will be sold and divided ... no one will have ears sharp enough to hear the Pillagers' low voices ... [and] the young ... [will] return from the government schools blinded and deafened" (204–5). But the final scene tempers this sense of loss by affirming Fleur's power and the agency of the land. It also overtly contradicts Pauline's prediction when, on the novel's final page, Lulu returns home from boarding school, her orange dress (the clothing of runaways) showing her persistent rebelliousness.[14] This promise plays itself out in subsequent novels[15] when the adult Lulu—significantly, a female character—follows in the footsteps of Nanapush and Fleur by herself becoming a "holdout."[16]

The end of *Tracks*, in other words, is the beginning of a story of ongoing land conflicts that unfolds throughout Erdrich's work and still rages throughout Native America. By revealing the destructiveness and ultimate failure of policies such as allotment, *Tracks* traces an alternative history of the assimilation era that overturns the universalist narrative of progress and protests settler colonial nation-building and resource exploitation on Native lands. By telling a story of Native histories on the land that culminate in survival, the novel engages in a process of "mapping by words" that answers the question of "who owns the land" in conflicts over territory and political control that remain ongoing. The past and present of colonial territorial conflicts, and the conflicting understandings of space at their center, are also the subject of Linda Hogan's *Solar Storms*. Like *Tracks*, Hogan's novel thematizes colonial cartography as a means to contrast Indigenous and settler spatial understandings and draw out their implications for territorial conflicts. *Solar Storms* also elaborates on the lethal connections between dispossession and gendered violence, and it offers a vision of resistance that centers Indigenous women in political transformation.

"THE TERRITORIES AND TRICKS AND LIES OF HISTORY": CARTOGRAPHY IN LINDA HOGAN'S *SOLAR STORMS*

Whereas *Tracks* takes as its subject dispossession at the turn of the twentieth century and its present-day aftermath, Hogan's novel centers on a contemporary conflict with deep historical roots. *Solar Storms* is a fictional rendering of the catastrophe that occurred in Canada when, in the early 1970s, the Hydro-Québec utility corporation diverted rivers flowing into James Bay to construct a massive hydroelectric project. The dams flooded traditional territories of Cree and Inuit communities, violating treaty rights, displacing entire communities, and destroying sacred sites. As rising waters submerged thousands of square miles of Native land, they drowned the animals on which the communities depended. "A project of this kind," explains Matthew Coon Come, grand chief of the Grand Council of the Crees, "involves the destruction and rearrangement of a vast landscape, literally reshaping the geography of the land. This is what I want you to understand: it is not a dam. It is a terrible and vast reduction of our entire world" (cited in Hellegers 2015, 1). The dam construction ignited a struggle between Indigenous groups and the Canadian government that continued for decades. *Solar Storms* presents the James Bay conflict as the most recent episode of European expansion in the north, showing that historical events such as explorers' journeys and the fur trade form "the old roots of these new events" (Hogan 1994, 301). In drawing these connections, Hogan's novel, in one critic's words, traces the "intergenerational life of capital" by "representing hydropower projects like James Bay I as an *effect* or culmination of capital—and political power—accumulated by corporations through Indigenous trade with Europeans" (Hellegers 2015, 2).[17]

Through the theme of cartography,[18] the novel limns the understandings that give rise to such exploitation of the land. "The Europeans called this world dangerous," reflects narrator and protagonist Angel Wing; "their legacy, I began to understand, had been the removal of spirit from everything"

(Hogan 1994, 180). As her story unfolds, Angel comes to view her homeland as "storied land, land where deities walked, where people traveled" (177)—in other words, as geographies of the sacred and lived experience. As the novel sets capitalist and colonial notions of land against traditional Indigenous understandings, it also illuminates how the destruction brought by the dam inevitably shatters Native communities, thus overturning the dominant view of the dam as "progress." In the histories traced in *Solar Storms*, the ravages of colonialism entail marginalizing and brutalizing Indigenous women, and this connection between dispossession and gendered violence underlies the Indigenous political project that takes shape at the novel's end.

At the novel's beginning, the teenaged protagonist Angel returns to her childhood home of Adam's Rib after traumatic years spent in foster homes. Her return is, in part, an endeavor to understand her own past, especially why she was sent away—"I wanted an unbroken line between me and the past," she explains (77)—and to uncover the mystery of the deep scars that mar her face. Soon after Angel's return to Adam's Rib, the elderly Dora-Rouge, Angel's great-great-grandmother, announces her wish to return to her home community in the North (Inuit territory) to die, and meanwhile, messengers from that area arrive to warn that flooding from newly constructed dams will soon devastate the land. Three women characters—Angel, Agnes (Dora-Rouge's daughter and Angel's great-grandmother), and Bush (Angel's adoptive grandmother)—accompany Dora-Rouge on a journey to her birthplace that entwines the novel's major themes. Paralleling Dora-Rouge's return home, Angel is drawn north in hopes of finding her mother, Hannah, who had abandoned her when she was an infant, while Bush wishes to join Native protests against the dams. Agnes accompanies them to care for her mother, Dora-Rouge. Through these relationships, the novel reconstructs intergenerational relationships among Native women and matriarchal kinship structures suppressed under colonialism. As the story unfolds, the women's journey brings together quests for identity, belonging, history, and political transformation, processes that all ultimately center on land.

By taking a water journey as its theme, *Solar Storms* reprises a dominant motif in the literature of imperialism, exemplified most famously by Joseph Conrad's 1899 *Heart of Darkness*. In Conrad's novella, the protagonist, Marlow, describes his boyhood "passion for maps," how he would "lose himself in all the glories of exploration" by studying the "blank spaces ... that looked particularly inviting on a map," vowing that "when I grow up I will go there" (Conrad 2008, 108). Lured by the "blank spaces" of colonial cartography, Marlow commences a river journey to the heart of Africa that reiterates tropes of savagery in historical explorers' narratives. The voyage motif, writes Edward Said, has historically played a prominent role in the "battle over projections and ideological images" of the colonized world, as explorers' narratives have represented desired territories as empty or untamed spaces requiring European control. (In this respect, such narratives play a role in expansion akin to that of landscape painting, discussed in chapter 4.) Consequently, voyages also constitute a common theme in literary critiques of imperialism, where they serve as a means of "reinscription," a "reclamation of fictive territory," and a "cultural effort to claim a restored and reinvigorated authority over the region" (Said 1994, 210, 212).

So it is in *Solar Storms*. Following the ancient maps of explorers, the women's journey north takes shape, in one sense, as a journey back in time that retraces European explorers' routes and brings to light the devastation that ensued from their arrival: the human and animal lives lost and environmental destruction brought by colonizers' relentless quest for wealth. (In Conrad's novella, too, Marlow's journey uncovers the brutality of imperialism, one meaning of "heart of darkness" in his story.) In *Solar Storms*, colonial violence entails gendered violence (an issue frequently overlooked in anti-imperial critiques, including those by Said), and Angel comes to understand the scars that mark her own body as emerging from the same histories that scarred the land. Thus commences a journey of transformation that entails cultural and political awakening. "My own people," Angel realizes, "had lived there [in the area of the dams] forever, for more than ten thousand years, and had been sustained by these lands that were now being called empty and useless" (Hogan 1994, 58). Traveling to her ancestral lands over ancient waterways, Angel learns from her grandmothers how her people had always lived in these places, along with the songs and stories that made them meaningful. This knowledge in turn catalyzes political transformation as the characters join the fight to reclaim their land, a narrative turn that fictionalizes Indigenous resistance to the James Bay project.

In *Solar Storms*, as in *Tracks*, colonial maps embody a colonial spatiality that renders land "empty and useless," a mere object for exploitation. To facilitate their use "as statements of territorial appropriation," as "devices by which a Native American presence could be silenced," argues Harley, maps have served as tools in the "the destruction of [Indigenous] names" and "the redescription of an anciently settled landscape." Through these processes, maps have constituted "part of a wider colonial discourse, one that helped to render Indian peoples invisible in their own land" (Harley 1992, 522; Harley 2002, 181, 188). Such maps, which reduce land to two-dimensional space devoid of history and cultural meanings, reflect the Enlightenment preoccupation with scientific rationalism. During this era, shifts in geographical thought, as geographer R. D. K. Herman describes them, entailed "the removal of any 'spiritual' aspect of the world—that is, a reduction of the world into pure mechanistic materiality," and this "bifurcation of humanity and nature poses a conceptual distance and detachment that allows for the commodification of the material world essential for capitalism" (Herman 2008, 74). In *Solar Storms*, when Angel, Dora-Rouge, Agnes, and Bush commence their journey north, they follow ancient maps created by European explorers that exemplify these traits. These are "incredible topographies, the territories and tricks and lies of history," created by "men possessed with the spoils of this land" whose legacy was "the removal of spirit from everything." As such, these maps erase "people [and] animal lives" as well as "the carnage" brought about by European settlement and the establishment of the fur trade (Hogan 1994, 122–23, 180). Three hundred years later, the hydroelectric proposal similarly represents land through "their figures, their measurements, and ledgers" as a "flat, two-dimensional world" (279), with the worth of all things assessed in "numbers, dollars, grams" (343). The undertaking exposes the collusion of colonialism and capitalism: "government and corporation officials . . . were clearly in cahoots and would go to unethical lengths to get what they wanted" (279). These correspondences between historical and contemporary cartographies underscore the continuities between early European exploration and the hydroelectric project, both facilitated by capitalist-colonial spatiality.

As the women follow the ancient routes and maps of explorers, their story unravels the colonial myths and spatialities that rationalize settler territorial claims. "We were undoing the routes of explorers," ruminates Angel, "taking apart the advance of commerce, narrowing down and distilling the truth out of history." Whereas colonial maps suppress history to depict vacant land available for appropriation ("their history had been emptied of us" [280]), "the waterways," in the novel's account, "had a history" (176, 21). Often carried in oral narratives rather than official documents, this history testifies both to an ongoing Indigenous presence and to obscured historical violence. Angel recalls, for instance, the story of the Indigenous woman who first encountered white men in the territory and saw "the wind-filled sails of [their] graceful boat of death," a "tormented world . . . its true cargo." Little did she know then that because of their arrival, "beloved children would be mutilated, women cut open and torn, that strong, brave men would die, and that even their gods would be massacred" (168). In the story, the waterways themselves bear evidence of the "French trappers and traders who emptied the land of beaver and fox" and whose "boats carried precious tons of fur to the trading post" (21), a history registered in the toponymy "Fur Island." In Native mapping practices, according to Margaret Wickens Pearce, toponyms typically refer to people who occupy the land, the ways they use it, or events that occurred in that place (M. W. Pearce 1988, 159). Reprising these traditions, place-names throughout *Solar Storm* are "like layers of time" (65) that make histories legible, including those of violence. Poison Road recalls the slaughter of wild animals by European settlers (historically, the slaughter caused widespread starvation among the James Bay Cree), whereas Bone Island, in another invocation of an historical event, holds the remains of victims of epidemics that annihilated entire Native communities (Hogan 1994, 24, 196). As the novel unravels settler narratives that erase Indigenous people, it exposes the "savagery of civilization" (65), the violence on the land that belies the ideological justification of expansion as progress.

In the novel's telling, land and Native women's bodies are twin sites of colonial violence. At the story's beginning, Angel returns to Adam's Rib, a name that signifies the denigration of Indigenous women in the historical context of the fur trade: "The first women at Adam's Rib had called themselves the Abandoned Ones. Born of the fur trade . . . [they had] traveled down with French fur trappers who were seeking their fortunes from the land. When the land was worn out, the beaver and wolf gone, mostly dead, the men moved on to what hadn't yet been destroyed, leaving their women and children behind, as if they too were used-up animals" (28). Here *Solar Storms* connects the worldview that understands land as an object for exploitation with the one that sees women as useless and disposable. As the place-name Adam's Rib also registers the feminization of land in colonial contexts, it implicates Christianity in the entanglements of gendered and colonial violence by invoking the Biblical story in which Adam gains dominion over the earth and over Eve. The place-names in turn links this Biblical story to that of the town, its houses built by missionaries and its main street (Poison Road) named for acts of destruction. This connection threads through the novel as women's bodies, like the land itself, are physically marked by colonial violence.

As Angel learns her peoples' history, she comes to understand the role of such violence in her own past. Agnes tells her about meeting the young

Loretta, who would later marry Agnes's son and become Angel's grandmother, and how her body, like the land, was scarred and poisoned:

> Loretta smelled of something sweet, an almond odor that I couldn't place until years later.... When I finally placed the odor, when I knew it was cyanide, I knew who she was, what people she came from. She came from the Elk Islanders, the people who became so hungry they ate the poisoned carcasses of deer that the settlers left out for the wolves.... The curse on that poor girl's life came from watching the desperate people of her tribe die.... After that, when she was still a girl, she'd been taken and used by men who fed her and beat her and forced her. (38–39)

Paralleling the commodification of land, Loretta was sold into prostitution, underscoring integral connections between gendered violence and exploitation of Native lands. Because of her experiences of torture, Loretta becomes "the one who hurt others" (39), and the story of her daughter Hannah (another Biblical name) repeats her own. When Hannah appears as a young child at Adam's Rib, she too exudes the smell of cyanide, a smell "deeper than skin... blood-deep... history-deep," and "her skin was a garment of scars," of "burns and incisions," the "signatures of torturers" (40, 99). Her body is "a battleground," a place where "time and history and genocide" meet—a description that resonates with the disputed territory in the story (99, 101). Angel's body, too, is marked and scarred, some of the wounds inflicted by her mother, Hannah. Emphasizing the link between gendered violence and territorial expansion, Angel realizes that "my beginning was Hannah's beginning, one of broken lives, gone animals, trees felled.... Our beginnings were intricately bound up in the history of the land... in the nooks of America" (39, 96).

As the women's journey progresses north, the novel engages in dual projects of remapping the land and redefining the social places of Indigenous women. Following the routes of explorers and fur traders, the women's itinerary brings to light the violent past and the ways current events repeat it. The women encounter not only evidence of historical destruction but also its repetition in the present, such as miners' frenzied search for Spanish silver at a trading post and, most centrally, the devastation brought by the dam. But, even as the journey calls up long histories of colonial destruction, it also "undo[es] the routes of explorers, tak[es] apart the advance of commerce" (176) by recovering the land's sacred meanings. Maps, declares Dora-Rouge, "are only masks over the face of God. There are other ways around the world"

(138). And, indeed, her own memory of the water routes proves more reliable than the map created by explorers. Eventually the explorers' map crumbles in Bush's hands, and the women uncover "a deeper map," the "map inside ourselves" drawn from "the old ways, the way we used to live" as remembered by Dora-Rouge (123, 17). This alternative spatiality revives the "ancient pact... humans had once made with animals" and recognizes "the world was alive and that all creatures were God" (139). Angel's transformation entails, among other things, learning the traditional uses of plants, their sacred meanings and curative applications, and the novel likens her drawings of them to "a map awaiting creation" (171).

By likening plant knowledge to cartography, the novel gestures to mapping projects by Indigenous communities in the North that began in the 1970s, the time frame of the story, to establish legal claims to land. During this era, the Canadian government initiated "use and occupancy studies" to establish the legitimacy of Aboriginal title. As in the James Bay dispute, these most often took shape as mapping projects that documented, through participation by Indigenous people, traditional uses of territories, place names, and subsistence and cultural practices. Such mapping projects provided powerful tools for legal claims to ancestral lands and securing continued use. Yet, in Canada and across the globe, such studies have neglected the gendered nature of land use, often documenting men's activities while leaving women "weakly represented" (Chapin, Lamb, and Threlkeld 2005, 630; see also D. Rose 1996). Such neglect calls for "countermaps" that document women's knowledge and uses of Indigenous lands to secure their own territorial rights and access to resources (see, for example, Rocheleau et al., 1995). A narrative thread in *Solar Storms* centers on plant knowledge (women's knowledge) in a way that resonates with such use and occupancy studies. Guided by Dora-Rouge, whose mother had been an "herb woman" (Hogan 1994, 171), Angel learns the medicinal uses of plants, and the narrative includes descriptions, sometimes drawings, of the plants and specifies their locations. In this way, too, *Solar Storms* constitutes a "countermap" by establishing women's histories on, uses of, and thus claims to Indigenous territories.

But in the novel, such Native uses of the land are threatened by changes brought by the dam. These changes expose another shortcoming of maps: their representation of land as inert and unchanging. "The cartographers thought if they mapped [the land], everything would remain the same," Angel reflects, "but it didn't... change was the one thing not accounted for." Like *Tracks*, Hogan's novel depicts land as agential, as "defiant land" that "had its own will" and "refused to be shaped by the makers of maps," in turn making it "difficult for them to claim title" (123). The story calls up this understanding when Dora-Rouge negotiates with the spirit of the water (interpreted by some critics as a manifestation of Misshepeshu, the spirit of the water described in *Tracks*[19]) to allow the women safe passage on their journey. Here and throughout the novel, the focus on water is significant: beyond exhibiting agency, water is an entity that cannot be bounded, easily controlled, or legally possessed. Change of another kind—change brought by colonial destruction—marks the women's journey as well. When they finally arrive at Dora-Rouge's birthplace, they find her childhood home obliterated. The place had been flooded by the hydroelectric project, with homes, landmarks, and animals disappeared, leaving the people "despondent" so that "in some cases, they had to be held back from killing themselves" (225). Here *Solar Storms* underscores interdependencies of the people and the land, so that "the devastation and ruin that had fallen over the land fell over the people, too," who "wept without end," and even "young children drank alcohol and sniffed glue," with no remedy for their grief because the healing plants had been destroyed (226). Angel likewise finds only disappointment on her arrival, as her mother, Hannah, shuns her and then dies soon after they meet. In this way, *Solar Storms* departs from an earlier generation of Native American novels by refusing the notion of a return to origins as restoration and reintegration.

Although return does not figure here as restoration, neither does it signal defeat. Instead, the specter of devastated land brings another transformation, this one related to political subjectivity. As the story presents an alternative spatiality, a notion of land as sacred that disputes claims of capital and the state, it marks out a central place for Indigenous women in political resistance. The novel counters colonial erasures of Indigenous women by making Angel, Bush, and Dora-Rouge (who survives until after her return home, though Agnes dies during the journey) the leaders in the fight against the dam. The women become enraged by the devastation and injustice, as well as by the media silence surrounding the effects of the hydroelectric project. Countering the colonial silencing of Indigenous women, Bush becomes a journalist whose stories and photographs find a place in national newspapers, while Angel testifies to the devastation of the dams on a radio program. Both events make the dam's devastation visible and draw support for the resistance. As the police grow ever more menacing, the women position themselves between armed soldiers and the homes that they threaten. Dora-Rouge, seated in her wheelchair, places herself on the railroad tracks as part of a blockade of the dam builders' supplies. Angel, taking a lesson from stories about wolverines, sabotages the workers' food supplies, making it difficult for them to remain in the area. The process of resistance helps unify the affected communities, just as it did in the actual James Bay conflict and, in this way, counters the fragmentation and brokenness brought by colonialism. In the novel, the community wins a victory against the dam, however partial, when a court halts construction of the dam project, but only after it has destroyed entire communities, including the houses at Adam's Rib. (Here, too, the novel roughly follows the historical conflict, though Indigenous activists won a more limited victory in the form of the 1975 James Bay and Northern Québec agreement, the first modern Canadian treaty with Native nations.)

By concluding with a scene centered on Indigenous women's voice and activism, *Solar Storms* inverts colonial narratives about Native women's complicity in conquest. It underscores this critique by gesturing to the ways that such notions have been internalized even by Native communities themselves to the detriment of Native women. In this scene, young Native men grow suspicious of Bush, mistaking her endeavor to protect the elderly Dora-Rouge from police violence for complicity with the dam builders. Alluding to the male-dominated activism of the 1970s (the period of the James Bay conflict), Hogan writes that it was "the young men who were quickest to accuse her... the ones from the city, the ones of uncertain identity who had names and categories for themselves, who wore braids" and admired masculinist aggressiveness rather than the quiet dignity of traditional leaders (316–17). If the settler colonial history traced by *Solar Storms* connects the exploitation of Native women and the exploitation of Native land, it follows that such connections must in turn underlie a genuinely anticolonial project. In the words of Indigenous activist Elsie B. RedBird, "If the erosion of sovereignty comes from disempowering women, its renewed strength will come from reempowering them" (RedBird 1995, 135). By foregrounding links between gendered violence and dispossession and then drawing out the implications for Indigenous politics, *Solar Storms* anticipates the contemporary era of Indigenous women's activism centered on gendered violence and resource extraction on Native lands, campaigns that are waged in part in the realm of culture.

. . .

In 2012, Louise Erdrich published *The Round House*, a novel that reads like a sequel to *Tracks* in that it illuminates connections between dispossession and sexual violence against Indigenous women in contemporary contexts. The story takes place a century after the passage of the General Allotment Act, the subject of *Tracks*, and like the earlier novel, it draws out the ongoing gendered effects of allotment on an Anishinaabe reservation near the fictional town of Argus, North Dakota. The novel opens with the brutal rape and attempted murder of Geraldine Coutts, tribal enrollment officer and wife of a tribal judge. The story about what happened—what brought Geraldine to the site of the rape, who attacked her, and why—unfolds as a mystery, disclosed piece by piece, that ultimately reveals the multiple ways the assault is embedded in ongoing settler colonization, especially land loss. As Erdrich explains in the afterword, she drew inspiration for the novel from alarmingly high rates of violence against Native women and legal barriers to prosecuting these crimes. In Geraldine's story, as in the real-life events that inspired it, the rape results from histories of dispossession along with other practices of colonial control. I conclude this chapter with a brief discussion of *The Round House* to call attention to the contemporary consequences for Native women of the spatial histories recounted in *Tracks* and *Solar Storms* and to set the stage for an analysis of Indigenous women artists' responses to the current crisis surrounding missing and murdered Indigenous women and girls (the subject of chapter 3).

Connections among women's bodies, land, and colonial power, particularly as they come to bear on law, drive Geraldine's story. "What needs to be emphasized about European invasion and colonization of the Americas," explains Eric Cheyfitz, "is that it began and continues under the name of law" (2004, ix). This holds true in *The Round House*, and the rape comes about in part because of jurisdictional problems that emerged in the aftermath of the General Allotment Act. As allotment enabled settlers and corporations to acquire reservation territory, the consequent checkerboard pattern of land ownership created a maze of jurisdictional problems that increased Native peoples' vulnerability to violence. Tribal, state, federal, and private land each fall under different jurisdictional authority, sometimes depending on the racial identities of the parties in the conflict (tribes have little or no legal authority over non-Native people, even on reservation land), and tribal legal authority in general remains limited. The limits on tribal jurisdiction bear on a range of crimes, but "the problem is greatest in the realm of sexual violence," explains legal scholar N. Bruce Duthu, "because rapes and other sexual assaults on American Indian women are overwhelmingly interracial," and so these crimes fall outside tribes' prosecutorial authority (2008, A17). As a result, sexual predators target Native women on reservations, knowing that they will likely face no consequences.

In *The Round House*, the rapist Linden Lark learns about the limits of tribal jurisdiction on the reservation and women's consequent vulnerability, and this emboldens him to attack Geraldine. The assault takes place at the round house, where state, federal, and tribal lands converge. The place, then, represents the long history of colonial dispossession as well as the diminishment of Native sovereignty, because here tribal legal powers, such as they are, come into conflict with those of state and federal governments. The novel cites the litany of legal cases—from the Marshall Trilogy to *Lone Wolf v. Hitchcock* to *Tee-Hit-Ton* (Erdrich 2012, 228–29)—that have advanced Indigenous dispossession and political disempowerment, threads that come together in the rape. Understanding the loopholes created by conflicting legal jurisdiction, Lark blindfolds Geraldine so that she is unaware of the location where the rape takes place, making the crime impossible to prosecute. In the story, then, Geraldine's rape is a consequence of histories of dispossession that also preclude the possibility of legal accountability in the aftermath of the violence. But the round house, the site of the rape, is significant for another reason as well. As the place for performing traditional ceremonies, it is a sacred place ordained as "the body of [our] mother" (214), its beginnings entwined with the origins of the tribe. The resonance with Geraldine, the primary mother figure in the novel, is unmistakable, so that the rape constitutes a violation of cultural traditions and an assault on the community itself. The rape, in other words, is not merely a *consequence* of historical assaults on land, culture, and political power but rather *the very paradigm* of ongoing colonial power enacted through gendered violence.

Together, *Tracks*, *Solar Storms*, and *The Round House* trace the entwined histories of dispossession and gendered violence that find roots in the earliest years of European expansion, extend through the assimilation era (the period of allotment), and manifest in violence against Indigenous women in the present day. As this violence has drawn increasingly widespread attention over the past two decades, it has also become an even more prominent theme in Indigenous women's culture. In the following chapter, I analyze Indigenous women artists' responses to the 2002 arrest and 2007 trial of serial murderer Robert Pickton in Vancouver, British Columbia, one of the first events to call widespread public attention to what has become known as the crisis of missing and murdered Indigenous women and girls (#MMIWG). Like Erdrich and Hogan, these artists demand attention to gendered violence along with its roots in ongoing dispossession as they create images of Indigenous women that challenge dominant media coverage and popular understandings rooted in colonial representations. But, whereas Erdrich and Hogan dispute dominant representations of Indigenous land and bodies by refuting the logic of the visual, these artists use visual forms to protest violence against Indigenous women and the histories in which it is embedded. In so doing, they endeavor to interrupt dominant visual iconographies (discussed in chapter 1) by transforming Indigenous women's bodies from figures of submission to figures of protest. At the same time, these artists draw on the imaginative possibilities of culture to lay a path toward a more just future for Indigenous women and Indigenous communities as a whole.

THREE

Scenes from the Fringe

GENDERED VIOLENCE AND THE GEOGRAPHIES OF INDIGENOUS FEMINISM

In 2007, in the wake of the most notorious serial murders in Canadian history, a photograph of a wounded female body appeared on a billboard in downtown Montreal. Anishinaabe artist Rebecca Belmore created the image, titled *Fringe*, in response to the arrest of Robert Pickton and his confession to killing forty-nine women, more than any other serial murderer in Canadian history (fig. 8). Pickton had sought his victims on Vancouver's impoverished Downtown Eastside, an area described in media accounts as "streets of fear" (MacQueen 2002), a "version of hell populated by prostitutes, drug addicts and pimps" (D. Brown 2004), a space of violence and death. Such descriptions naturalize the violence that occurs in impoverished neighborhoods, attributing it to the degeneracy of the inhabitants and the inevitable perils of life on the street (Jiwani and Young 2006).[1] This explains in part why the disappearances of Native women initially drew little public attention and long went uninvestigated by police. When Pickton was finally arrested, more than a decade after his first murder, the event prompted an international media spectacle because of the number of killings and their brutality. As lurid details came to light, the crimes appeared to be the deviant work of a psychopath with no connections to structural violence. Outside Indigenous communities, few noticed that as many as half of Pickton's victims were Aboriginal, even though Aboriginal people represent only about 3 percent of the total population of Vancouver.

Yet the overrepresentation of Aboriginal women was no accident. Conversations surrounding gendered violence—including those in the #MeToo movement—often presuppose that women's vulnerability cuts across boundaries of race and class. But Indigenous women in Canada and the United States fall prey to violence at far higher rates than women in any

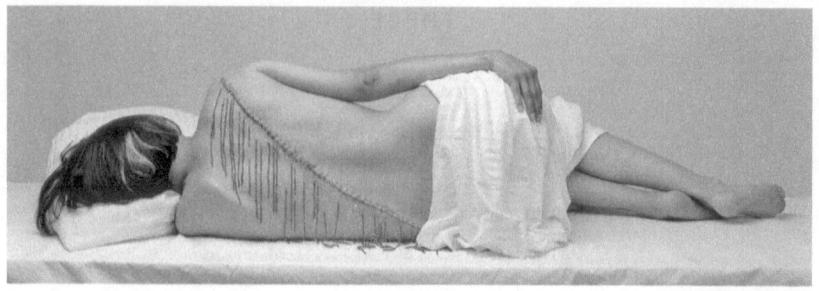

FIGURE 8. Rebecca Belmore, *Fringe*, 2007. Collection of the National Gallery of Canada. Reprinted by permission of the artist.

other group (see, e.g., Amnesty International 2004, 2007; Rosay 2016). The statistics are sobering. In Canada, Aboriginal women are three times more likely to experience violence, and six times more likely to be murdered, than non-Aboriginal women (Beattie, David, and Roy 2018). In the United States more than one in three Native women will be raped during her lifetime, according to the National Congress of American Indians (NCAI) Policy Research Center (2013), but a study by the American Indian Women's Chemical Health Project places the risk even higher, indicating that 75 percent of Native women report a history of sexual assault, while acknowledging that most violence goes unreported (National Sexual Violence Resource Center 2000, 4–5). Legal scholar Sarah Deer contends that even these numbers fall short: "Through my work in Native communities, I heard more than once, I don't know any woman in my community who has not been raped" (2015, 5). Beyond sheer numbers, other factors distinguish violence against Indigenous women. Whereas most violence is intraracial, in the United States, 96 percent of Native women who report experiencing violence name a non-Native perpetrator, and assaults on Native women are far more likely to be brutal or deadly (Rosay 2016, 19, 48).

The reasons for Indigenous women's vulnerability are complicated and hard to pin down, but they are inevitably tied up with history. Colonial policies of dispossession have disproportionately affected Native women, driving them to impoverished neighborhoods in urban centers, such as Vancouver's Downtown Eastside, where they become vulnerable to violence. In Canada, when in 1876 the Indian Act disenfranchised Aboriginal women who married non-Aboriginal men, it forced them from their home communities and replaced traditional (often matriarchal) kinship systems with patriarchal family structures. The residential (or boarding) school system, which continued in Canada until 1996, reinforced women's subjugation and economic marginalization, in part by training them for domestic labor.[2] The systematic dismantling of tribal legal authority renders communities virtually powerless to prosecute assailants, and government authorities seldom investigate, let alone prosecute, assaults when the victim is Native. As a result, sexual predators target Native women, especially on tribal lands (Duthu 2008). In this way, contends an Amnesty International exposé (2004, 10), sexual violence against Indigenous women is a "legacy of history" brought about by colonial policies and practices. Understanding violence against Indigenous women, then, entails confronting not only patriarchy but also white supremacy, and addressing the ways that ongoing settler colonialism makes Native women targets of violence, usually with no consequences for perpetrators.

The Pickton murders disclosed the heightened vulnerability of Native women and the reasons why the racial dimensions of the murders escaped public notice.[3] For many non-Indigenous people, it was impossible to see the Aboriginality of the missing women because they could not see Aboriginal people at all. Colonial discourses define "Indianness" as existing only in the historical past, doomed to disappearance or relegated to the anachronistic space of the reserve (reservation). Consequently, contemporary Native people confront nearly complete social invisibility, especially in cities. According to a statement by the Native Council of Canada, there remains "a strong, sometimes racist perception that being Aboriginal and being urban are mutually exclusive" (Native Council of Canada 1992, 10). The stakes of social erasure emerge from the unique legal and political challenges represented by Indigenous communities: claims to political autonomy and territorial rights that controvert the claims of colonial nation-states and motivate the settler-colonial imperative to eliminate the Native (see introduction). Contemporary violence, including gendered violence, enacted on Indigenous bodies extends from and repeats the colonial subjugation of Indigenous communities and their eviction from traditional homelands, part of the histories that transformed Indigenous territories into cities where Indigenous populations persist as small, often segregated minorities. Just as the social invisibility of Native people obscures the challenges that Indigeneity poses to the political order, it also conceals the violence that ensues from dispossession. In the political dynamics that surround the murders, then, Indigenous women's bodies and land figure as intersecting sites of colonial power, thus underscoring the centrality of gendered violence in ongoing contests over territorial and political control.

In representations of the Pickton murders, the Indigenous woman's body became a site of contestation, its meanings bound up with the political significance of the killings. Media accounts sensationalized the murders by fixating on their brutality and, when the identities of the women eventually became clear, by playing on stereotypes about Aboriginal degeneracy. The dominant framing characterized the missing women as drug-addicted sex workers, as "blameworthy," thereby deflecting attention from the structural dimensions of the violence (Jiwani and Young 2006, 901). This attitude extended even to those missing women who did not engage in sex work (M. Pearce 2013). The "conflation of Aboriginal woman and prostitute," explains Sherene Razack, creates "an accompanying belief that when they encountered violence, Aboriginal women simply got what they deserved" (Razack 2002, 131).

As the murders became front-page news, they emerged as an urgent subject of Indigenous women artists who demanded attention to the Aboriginality of the missing women, the reasons for their vulnerability, and connections between gendered violence and ongoing settler colonialism.[4] In the billboard created by Belmore, the fringe of red beads that cuts across the model's back is a racial signifier that marks this body as Indigenous, and because the fringe resembles streams of blood, it also represents violence. Just as Indigeneity and violence are bound together in a single signifier, so too is it impossible to comprehend the murders apart from their racial dimensions.

To explain why so many Aboriginal women fell prey to a serial killer, we must ask what drew these women to Vancouver's Downtown Eastside, where Pickton sought his victims, what led some to sex work and drug addiction, and why police and non-Native community members initially paid no heed to their disappearances and saw their lives and deaths as matters of little consequence. The questions alone expose injustices that create social marginality registered in the term "fringe." The answers reveal how contemporary sexual violence is bound up with histories of dispossessing and disempowering Indigenous peoples. By representing brutality enacted on the body of an Aboriginal woman, then, *Fringe* condemns not only the murders themselves but also the colonial dynamics and acts of dispossession in which they are embedded.

By elucidating connections among gendered violence, settler colonialism, and patriarchy, Native women artists, in my reading, advance an Indigenous feminist practice that centers on culture.[5] Indigenous feminism, in Cheryl Suzack's words, "represents a critical paradigm . . . [that] focuses on the intersections between colonialism and patriarchy to examine how race and gender systems overlap to create conditions in which Indigenous women are subjected to forms of social disempowerment that arise out of historical and contemporary practices of colonialism, racism, sexism, and patriarchy leading to social patterns of 'discrimination within discrimination'" (Suzack 2015, 261). Since the Pickton murders brought widespread public attention for the first time to Native women's heightened vulnerability, Native community activism has given rise to social movements in Canada and the United States to demand justice for missing and murdered Indigenous women and girls. The objective of an Indigenous feminist project, writes Suzack, "is to achieve 'gender justice'" (2015, 261). In the case of missing and murdered Indigenous women and girls, this objective entails addressing ongoing dynamics of settler colonialism and patriarchy that cause Native women to go missing, render their disappearances invisible, and preclude legal and other forms of accountability.

In addition, by bringing to light the entanglements of patriarchy and settler colonialism, Indigenous women artists' responses to the Pickton murders underscore intrinsic connections between the politics of gender and those of land and sovereignty. Attention to spatiality in their work, I argue, shows that gendered violence is not merely a consequence of colonial assaults on land, culture, and political power but is the very paradigm of those assaults. As these artists' work thus challenges mythologies of expansion and iconographies of Native women's bodies analyzed in chapter 1, they attest to the contemporary consequences of dispossession for Native women and tie protests against the murders to acts of territorial reclamation in urban and rural spaces alike. These artworks redraw colonial geographies in other ways as well. Because of the geographical ubiquity of violence against Native women—the fact that it cuts across boundaries of Indigenous communities and colonial nation-states—these artists limn the distinctive contours of a transnational Indigenous feminist project while also facilitating a feminist rethinking of Native land claims that insists on the urgency of gender. This Indigenous feminist critique in turn levels a forceful challenge to colonial nation-states by exposing the dire conditions they have created for Native communities, the presence of the "Third World" within the "First World" that attests to settler colonialism as ongoing process.

SEXUAL VIOLENCE, ACTIVISM, AND ART

Although the Pickton murders count among the events that initially drew widespread public awareness to violence against Indigenous women,[6] this issue had long been the focus of Native women's activism. Native women have always played vital roles in Indigenous social movements (see, for example, Langston 2003), but in the 1970s, major local and national organizations emerged to address issues specific to Native women. Initially these issues primarily included forced sterilization, environmental justice, child welfare, and public policies with special relevance to women. The Native Women's Association of Canada (NWAC), to take a prominent example, was founded in 1974 to address gender inequalities in the Indian Act, and in the United States, Women of All Red Nations formed the same year to support women's health, child welfare, and broader campaigns for sovereignty, land rights, and environmental justice. Beginning in the 1980s and 1990s, sexual violence became a major focus of Native women's activism. During this time, NWAC expanded its mission to encompass a host of social and policy issues affecting Indigenous women. In 2004 it launched the "Sisters in Spirit" initiative to track for the first time the numbers of missing and murdered Aboriginal women, identify the causes of the violence, and create programs to address them. The initiative holds annual vigils across Canada to honor the lives of missing and murdered Indigenous women and support grieving families. Similarly, since its founding in 1984, Pauktuutit, an organization that represents Inuit women in Canada, has focused on sexual abuse and gendered violence. In the United States, issues concerning gender have historically been less central in Indigenous social organizing, and widespread public awareness of missing and murdered Indigenous women came later, largely as a result of Native activism and independent Native media coverage of individual disappearances rather than a high-profile event like the Pickton murders. But in recent years a number of US organizations, both national and local, have begun to address gendered violence broadly, including missing and murdered Indigenous women.[7] In both Canadian and US contexts, these organizations confront a lack of data as violence often goes unreported, record keeping typically fails to track violence against Indigenous people, and mainstream media coverage is minimal or nonexistent when women and girls go missing (see, for example, Urban Indian Health Institute 2018). Consequently, activism around violence against Indigenous women has often taken the form of gathering information about the extent of the violence, raising public awareness, and honoring missing women.

Vancouver's Downtown Eastside, the neighborhood where many women have disappeared and Pickton sought his victims, has been a locus of such activism (see Culhane 2003; Martin and Harsha 2019). The Downtown

Eastside counts among the poorest neighborhoods in Canada, with many residents experiencing homelessness, poverty, mental and physical health problems, and substance addiction. Around 10 percent of its residents are Aboriginal (see Leo et al. 2018, 3–4). Women began to disappear from the neighborhood in the 1980s, with numbers increasing in the years prior to Pickton's arrest in 2002. Nevertheless, community suspicions about a serial killer went unheeded by police. The Downtown Eastside has a long history of feminist and labor organizing, and in 1991, women's groups designated February 14 as a day of remembrance for women (both Aboriginal and non-Aboriginal) who had disappeared from the neighborhood.[8] On that day every year, the community holds the Women's Memorial March, an event that draws residents as well as family, friends, and allies. The march has become an occasion not only for collective grief but also for protests against the conditions of racism and poverty that render women vulnerable and for challenging dominant understandings that these women somehow brought about their own fates. In this way, explains Dara Culhane, "the families of the missing women and their supporters have claimed a space of dignity for the poorest and most marginalized women in Canada and have achieved some degree of victory in setting the terms and conditions under which a previously invisible population has entered public discourse" (2003, 603). In the words of one speaker, "These women are mothers, sisters, aunts. They are human beings" (594–95). The fact that the annual march is held on Valentine's Day emphasizes that the missing women are beloved and their losses are tragic.

National Native women's groups have also aimed to change public policy and, along with it, the material conditions that create social precarity. From the beginning, Native women's groups in Canada contended that government officials had long known about missing Indigenous women but taken no action.[9] When asked in 2014 about the possibility of a national inquiry into the problem, Prime Minister Stephen Harper replied, "It isn't really high on our radar," revealing the extent of government indifference (Kappo 2014). As organizations such as the Native Women's Association of Canada began to track numbers of missing women, however, the figures climbed into the thousands and prompted far-reaching calls for action. The tide turned when the murder of fifteen-year-old Tina Fontaine incited Indigenous grassroots movements, highly publicized marches, and national outrage. In 2016, the Canadian government launched the National Inquiry into Missing and Murdered Indigenous Women and Girls. Over the course of nearly three years, the National Inquiry held hearings and gathered testimony from family members of missing women, survivors of violence, traditional knowledge keepers, and other experts and officials. The Inquiry, though, was beset by controversy over the project's structure and process, leading to multiple resignations of high-profile staff. In 2019, the Inquiry issued a lengthy final report concluding that violence against Indigenous women and state responses to it are "rooted in colonialism and colonial ideologies, built on the presumption of superiority, and utilized to maintain power and control over the land and the people by oppression and, in many cases, by eliminating them" (see National Inquiry 2019, 54). Violence against Indigenous women, the report concluded, constitutes a Canadian "genocide."

In the United States, as is typical with Indigenous issues there, action surrounding missing Indigenous women has emerged more slowly and been lower in profile. In 2017, in response to pressure from Native women's groups, the US Congress designated May 5 as National Day of Awareness for Missing and Murdered Native Women and Girls.[10] The following year, several states began to build databases on missing Indigenous women that broadened attention to the problem, and an initial version of Savanna's Act, also called the #MMIW Act, passed the US Senate in 2018. Named for Savanna LaFontaine-Greywind, a Spirit Lake Sioux woman who was eight months pregnant when she was murdered, the act improves data collection on missing Indigenous women and provides tribal law enforcement with access to federal databases.[11] In late 2019, President Donald Trump established a federal task force on missing and murdered American Indians and Alaska Natives. Unlike the National Inquiry in Canada, the task force and its work have received little press coverage or attention outside Native circles.

From the outset, Native women artists and writers have contributed to such activist projects by demanding attention to violence against Indigenous women and bringing to light the roots of the violence in the ongoing dispossession and disempowerment of Indigenous communities. Over well more than a decade, Métis artist Jaime Black's REDress Project has appeared in high-profile Canadian and US museums, universities, and other exhibition sites. The public installation of red dresses, some donated by families of missing women, draws attention at once to the violence and to its social erasure while also claiming social space for Indigenous women's issues. Louise Erdrich's 2012 novel *The Round House* (discussed briefly in chapter 2) explores the interconnections among dispossession, political disempowerment, and sexual violence on contemporary US reservations, focusing particularly on the outcomes when legal loopholes surrounding territorial jurisdiction render Native women vulnerable. As part of Canada's National Inquiry into Missing and Murdered Indigenous Women and Girls, 819 people contributed creative artistic expressions to the Inquiry's Legacy Archive, deepening awareness of the missing women's humanity and the pain that has ensued from their loss. Superstar Inuk throat singer Tanya Tagaq has honored missing women in her performances, including a composition titled "Qiksaaktuq" ("grief" in Inuktitut), and other Inuit women have memorialized missing women with *inuksuit* stone structures typically used as landmarks, using their likeness to human figures to invoke the physical presence of the women. Walking with Our Sisters, initiated by Métis artist Christi Belcourt, is a commemorative art project composed of 1,800 beaded moccasin vamps (moccasin tops) donated by family, friends, and allies, each one commemorating a missing woman. The installation recalls, deliberately or not, a display of victims' shoes in the US Holocaust Memorial Museum, a poignant reminder of individual lives cut short by genocide.

Indigenous women artists' responses to the Pickton murders count among the first and most prominent cultural engagements with violence against Indigenous women, and their work complements the projects of activists by demanding attention to the violence, its roots in ongoing dispossession and settler colonialism, and the dignity and humanity of the missing women. In the following pages of this chapter, I analyze three visual works created to protest the murders: Anishinaabe artist Rebecca Belmore's photograph *Fringe* (2007) and street performance *Vigil* (2002), along with Métis filmmaker Christine Welsh's documentary *Finding Dawn* (2006). These artists interrupt a colonial history of representation (discussed in chapter 1) by positioning the Indigenous woman's body as *anti-allegory*—that is, as a figure that demands attention to gendered colonial violence to protest settler colonial authority and territorial claims. But by transforming the Native women's body from a figure of submission into a figure of protest, these artists inevitably confront the paradoxes of visuality in Indigenous contexts and the enduring force of colonial discourses that sexualize, objectify, and silence Indigenous women, thus threatening to mute subversive meanings. This force includes a long history of images that conflate Indigenous women's bodies with land in order to rationalize European expansion. On one hand, visuality offers a powerful means to counter the social invisibility of Native people and violence against them; on the other hand, these artists' work inevitably calls up the hypervisibility of Indigenous people as deviant bodies, along with longstanding images of racialized and gendered bodies rendered mute and reduced to the flesh. In Native contexts, the hypervisibility of Indigenous people as "savage" or "deviant" underlies an abiding social invisibility, the erasure of contemporary Indigenous people that undermines their political and territorial claims. Belmore's and Welsh's work challenges this history of representation, probing the limits and possibilities of visual images to enable their viewers to see Native women differently and thus comprehend the political significance of the murders, including the ongoing settler colonial dynamics and processes of dispossession that enable them. By connecting colonialism and gendered violence, these artists offer a vision of political engagement that ties gender justice to justice for Indigenous communities as a whole.

PICTURING THE INDIGENOUS BODY:
REBECCA BELMORE'S *FRINGE*

Among the best-known contemporary Indigenous artists, Rebecca Belmore uses her work to engage such pressing political issues as territorial conflicts, colonial histories, environmental destruction, and violence against Indigenous people. The politics of representation and the entwined symbolic and material dimensions of violence are persistent themes in her art. In these projects, the body—often her own body—provides her most crucial tool for political expression. "I have always had an awareness of my body as a place from which to address the whole notion of history and what has happened to us as Aboriginal people," she said. "I am very much aware of myself as a politicized body" (cited in Bell 2009, 35). The utility of the body, as she has described it, emerges from "being an Aboriginal person and how my body speaks for itself. . . . It's the body that didn't disappear. So it means a lot in terms of the presence of the Aboriginal body in the work. And the female body, particularly" (cited in Ritter 2008, 55). This focus distinguishes Belmore from other artists. Responding, perhaps, to the persistence of colonial meanings assigned to Indigenous bodies, many other artists have tended to address the topic of gendered violence by featuring the absence, rather than presence, of women's bodies or by supplementing images with text so as to limit possible misinterpretations. Belmore's art, by contrast, uses images (without text) of the Indigenous female body—the "politicized body," the "body that didn't disappear"—to assert Native presence, bring to light histories that bear on the body, and scrutinize conventional images. Tensions between subversive and colonial meanings animate *Fringe* as the photograph calls up conventional images in order to displace them. By bringing into play multiple, contradictory meanings of Indigenous bodies, the photograph underscores the status of images as *representations*, as social constructions, so as to denaturalize conventional images and expose their connections to power.

For Belmore, photography offers a powerful tool for heightening the visibility of Native people—and by extension, drawing attention to the racial dimensions of the Pickton murders—in part because of the reality effect of the image, what Roland Barthes labeled its "evidential force." Photography, Barthes famously claimed, "is literally an emanation of the referent. From a real body, which was there, proceed radiations which ultimately touch me, who am here" (Barthes [1980] 2010, 80). After the death of his mother, as Barthes poignantly describes, photography assuaged his sense of loss. The reality effect of the photograph, however problematic, provided "a certificate of presence," an assurance that *"the thing has been there"* (87, 76), even if it is there no longer. This "evidential force" carries particular weight for representing Indigenous women who have been rendered invisible in life as well as in death. In the context of the murders, denials that the women *had been there* at all fueled denials of the violence itself. For some victims, their participation in sex work further contributed to their social invisibility, beyond their Indigeneity. "Vancouver's sex workers," writes Claudette Lauzon, were "invisible long before they began to disappear"; they were "always already absent presences—invisible but for (and due to) their *hyper*visibility as objects of a simultaneously fascinated and horrified normative gaze" (Lauzon 2008, 157). Social invisibility delayed an investigation of the murders until long after women began to go missing, and when confronted with the facts of the disappearances, police responded that there were no bodies or that these women led transient lives and so were "impossible to trace" (Watson 2003, 7). In one journalist's words, "It's as though they passed through life without leaving footprints" (MacQueen 2002). That Pickton disposed of his victims in a way that left scant evidence seems overdetermined, making literal their invisibility in death. Staging a photograph of an Indigenous body on a billboard, a medium designed to promote visibility, confronts viewers with the fact that the women *had been there* and thus with the reality of their murders. In *Fringe*, the image of a material female body becomes a surrogate for those Native women who vanished without a trace and whose bodies have no materiality, and offers a focal point for grief and mourning.

As social visibility makes it possible to perceive violence enacted on Native bodies in urban spaces, it transforms the meanings of those spaces by bringing to bear collective histories and political claims. *Fringe* first appeared as a billboard above the downtown Montreal location of the Grand Council of the Crees,[12] an organization that promotes the political interests, treaty rights, and contemporary land claims of Cree Nation. In a timeline on its website, Cree Nation traces its "remarkable journey toward Indigenous Nation-Building" through struggles over land, most recently in the thirty-year controversy, beginning in the 1970s, surrounding the James Bay hydroelectric project (Grand Council of the Crees [Eeyou Istchee] n.d.). As this controversy exemplifies how land conflicts endure in the present, the urban location of the Grand Council defines the city as a place where Native people reside and assert political claims, thus undermining antinomies between the city and the reserve as Native space. An ongoing Native presence, in turn, invokes histories of how urban spaces came to be, the processes of dispossession that transformed Indigenous territories into cities, and the connections between these histories and contemporary violence. Within Indigenous communities, the placement of the billboard above the Grand Council insists on the centrality of gendered violence in struggles over land and sovereignty.

As *Fringe* draws on photographic realism to make Native bodies visible, it simultaneously unsettles the reality effect of images to elucidate their relationship to material violence. This photograph, unlike that of Barthes's mother, does not depict its referent. Rather, the body in Belmore's photograph stands in for women who disappeared, who were rendered invisible in life and in death, whose bodies can never be seen. The gap between image and referent emphasizes that the photograph is a work of art rather than a document and that, as such, it carries no "evidential force." Realism, scholars have long argued, is bound up not only with social justice projects but also with uses of photography as an instrument of surveillance and social control. The notion that "a photograph can come to stand as *evidence*," John Tagg has written, "rests not on a natural or existential fact, but on a social, semiotic process" that emerges from changing relations of power (Tagg 1993, 4). Beginning in the nineteenth century, the changing nature of social power required "disciplinary apparatuses" that were "closely linked . . . to the formation of new social and anthropological sciences" centered on the body. The "rhetoric of photographic documentation" facilitated projects of social reform while constituting "the working classes, colonised peoples, the criminal, poor, ill-housed, sick or insane" as "passive—or, in this structure, 'feminised'—objects of knowledge . . . incapable of speaking, acting or organising for themselves"[13] (Tagg 1993, 4–5, 11; see also Sekula 1986). In

Indigenous contexts, photographs have played other roles as well, positioning Native people as objects of tourist consumption and symbols of colonial national identity, while locating them in the historical past so as to obscure their contemporary presence and political claims. In these ways, photographs, in Amber-Rose Bear Robe's words, "convey an idealized and romantic representation of the savage or stoic and 'vanishing Indian' to the larger public" (Bear Robe 2013, n.p.). Thus, writes James Faris, photography "became symbolic in the West's history of conquest, of defeat, of assimilation or disappearance, a force by which white men's power was validated" (Faris 2003, 14). Because *Fringe* is clearly staged, it undermines the reality effect on which such social uses of photography depend, instead calling attention to the constructed nature of the image, its semantic ambiguity, and its relationship to social power. The image unsettles the reality effect of conventional representations by bringing into play three photographic genres (the nude, the forensic, and the ethnographic), drawing connections among them, and reworking their conventions.

In terms of genre, *Fringe* falls most obviously within the realm of nude photography. The female nude, argues art critic Lynda Nead, expresses the "hidden properties of patriarchal culture, that is, possession, power, and subordination," that constitute "patriarchal understandings of female sexuality and femininity" (Nead 1990, 326). *Fringe* mobilizes such fantasies of power and possession because the model has a conventionally beautiful body and she lies in a prone position, appearing as desirable and potentially available. The formal dimensions of the photograph amplify the sense of visual mastery through distance, employing the fantasy, in art critic Griselda Pollock's words, of the "disembodied eye, detached from time and space, able to explore fantasmatically every aspect of the discovered other" (Pollock 2003, 183). Staging *Fringe* as a billboard registers the hypervisibility of the sexualized Indigenous body, rendered as a commodity to be acquired and possessed. In addition to invoking the fact that some of Pickton's victims were sex workers whose bodies functioned as commodities, the billboard form iterates the conflation of Indigenous women's sexuality with sex work. In Indigenous contexts, as discussed in chapter 1, such fantasies of sexual availability are associated with colonial power and territorial dispossession: Belmore, in Jolene Rickard's words, "uses her body to signify the ongoing colonization of the Americas, which is in keeping with the use of a native woman's body as 'trope' ... for the desired occupation or ownership of land" (Rickard 2005, 71). Belmore's art, in other words, calls up colonial tropes that associate the Native woman's body with land, but by exposing rather than obscuring colonial violence, it challenges settler appropriations of Indigenous land.

Fringe calls up these powerful patriarchal and colonial fantasies only to interrupt them by bringing into play another photographic genre: the forensic. The clinical setting—a table covered with a white sheet in a white room—suggests that the injured woman in the photograph has experienced violence, thus countering insinuations, prevalent in popular media, that Pickton's victims somehow brought on their own fates. As the billboard brings visibility to violence against Indigenous women, because it is a form of mass media, it implies a critique of the fact that media coverage, when it eventually acknowledged the overrepresentation of Native women among Pickton's victims, presented Aboriginal pain and death as a spectacle for public consumption. But, rather than restaging this spectacle, the photograph disrupts the power of the gaze, the pleasure of viewing and sense of visual mastery over the woman's body. The wound that runs across the model's back mars her physical beauty and diverts attention away from her sexuality while also linking sexualization to violence. Further, the model's pose subverts the fantasy of possession through postures that denote refusal rather than submission. She is turned away from the camera, and she holds in place a white sheet that conceals her body from view. In these ways, the image transforms the woman's body from a source of voyeuristic sexual pleasure, associated in Native contexts with colonial mastery, into an indictment of sexualization and its connection to material violence.

While the juxtaposition of these genres connects the sexualization of Indigenous women with material violence, the third visual genre—the ethnographic, still the dominant interpretive framework for Indigeneity—underscores the significance of racialization in the murders. Visual technologies have played a crucial role in constructing Native invisibility by defining social identities in terms of physical or cultural attributes that are readable on the body. The body, in the words of art historian Jennifer González, "is the site where race discourse is seen to play out because it is where race is presumed to reside," and in this way images have played a key role in creating the "'raced' body" as a "reified body" (2011, 4). Historically, the visual underpinnings of racial ideology, or the idea that appearances reveal underlying traits, have enabled images to establish the differences that naturalized inequalities. Beginning in the nineteenth century, photography became "productive of racial ideas and orders," explains anthropologist Deborah Poole, and "photographs themselves came to constitute the facts of anthropology" by positioning bodies in a classificatory order that underpinned social hierarchies (Poole 2005, 160, 163). Such hierarchies carried unique implications for Native communities by defining them not only as inferior but also as "disappearing," as a "vanishing race" confined safely to the historical past. Ethnographic discourse, in Johannes Fabian's classic formulation, has conventionally "construe[d] the Other in terms of distance, spatial and temporal," thereby turning "the Other's empirical presence into his [sic] theoretical absence" (Fabian 1983, xi). What Fabian labeled the "denial of coevalness" situates Indigenous people outside the time and space of modernity, thus contributing to their social invisibility. Invisibility denies Indigenous people a contemporary social presence and, by extension, political and territorial claims.

Fringe employs the instability at the heart of ethnographic photography to destabilize the meanings of the racialized body and the photographic encounter. The history of the genre, Poole contends, "is clearly as much about the instability of the photograph as ethnological evidence and the unshakeable suspicion that perhaps things are not what they appear to be as it is about fixing the native subject as a particular racial type . . . photography simultaneously sediments and fractures the solidity of 'race' as a visual and conceptual fact" (2005, 165). This instability emerges from the "twin menace of intimacy and contingency" that registers "the coevalness and, thus, the humanity of [the photograph's] racial subjects" (164). In *Fringe*, Belmore presents the model in a way that emphasizes her humanity and contemporaneity. The distinctiveness of her pose—the fall of her arm and hair, the arrangement of her feet—denotes interiority, and the fact that this is a light-skinned and racially ambiguous body subverts the classificatory purpose of "type" photography. Rather than situating its Native subject in the past, the photograph is emphatically contemporary (the model's hair is cut short in a decidedly modern style). As it compels the viewer to recognize the woman's humanity rather than see her as a type, the photograph reframes the act of viewing as an encounter fraught with power, thereby undercutting the illusion of scientific objectivity and neutrality.[14] By drawing together the genre of ethnographic photography with those of the nude and the forensic, the image in turn implicates ethnographic images in the violence of the gaze, the ways that spectatorship objectifies and dehumanizes racialized peoples. Whereas ethnographic photography is conventionally frontal photography—that is, it pictures the subject facing the camera, rendered submissive and available for scrutiny—here the woman faces away from the camera, thwarting the viewer's desire to see and to know. In these ways *Fringe* defies the ethnographic imperative to fix the racialized subject and exposes the entanglements of looking, authority, and control.

Fringe therefore compels the viewer to question conventional ways of seeing the Indigenous woman's body, and the fact that an Indigenous woman created the image further undercuts the erasure of Native people and the structures of authority that situate Indigenous people as objects, but never creators, of representation. Unsettling the meaning of the Indigenous woman's body also unsettles assumptions about the murders and demands attention to the reasons for ongoing violence. Yet, in some ways, *Fringe* remains confined within the conventions that it aims to subvert. By bringing into play colonial representations, however critically, *Fringe* attests to the enduring power of those representations, the ways that ongoing colonialism continues to shape the meanings and social places of Native bodies. The woman in *Fringe*, after all, remains faceless and nameless, her body brutalized, a figure of silence and absence even as she is also a figure of protest. In *Vigil*, created in the aftermath of Pickton's arrest, Belmore explores the possibility of performance, of viewers' engagement with an Aboriginal woman in performance space, to assign other meanings to the Indigenous woman's body that call into question settler-Indigenous relations.

RESIGNIFYING THE INDIGENOUS WOMAN'S BODY: BELMORE'S *VIGIL*

In 2002, in the aftermath of Pickton's arrest, Rebecca Belmore performed *Vigil* on a street corner in Vancouver's Downtown Eastside, near where many Native women had disappeared. Originally commissioned by the Talking Stick Festival, an annual event featuring Indigenous culture, the performance subsequently appeared as a video loop in *The Named and the Unnamed*, an installation of Belmore's work at the Belkin Gallery at the University of British Columbia. In *Vigil*, Belmore honors the missing women who disappeared from the Downtown Eastside, grieves their loss, and, in so doing, challenges dominant perceptions of both the women and the place they inhabited. Arguably in *Fringe*, the intransigence of colonial meanings, the indelible silence and passivity of the figure of the woman, emerges in part from the photographic form itself. The woman in the picture can never return the gaze, nor can she step outside the frame to challenge the spectator so that the encounter with the Native takes shape on equal footing. Instead, the body in the photograph forever remains the mute object of the gaze in a dynamic that risks reproducing colonial hierarchies. The "'primitive body' as object," explains Diana Taylor, "reaffirms the cultural supremacy and authority of the viewing subject, the one who is free to come and go (while the native stays fixed in place and time), the one who sees, interprets, and records. The native is the show; the civilized observer the privileged spectator" (Taylor 2003, 64). Indeed, as I have argued, *Fringe* restages these dynamics of spectatorship to expose the entanglements of representation and colonial violence.

In *Vigil*, by contrast, Belmore turns to the medium of performance to subvert conventional representations of Indigenous women and the dynamics of spectatorship. Performance heightens critical attention to and potentially denaturalizes social inscriptions of bodies. By shifting attention from "authority to effect, from text to body, to the spectator's freedom to make and transform meanings," in Elin Diamond's words, performance can "enable new subject positions and new perspectives to emerge" (1996, 3, 6). The transformative power of performance emerges in part from its ability to disrupt the dynamics of spectatorship. Engagement with the performer, as active being rather than static object, disallows spectatorial detachment, and in *Vigil*, such engagement brings into the frame audience members' relationship to Aboriginal bodies and histories, so that the performance not only deepens understanding of the structural dimensions of the murders but also underscores the accountability of witnesses—and, by extension, settler colonial society—in bringing about political change.

At the beginning of *Vigil*, Belmore silently takes up bucket and sponge, then scrubs the street on her hands and knees. Describing her own penchant for performance, Belmore relates that it comes from "my own specific aboriginal body" and having "a particular political history," being "born into a political situation" (cited in Watson 2005, 24). In *Vigil*, the act of scrubbing recalls histories that bear on Indigenous women's bodies, especially the colonial imposition of patriarchal gender roles that have relegated Indigenous women to domestic labor and confined them to domestic space, thereby contributing to their social vulnerability (Lomawaima 1994; Barman 1997–98). Scrubbing the street also summons the multiple, intersecting histories that render the place in need of cleansing and purification: the violence that transformed Indigenous territories into urban spaces, the eviction (past and present) of Native people from those spaces, and the brutality enacted on women's bodies in these processes. Yet, at the same time, Belmore's presence on the street resists the subordination and removals of Indigenous people, and the domestic act of cleansing reclaims the street as an Indigenous home. Performance, in Belmore's words, provides a means of "renegotiating space and occupying it" (cited in Watson 2005, 24). *Vigil* straddles the boundary between art and ceremony, mourning the missing women and transforming the site of their disappearance into sacred Indigenous space. (In 2014, the city of Vancouver officially acknowledged that it sits on unceded territory of Musqueam, Squamish, and Tsleil-Waututh First Nations.) By invoking the imposition of patriarchy and territorial conflicts in a single act, the performance calls attention to connections between these histories and their roles in ongoing violence against Native women.

As Belmore's presence transforms the meaning of the street, it alters the meanings of the people who inhabit it as well. When the Aboriginality of Pickton's victims became clear, the fact that they had resided in the Downtown Eastside contributed to perceptions that they brought about their own fates. "Degenerate space," argues Sherene Razack, seems "innately given to illicit and sexual activity," and "bodies in degenerate spaces lose their entitlement to personhood" (2002, 155). There, as a result, "violence may occur with impunity" (143). Conversely, cleansing the street and casting it as sacred space, as an Indigenous place of home, entails acknowledging the personhood of its inhabitants. After Belmore scrubs the street, she solemnly lights a candle for each of the missing women, and one by one calls out their names. These acts of mourning and commemoration demand attention to the women's humanity and in turn emphasize the injustice of the murders. Here Belmore draws on the multiple meanings of "vigil": the performance is at once an act of mourning and of commemoration, a protest against social injustice, and a call for watchfulness to guard against future harm.[15] Belmore solicits the help of a male spectator in the task of lighting candles, calling on him—and, by extension, other audience members—to share her grief and protest the violence. In this way, the performance subverts the dynamics of colonial spectatorship by connecting audience members to the missing women. At the same time, the performance makes visible Aboriginal and non-Aboriginal bodies together in the performance space, presented here as contested land. These proximities focus attention on interrelationships among the performer, audience members, and the missing women, and thus on their respective relationships to ongoing colonial dynamics that give rise to violence.

Tensions between speaking and silence, presence and absence animate *Vigil*. In press accounts of the murders, the missing women, when they were

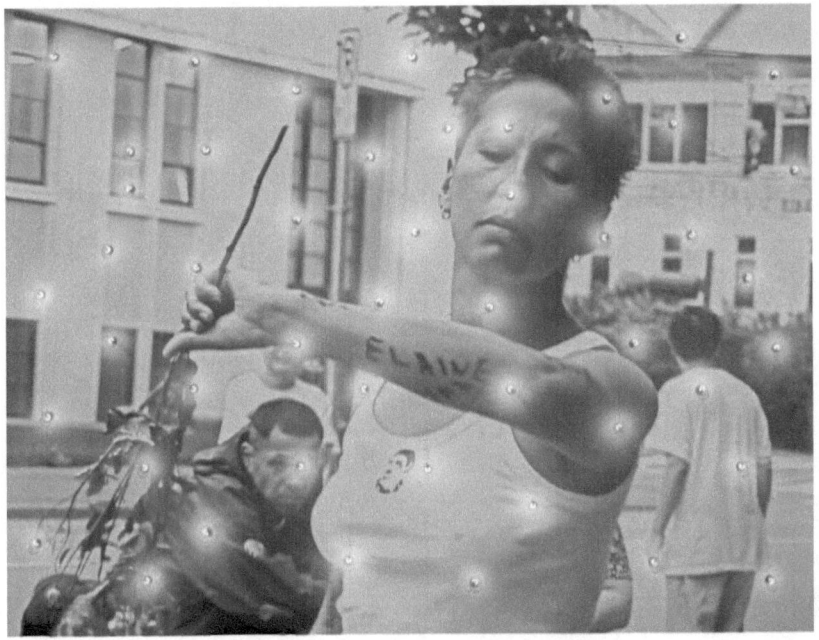

FIGURE 9. Scene from *Vigil*. Rebecca Belmore, *The Named and the Unnamed*, 2002. Collection of the Morris and Helen Belkin Art Gallery, University of British Columbia, purchased with the support of the Canada Council for the Arts Acquisition Assistance Program and the Morris and Helen Belkin Foundation, 2005. Photo by Howard Ursuliak. Reprinted with permission.

mentioned at all, went unnamed, invisible in death as they had been in life. Standing on the street and calling out their names, Belmore counters the social invisibility of the women and exposes the unacknowledged violence against them, thus speaking the unspoken, naming the unnamed (fig. 9). The names—Sarah, Helen, Andrea, Theresa, Brenda, Francis, and others—register their humanity, declaring their lives as beloved friends and family members irreducible to mere crime statistics. (The title of the exhibit in which a video loop of *Vigil* appeared—*The Named and the Unnamed*—emphasizes the importance of silencing and naming in the work.) Throughout the performance, Belmore's body itself becomes the site where struggles over meaning and control are waged. As she calls each name, she shreds a red rose with her teeth, clearly inflicting pain in the process. The missing women's names are written on her skin, grave reminders that the forces that brought about their fates inscribe her own Aboriginal body. Her body thus becomes at once a surrogate for the missing women and a synecdoche for the collective subjectivity of Indigenous women, who are drawn

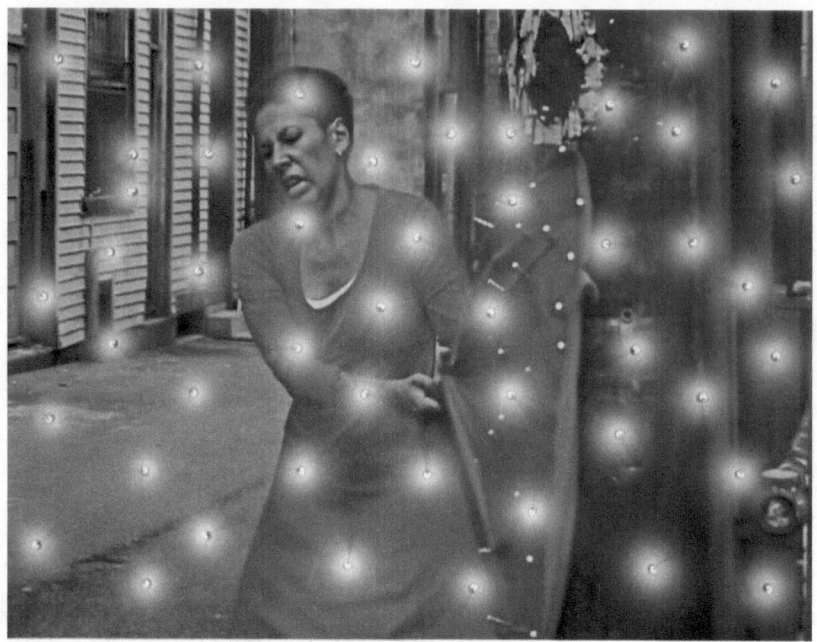

FIGURE 10. Scene from *Vigil*. Rebecca Belmore, *The Named and the Unnamed*, 2002. Collection of the Morris and Helen Belkin Art Gallery, University of British Columbia, purchased with the support of the Canada Council for the Arts Acquisition Assistance Program and the Morris and Helen Belkin Foundation, 2005. Photo by Howard Ursuliak. Reprinted with permission.

together by a shared colonial predicament. And yet, because Belmore can never call the missing women back, her presence registers the permanence of their absence, just as her words make their silence legible. Significantly, the missing women's names are the *only* spoken words in *Vigil*, a disturbing invocation of the silence surrounding the murders and the persistence of colonial tendencies to represent the Indigenous body only in death.

The remainder of the performance invokes the histories that led the missing women to their fates, histories that are borne by the body but usually remain unspoken. After she calls out the missing women's names, Belmore dons a red evening dress and nails it to a telephone pole, ensnaring her own body in the process (fig. 10). The dress is a multivalent symbol, its contradictory meanings expressing the social conflicts that bear on Indigenous women's bodies. It recalls, among other things, the sexualization of Indigenous women and the conflation of Aboriginality with prostitution. Red is a racial signifier and the color of blood, so that the dress also signifies racialized violence (as do the red beads in *Fringe*). Whereas colonial discourse represents Indigenous women as inherently hypersexual in order to naturalize violence, *Vigil*, by contrast, presents the red dress as a constraint from which Belmore tries to break free: she struggles fiercely, and at first futilely, to free herself, ripping the dress piece by piece from the nails that shackle her to the utility pole. Her struggle is a painful invocation of the murder scenes that elicits sympathy for the missing women, further underscoring their humanity as it casts them as resisting, rather than complicit in, their fates. Belmore's clothing—the red dress reveals a white tank top underneath—also matches the colors of the Canadian national flag (a frequent symbol in Belmore's work) and so casts the murders as bound up with state violence. But the red dress carries other, contrary meanings as well. Because red is a sacred color in many Indigenous societies, the red dress has become a symbol for commemorating missing Indigenous women and protesting sexual violence in art and activism alike.[16] In *Vigil*, the multiplicity of meanings bears on the project of the performance itself: it recalls an array of colonial meanings to denaturize them while also gesturing to other signifying possibilities.

In the final scene of *Vigil*, Belmore's body becomes subject to the forms of violence that it protests. Her fierce struggle to break free from the red dress nailed to the utility pole leaves her exposed and vulnerable, standing on the street in only her underclothes. As the performance closes, in another chilling invocation of the missing women's final moments, she enters a pickup truck with James Brown's song "It's a Man's Man's Man's World" playing on the radio. The performance, then, offers no resolution to the violence but instead constitutes a traumatic repetition of the women's disappearances, registering the ongoing vulnerability of Indigenous women who continue to disappear. Even so, the performance does not present ongoing violence as inevitable. By positioning audience members as witnesses, *Vigil* also calls on them to act. Because the performance space is at once contested land and the place where the women disappeared, *Vigil* brings into focus the histories that create Native women's vulnerability, so that action to stop the murders necessarily entails addressing colonial structures and histories of dispossession. In these ways, Belmore's performance calls for accountability as it counters the social invisibility and apathy that have enabled the violence to continue relentlessly.

Like Belmore, filmmaker Christine Welsh probes the entanglements of representation, spatiality, and gendered violence in creating the conditions for and understandings of the Pickton murders. The documentary *Finding Dawn* draws on the power of photography to situate its subjects in the social field, in part through location in geographical space, while the narrative dimensions of film embed the murders in the histories and political dynamics that render Indigenous women vulnerable. At the same time, the film probes the limits and possibilities of domesticity—as the geographical place of "home," social relationship, and nexus of colonial policies—as a means of transforming understandings of the murders and ultimately asserting Native territorial claims, a process in which Indigenous women play crucial roles.

VISIONS OF HOME: CHRISTINE WELSH'S *FINDING DAWN*

For Native artists, writers, and activists, the notoriety of the Pickton murders provided an opportunity to bring attention to broader patterns of violence against Indigenous women. Christine Welsh's influential 2006 documentary, *Finding Dawn*, takes the murders as a starting point for a story about countless Aboriginal women who went missing across Canada in the twenty years preceding Pickton's arrest.[17] Distributed by the National Film Board of Canada, the film garnered multiple awards and circulated widely on the independent film circuit and during human rights–focused events (including the Amnesty International Film Festival and a session of the United Nations Commission on the Status of Women). In *Finding Dawn*, interviewees from across Canada describe how Native women's vulnerability emerged from histories of dispossession and dislocation, the dismantling of tribal economies, assaults on traditional kinship structures, and forced removals of children to residential schools and foster homes. By thus connecting acts of violence across time and geographical places, the film depicts the Pickton murders not as an anomaly but rather as part of an ominous pattern. For Welsh, photography provides a crucial strategy for memorializing and conveying the humanity of murdered Indigenous women and linking acts of violence across time and place into a coherent whole.[18] The narrative dimensions of film embed the photographs in histories and social dynamics so as to draw out their political meanings, while the authority of documentary, its status as evidence and its long-standing role in social justice endeavors, positions the film in campaigns for political change.

The film begins with the story of Dawn Crey, one of the Indigenous women whose remains were found on Pickton's farm. Because of the way Pickton disposed of his victims' bodies, not enough of Crey's DNA remained to enable the state to bring charges for her murder. She thus counts among the many women whose deaths find no legal reckoning and who risk being forgotten. In

Finding Dawn, family members recount poignant stories about Crey, happy times during her childhood along with sobering events that eventually led to her demise. By featuring photographs of her, together with those of other missing women, the film rallies the power of the image to bring past into present, to invoke bodily presence, to call up the dead. Whereas mainstream news accounts lingered on Pickton's depravity, Welsh's film, by contrast, neglects even to name Pickton and instead focuses on the lives of the women, starting with Crey. "Like all the others," Welsh begins, "she is much more than a number. She has a name.... I need to put a human face to what's happened to so many of my sisters.... Who was she, and how did we lose her?" Answering these questions entails placing the murders within broader histories so that Crey's story, in Welsh's words, "is part of a much bigger picture" of the "Native women [who] have gone missing or been murdered across Canada." To "put a human face to what's happened" and compel action on the women's behalf, Welsh presents them as relatable and sympathetic. Her use of the term "sisters" portends her strategy throughout the film: to situate the women in the realm of the familial, the domestic, and to call upon the power of sentiment, a project that unfolds in part through the use of photography.

As *Finding Dawn* opens, the sixty women who went missing from Vancouver's Downtown Eastside appear first in police photographs (including mugshots) arranged in a grid, taken from the "Missing Downtown Eastside Women" poster.[19] The grid appears three times, as if to highlight the discourse of criminality that frames popular understandings of the women. In the years leading up to the Pickton murders, political and media discourse increasingly criminalized sex workers and thereby heightened their vulnerability to violence. Beginning in the 1980s, explains criminologist John Lowman, the "'discourse of disposal'—that is, media descriptions of the ongoing attempts of politicians, police, and residents' groups to 'get rid' of street prostitution ... contributed to a sharp increase in murders of street prostitutes." In turn, police became less likely to investigate or prosecute disappearances because of the notion that victims were "throwaway people" whose risky behavior ostensibly led to their fates (Lowman 2000, 988, 995). The conflation of Aboriginal woman and prostitute heightened such attitudes even for Aboriginal women who were not engaged in sex work. In the case of Pickton's victims, the circulation of police photographs called up such discourses of criminality along with historical uses of photography to situate "othered" bodies in the social field. In the nineteenth century, explains photographer and critic Allan Sekula, "photography came to establish and delimit the terrain of the *other*, to define both the *generalized* look—the typology—and the *contingent instance* of deviance and social pathology" (1986, 7). Through such projects as photographic documentation of prisoners, images defined the "criminal body" and in turn delineated the boundaries of respectability. The criminalized body is also a racialized body, so that the police photographs in *Finding Dawn* situate the women in the realm of otherness, distant and distinct from the "respectable" viewer and therefore unworthy of concern. The boundary between respectability and criminality hinges not only on the ostensible legibility of bodies but also on geographical segregation, so that the meanings of bodies emerge in part from the spaces they inhabit. By situating the murdered women in "degenerate space" (the streets of Vancouver's Downtown Eastside, Pickton's farm), media accounts further naturalized the violence against them. In Welsh's film, Ernie Crey (Dawn's brother) draws out the consequences of spatial location for public and police responses to the murders:

> If these women had been from a wealthier part of Vancouver ... some upscale, tonier neighborhood of Vancouver, and [the murders] involved largely white women ... the investigation would have been thoroughgoing, it would have been well financed, and there would have been a lot of police officers ... we would very likely have had a suspect in jail far earlier.... What [the victims] have in common ... is they were all poor, living in a poor community in Vancouver, the Downtown Eastside, probably drug dependent, and having to resort to prostitution.... Those are not powerful people in this society, we can't pretend they are, and we can't pretend that the police are equally responsive to different parts of the society.

To counter notions that the missing women somehow deserved their fates, *Finding Dawn* situates the missing women in "respectable" rather than "degenerate" spaces, especially domestic spaces. The street and Pickton's farm appear in the film's opening scenes, but only fleetingly. Most subsequent scenes involve interviews with family members that take place in their homes.

As the film sites the missing women in domestic spaces, it rallies the power of photography—specifically domestic photography—to reposition the women in the social field and redefine their relationship with presumed viewers. Whereas criminal photography defines its subject as deviant other, domestic photography creates a sense of identification so as to facilitate empathy. Identification in turn alters the meanings of political events. When domestic photographs of the dead enter the public sphere, according to Gillian Rose, they "erase any differences between us ... and them, the dead.

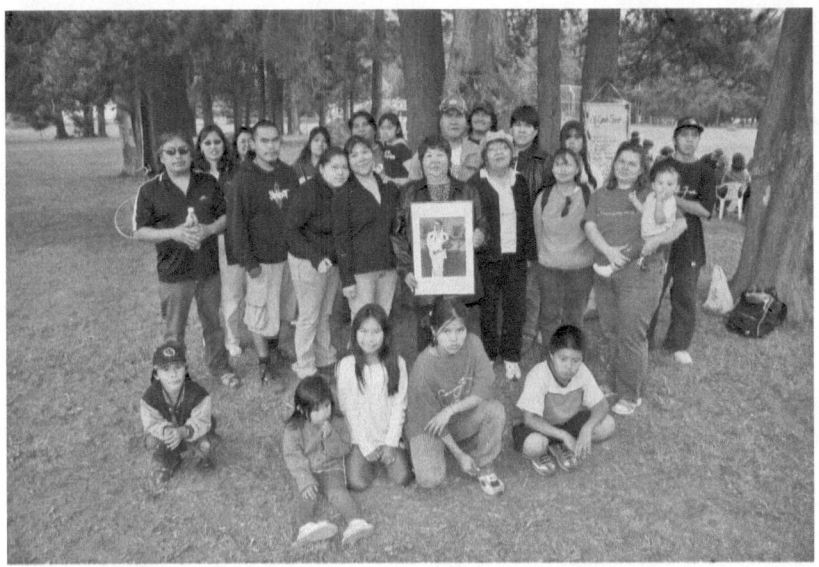

FIGURE 11. Scene from *Finding Dawn*, directed by Christine Welsh, produced by Svend-Erik Eriksen, National Film Board of Canada, 2006. Photo by Jessica Wood. Reprinted with permission.

They look like us, they lived like us: the only difference between us and them is that they died and we are still alive" (2010, 99). For this reason, family photographs of crime victims frequently circulate publicly so as to create a sense of common humanity and make the deaths seem "moving and poignant" (80). Similarly, *Finding Dawn* uses domestic photographs to highlight the missing women's roles as mothers, sisters, and daughters (fig. 11). During interview scenes, family members appear surrounded by domestic photographs as they tell about missing loved ones. At the film's beginning, for instance, Crey's siblings recount events in Dawn's life—the sudden death of their father when Dawn was a young child, her forced removal to foster homes where she experienced abuse, and in early adulthood, her eventual move from the reserve to Vancouver—while the film features photographs of Crey posing with her biological and foster families, laughing with her siblings, holding a kitten. Domestic photographs appear prominently in subsequent interview scenes, as other grieving families tell about their own missing relatives. We see missing teenager Ramona Wilson as an adorable toddler, hands clasped together while standing on the family's front porch, then smiling broadly in a high school photograph; Daleen Bosse, described as a young mother and university student, appears in photographs taken in her parents' home as her father reminisces about her love of singing. In stark contrast to the police photographs at the film's beginning, the family photographs depict the missing women as belonging to families and communities, as lovable and loved, as relatable so that the families' grief becomes the viewer's own.

Yet, in the film and elsewhere, such uses of domesticity represent a vexed strategy, in part because they reinforce the normativity of racial whiteness and patriarchal family structures.[20] When family photographs of white victims circulate publicly, for example, they can help to racialize alleged criminal perpetrators and hence amplify public outrage (see, for example, G. Rose 2010, 100–104).[21] *Finding Dawn* strategically inverts this racial logic by associating racialized women with domesticity. Beyond soliciting sympathy for the missing women, this association carries political meanings by stressing the injustice of removing Indigenous children from their families to residential schools and foster homes. But, at the same time, the film risks effacing social differences that underlie Indigenous women's vulnerability, obscuring viewers' potential complicity in the social dynamics under scrutiny, and paradoxically reinforcing the patriarchal, colonial structures that imperil Indigenous women. Domestic photography emerged with bourgeois domestic ideologies in the nineteenth century (see Sekula 1986), and it remains tied to bourgeois gender ideals that relegate women to domestic labor and confine them to the space of the home. Family photographs, feminist critics have argued, idealize the nuclear family by erasing domestic labor, concealing women's physical and emotional exploitation, and obscuring the classed and racialized dimensions of domesticity (G. Rose 2010, 8, 11). The reality effect of the image further enhances the power of such images. "Photography's social functions are integrally tied to the ideology of the modern family," writes feminist cultural critic Marianne Hirsch, in part because "the photograph gives the illusion of being a simple transcription of the real" so that "it has the effect of naturalizing cultural practices and of disguising their stereotyped and coded characteristics" (1997, 7).[22] Arguably, this holds especially true for family photographs, which often appear to be unstaged and free from artifice. In addition to the ways that images signify, domestic photography carries material effects as a social practice. It is crucial, among other purposes, to the production of domestic space, the "transformation of a house into a 'home'" (Rose 2010, 41, 45). The production of domestic space in turn reinforces feminine roles by facilitating the physical containment and control of women. These dynamics of containment extend beyond the home into the public sphere. When family photographs of the dead and missing appear in the media, explains Rose, they substitute passive emotional response for political action so that viewers are asked to do no more than "watch the horror and weep" (G. Rose 2010, 99; Hirsch 1997, 7). Perhaps most critically in this context, domesticity has long served as an instrument for disempowering and dispossessing Native communities through the marginalization of Native women (see chapter 1).

Finding Dawn, however, scrutinizes the interrelationships of domesticity and the sexual violence associated with colonialism, thus showing domesticity to be a site of conflict and making it an object of critique as much as a strategy for humanizing missing women. In the opening scenes, the film features another kind of domestic photograph: a historical image of women from Sto:lo Nation (Dawn Crey's home community), wrapped in blankets, most of them holding young children. The image invokes a traditional model of kinship based on extended families that colonial officials sought to replace with European domesticity, and the film narrates histories that join together assaults on Native families and territories. Within four generations of the arrival of Europeans, as Welsh describes, the Sto:lo Nation "lost much of what they held dear: their land, their livelihood, and even their children, who were taken away first to residential schools and then to foster homes," where they experienced abuse and neglect. After recounting these collective losses, the film cuts to a black-and-white image of Crey as a young child with her father and siblings, as Welsh recounts the sudden death of their father, an event that led to Crey's removal to foster homes where she experienced abuse that haunted her for the remainder of her life. The juxtaposition of these two stories about loss, along with the visual similarity of the historical photograph and the Crey family photograph, register that Dawn's story extends a long history of state violence against Native families. In Canada, because their domestic situations are deemed to be unfit, Aboriginal children are dramatically overrepresented in foster care to the extent that, in the words of one First Nations leader, the system is "truly looking more and more like a second generation of residential school" (Edwards 2018). Statistically, Native children who spend time in foster homes are more likely to resort to sex work and drug addiction as adults (Native Women's Association of Canada 2015, 4). These patterns held true in Crey's life, and her story exemplifies how colonial policies continue to endanger Native women.

The remaining scenes foreground the spatiality of colonialism and its role in ongoing gendered violence. The film features geographical spaces—church, school, home—that together served as colonial instruments to instill patriarchy, thus heightening women's vulnerability even in their home communities. Domestic space in particular figures heavily as a site of sexual violence. Janice

Acoose, a professor and journalist, and Fay Blaney, an activist for Aboriginal women's rights, each remember witnessing their mothers being brutally raped in their own homes. As the camera pans across wedding photographs of Blaney's mother, she recalls, "My mom left when I was about five years old . . . she had a permanent bruise on top of her eye, and she was telling me that my father did that to her . . . after [my father] drowned, she was being sexually assaulted in her own home . . . from where I sit now as an adult, I recognize that she really had no choice but to try and make her escape." In *Finding Dawn*, then, even as the domestic sphere figures as a means of depicting missing women as "grievable lives,"[23] it is also a space where patriarchal power manifests in sexual violence. Distinguishing the colonized space of the domestic home from Indigenous space, Acoose tells how her great-grandmother "refused to take a house, a government-issue house, because she loved that old [mud] house that she lived in—you know, she could still see the earth in her house and she loved that."

In *Finding Dawn*, such refusals extend to the patriarchal gender roles assigned to Native women under settler colonialism. Countering the silencing and invisibility of Native women, the film thematizes the voices of women such as radio broadcaster Lynn Terbasket and journalist and professor Janice Acoose, and the political leadership of Indigenous women, including Fay Blaney, who work at the national and community levels for Indigenous women's rights. Inevitably those reform efforts extend to land. Blaney describes how she fled from "the violence that had overtaken a once healthy and self-sufficient community, violence that came with the destruction of a way of life," caused in part by federal prohibitions on fishing practices that sustained the community. "Government policies, residential schools, and the loss of their traditional economy all took their toll," Welsh narrates, eventually forcing the community to abandon its traditional territory. Here Welsh underscores connections between gendered violence and the dislocations and losses of colonialism, and the film shows Blaney, among other figures, returning home to her community's traditional territory to recount their history in that place. In her story, reclaiming cultural traditions that command respect for women "means reclaiming Aboriginal rights and title to the land so that her people have the foundations they need to build a healthier community." The film itself engages in a kind of remapping project, picturing Native histories on the land that underlie legal claims. In the beginning scenes, Welsh describes how "Dawn came from the Sto:lo Nation, whose traditional territory starts at the mouth of the Fraser River and extends deep into the canyons of the coastal mountains." As she speaks, the

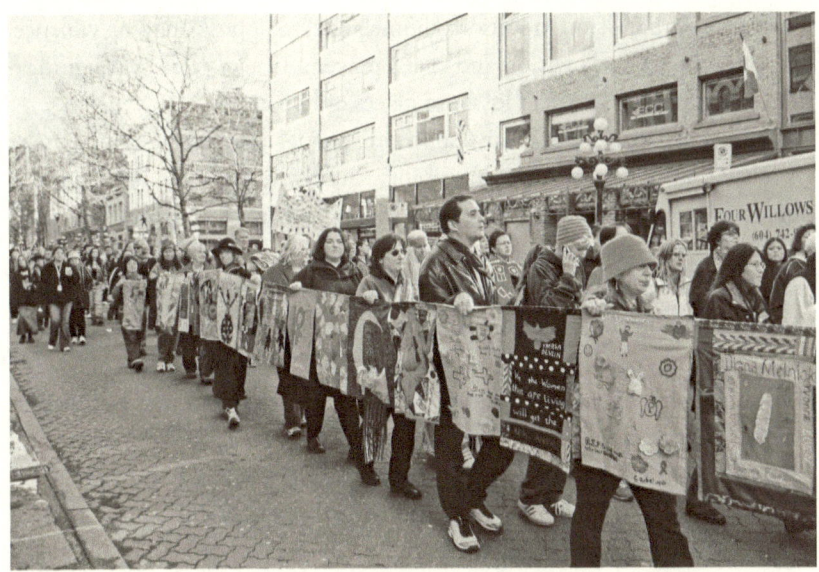

FIGURE 12. Scene from *Finding Dawn*, directed by Christine Welsh, produced by Svend-Erik Eriksen, National Film Board of Canada, 2006. Photo by Jessica Wood. Reprinted with permission.

film features images of the lands, the river, and mountains that mark the boundaries of Sto:lo territory. "All of us are quite proud of our tribal ancestry," continues Ernie Crey; "we're the Sto:lo people, the people of the river; we're a fishing community, a community that has lived here ... probably for as long as 9,000 years, certainly since the last ice age. This is the place we call home, and we grew up here." Here the film deploys the rhetoric of domesticity in the service of Native claims to traditional territories.

But even as the film asserts claims to traditional territories, it challenges the notion that Native peoples properly belong only to the space of the reserve, just as it also resists Native women's containment in domestic space. *Finding Dawn* takes shape as a film about mobility that is, in a sense, a road movie. In transitional segments between individual women's stories, Welsh drives from location to location, from the city to the reserve and back, journeys that bind the women's stories into a coherent whole in which the reserve and the city figure equally as Native space. Indeed, each segment of the film depicts a Native reoccupation of territories, rural and urban alike: the annual march on Vancouver's Downtown Eastside to memorialize the missing women (fig. 12); the Ramona Wilson memorial walk on the rural "Highway of Tears," where many Native women have disappeared; community searches in fields near Saskatoon, Saskatchewan; and women's returns to places of trauma (the urban stroll, traditional homelands) to oppose ongoing violence. These are acts of reclamation and social power as well as acts of resignification, transforming spaces of loss into places of home.

These reoccupations of Native spaces are partial and fleeting, moments of visibility that puncture social invisibility. But, by bringing to light connections between gendered violence and colonialism, *Finding Dawn* positions Indigenous women as agents of social change. As the film emphasizes women's voices and political agency, so too does it emphasize their leadership in the reoccupations of space that bring visibility to gendered violence and to the continuing presence of Native people on the land. In the words of Maddy Wilson, whose teenaged daughter, Ramona, counts among the Indigenous women murdered along the so-called Highway of Tears, "We're showing people that we are not afraid, we will never be afraid, that we are here, we'll always be here ... we shall never forget the loved ones who were murdered along ... the Highway of Tears." As these occupations call attention to the Native past, they also gesture toward a Native future in which struggles over the meanings of Indigenous women's bodies are no less than struggles over the meanings of history, the places we inhabit, and social power.

FOUR

Contested Landscapes

KENT MONKMAN, ZACHARIAS KUNUK, AND
THE ART OF INDIGENOUS HISTORY

In 1991, the year preceding the Columbus quincentennial, *The West as America: Reinterpreting Images of the Frontier, 1820–1920* opened at the Smithsonian's National Museum of American Art.[1] The exhibition featured iconic paintings, sculptures, and photographs that glorify westward expansion as progress of a superior civilization. But rather than advancing a heroic notion of settler history, *The West as America* aimed, in the curator's words, to "dispel traditional ideas about images of the West, to place them in a new context designed to question past interpretations" (Treuttner 1991, xi). Wall texts called attention to the violent effects of western expansion on Native people and the land, along with the ways that racial ideologies have shaped western art. The Smithsonian exhibit was not alone in rethinking popular understandings of the West. Beginning in the 1980s, the "New Western History" focused academic attention on power relations—especially those of race, class, and gender, along with environmental exploitation—in US expansion, and other museums had previously organized exhibits that similarly criticized western mythologies. But no prior event had generated the momentous backlash that befell *The West as America*. The exhibit caught the attention of journalists and commentators, prompting a slew of detracting commentaries. A review in the *Wall Street Journal* titled "Pilgrims and Other Imperialists" reported that the "main point" of the exhibition was that "the nation was founded as an imperialist venture, that it so continued throughout a rapacious expansion, driven by 'capitalists in the East,' and that artists of the West glorified these evils." *The West as America*, the review concluded, was "an entirely hostile ideological assault on the nation's founding and history" ("Pilgrims and Other Imperialists" 1991, A14). Drawn by the controversy, visitors attended the exhibit in droves, often waiting in long lines to write in comment books that exhibition organizers characterized as a "battleground" (Treuttner and Nemerov 1992, 70). In response, the US Senate launched an investigation into the Smithsonian's budget and threatened to eliminate its funding, warning its leadership never to allow such an exhibition again (Massip 2011, 12). Within a month after the exhibition's opening, the curator changed the wall texts that had prompted the most public outrage. Later, although *The West as America* had drawn vast crowds, the traveling exhibit was canceled, reportedly for financial reasons.

What is at stake in representations of the US West, and why would a revisionist art exhibition generate such controversy? As the exhibition's title signals, the West as geographical place has long been tied up with US national identity. The myth of the frontier, explained historian Richard Slotkin in a classic text, "is our oldest and most characteristic myth" with roots in the origins of the United States as a settler nation (1992, 10). In the American cultural imagination, "the conquest of the wilderness and the subjugation or displacement of the Native Americans who originally inhabited it," in Slotkin's words, "have been the means to our achievement of a national identity, a democratic polity, an ever-expanding economy, and a phenomenally dynamic and 'progressive' civilization" (10–11). Although its initial task was to justify the establishment of colonies on Indigenous lands, the myth of civilization's triumph over savagery has endured for centuries as an ideological framework for a range of social conflicts, including those surrounding labor, migration, economic development, and military campaigns such as the war in Vietnam. So close have been the ties that bind westward expansion with national identity that, after the director of the US Census Bureau announced in 1890 that the frontier was closed, historian Frederick Jackson Turner famously predicted in his "frontier thesis" speech a crisis for American democracy.[2] For these reasons, images of the West constitute "national pictures" that are often prominently displayed in sites of government, including the US Capitol Rotunda. *The West as America* featured many of these national pictures, including such monumental landscapes as those painted by Albert Bierstadt, Thomas Cole, and Frederic E. Church, that have long been associated with US national identity. But by bringing to light the violence of territorial conquest, the exhibition disputed the "sacred premise"[3] of westward expansion as civilized progress and thus seemed to undermine "America's creation myth," an effect augmented by the staging of the exhibition at the Smithsonian, the premiere national museum. According to one critic, "The very concept of an American national identity was here at stake" (Massip 2011, 16).

Ultimately, though, western mythologies center on who holds rights to the land. Western history, writes historian Patricia Nelson Limerick, "has been an ongoing competition for legitimacy—for the right to claim ... the status of legitimate beneficiary of Western resources" in a "contest for property and profit" (Limerick 1987, 27). During the era of westward expansion, Western art, such as the landscape paintings featured in *The West as America*, helped nineteenth-century Americans envision newly conquered places and imagine them as their own. In the decades since, stories about the frontier have been told and retold in Western novels and films, the quintessential American genre that still shapes popular understandings of US national history and identity. Typically, such narratives erase Native people altogether, or they mobilize the paradigmatic encounter between savagism and civilization to advance the idea of settler territorial expansion as the "manifest destiny" of a superior society. By scrutinizing the racialized notion of progress, *The West as America* called into question not only colonial national identity but also the idea that dispossession of Native peoples was just and inevitable. "Inventing 'the Indian,'" one of the most controversial sections of the displays, identified racism and violence as enabling US expansion. One original wall text (later removed) read, "The predominance of negative and violent views was a manifestation of Indian hatred, a largely manufactured, calculated reversal of the basic facts of white encroachment and deceit" (Gulliford 1992, 203). The implications for land title were not lost on visitors. Responses to the exhibit, in the curator's words, showed that "that the American West is still a territory as hotly disputed as any that appears in the paintings of Frederic Remington, Charles M. Russell, and other western artists" (Treuttner and Nemerov 1992, 70).

Yet, despite the significance of this critique, the exhibition's vision was limited, trapped in some ways within the very ideologies it contested. It featured only work by canonical (white) artists devoid of alternative social and spatial imaginaries that might present a more foundational challenge to colonial mythologies. Within *The West as America*, "the Indian" remained a settler invention, confined within the dehumanizing category of savagery and the prediction of inevitable disappearance, so that the exhibition proved unable to draw out the implications of contested land in the past or present.

Since the 1960s, Native artists, filmmakers, and writers have turned to the Western genre to challenge settler national mythologies and territorial possession promoted in canonical images, in part by foregrounding the gendered violence of expansion. As they endeavor to displace dominant ways of seeing, they rework conventions of the genre to represent Indigenous histories on and meanings of western places so as to support their own claims to contested land, projects central to this era of Indigenous activism.[4] This chapter analyzes two Indigenous remakes of iconic visual narratives of the West: Kent Monkman's painting *History Is Painted by the Victors* (2013), a revision of Albert Bierstadt's celebrated nineteenth-century landscape *Mount Corcoran* (1876–77), and Zacharias Kunuk's film *Maliglutit (Searchers)* (2016), a remake of John Ford's acclaimed Western film *The Searchers* (1956). Monkman is best known for remaking nineteenth-century landscape paintings, which he has described as "billboard[s] for the expansion of the West." In *History Is Painted by the Victors*, he populates Bierstadt's empty landscape to make visible Native histories on the land and the violent territorial conflicts obscured in canonical paintings. He also "queers" the landscape, calling attention to sexuality as both a site of colonial violence and a means for reconceiving the past and future of contested lands. Like Monkman's painting, Kunuk's film *Maliglutit (Searchers)* subverts settler mythologies of expansion, in this case by revising Ford's film about the US West to relate an alternative history of the Arctic, a parallel "frontier" that embodies Canadian national identity. As part of its project of critique, *Maliglutit* calls up the suppressed colonial history of violence against Inuit women, exposing the social ruptures and brutality brought by settler expansion in the Arctic. At the same time, the film foregrounds Inuit presence and the Inuit gaze, offering a vision of social restoration premised on traditional Inuit values, including those involving gender, in the aftermath of the historic 1993 Nunavut Land Claim Agreement.

The West as America was staged at a significant historical moment, when the United States and communities throughout the hemisphere were contending with the meaning of the Columbus quincentenary. Monkman and Kunuk created visual narratives of the West during a parallel period of national reckoning in Canada. In the 2010s, a series of high-profile inquiries—the government-sponsored Truth and Reconciliation Commission on Native residential schools (2008–15) and National Inquiry into Missing and Murdered Indigenous Women and Girls (2016–19), along with the 2010 report of the independent Qikiqtani Truth Commission—exposed the devastation caused by the nation's colonial policies and their enduring effects on Native communities. In the years surrounding the 2017 sesquicentennial of Canadian confederation, the histories revealed by these inquiries undermined the nation's founding mythologies and its self-proclaimed identity as a tolerant, democratic, and multicultural society. At the same time, Native land claims challenged the nation's geographical coherence as Canada negotiated new Indigenous settlements in the aftermath of the 1973 *Calder* decision (see the introduction). In the context of upheavals surrounding national history, identity, territorial possession, and the place of Indigenous people in the contemporary social order, Monkman and Kunuk adapted Western representations so as to dismantle conventional visual narratives of the West and open a space for Indigenous projects of nation-building and territorial claims (the ideological terrain of western images). After exploring the ways that western landscape painting and films have historically contributed to dispossession, this chapter analyzes how Monkman and Kunuk rework these visual genres to subvert settler mythologies and envision an Indigenous future premised on gender equity.

QUEERING THE LANDSCAPE: KENT MONKMAN'S WESTERN HISTORIES

At first glance, Cree artist Kent Monkman's monumental landscape *History Is Painted by the Victors* (2013) appears as both familiar and surprising. The painting reworks Albert Bierstadt's *Mount Corcoran*, a classic example of nineteenth-century US landscape painting, by populating Bierstadt's sublime vista with nude men, some engaged in erotic play. A painter, performance artist, and filmmaker, Monkman, as his website explains, takes as his subjects "colonization, sexuality, loss, and resilience—the complexities of historic[al] and contemporary Indigenous experiences"—in part by critically engaging Western art history. His focus, in other words, encompasses not only Indigenous experiences but also their renderings in dominant art traditions—the ways that colonial practices are bound up with representations of Indigenous peoples and territories. Monkman, dubbed as the "rock star" of Indigenous art in Canada,[5] is perhaps best known for revising iconic western landscape paintings—such as those by George Catlin and the artists associated with the US Hudson River School and Canada's Group of Seven—in order to scrutinize visual narratives of western expansion. "Europeans in North America," says Monkman, "had stolen our land. They created this whole document called 'art history' around their exploits.... I felt that borrowing from their landscape paintings would be a way of reclaiming some of the land they had stolen from us" (cited in Morris 2019, 133). Monkman's art critically engages the contributions that landscape paintings made to consolidating settler territorial claims and national identities, in part by erasing Native peoples. But beyond offering a critique of art history, Monkman's landscapes present an alternative visual narrative of westward expansion that counters Indigenous erasures and the temporalities that cast colonialism as progress. In these ways, Monkman's "borrowing" of western landscape paintings constitutes a cultural appropriation that undermines settler possession and asserts Indigenous claims to contested territories.

By reworking Bierstadt's *Mount Corcoran*, Monkman calls up the history of landscape painting and its connections to westward expansion in the United States, where landscape became the dominant art genre from around 1820 until 1880.[6] Significantly, these decades were marked by Native removals, settler migrations along the Oregon and California trails, the California gold rush, and the Indian Wars on the Great Plains. Throughout this period, painters and photographers created images of a vast, sublime frontier that became synonymous with colonial national identity. Landscape imagery provided a sense of familiarity with and ownership of newly acquired and little-known territories, an effect augmented when these paintings became available for purchase. Artists associated with the Hudson River School in particular created monumental works to capture the expansiveness of the land, and their realism encouraged buyers' sense of vicarious ownership. Native people seldom appeared in these images, and when they did, they seemed continuous with the landscape, part of the wilderness to be conquered in the name of progress. Westward expansion in turn set the stage for the resource exploitation necessary for industrialization. Landscape imagery played a crucial role in making the US West, in one art historian's words, "both an iconic symbol of national identity and a resource to be used in transforming the nation from a wilderness republic into a national power." Typically, western landscapes presented these as compatible goals, rarely depicting the environmental destruction wrought by "progress" or the threat it posed to wilderness that now represented US national identity (Anderson 1991, 240–41). By erasing Native presence and the destruction enacted in the name of progress, nineteenth-century landscapes presented a fantasy of unfettered access to the land and boundless possibilities for development.

Such uses of landscape emerge from the origins of the genre in the transitions to capitalism and imperialism. In early modern Europe, landscape arose from shifts in conceptions and representations of space, including the development of perspective in painting, associated with the first commercial uses of land as property. "Landscape was a 'way of seeing,'" writes geographer Denis Cosgrove, "that was bourgeois, individualist and related to the exercise of power over space" (1985, 45).[7] Perspective created a sense of depth and with it the illusion of realism, the fantasy of gazing at the land itself rather than at its aesthetic rendering. It also placed the spectator-landowner at the center of the field of vision, enabling a sense of mastery that Cosgrove labels the "visual appropriation of space": "Realist representation ... through linear perspective directs the external world towards the individual located outside that space. It gives the eye absolute mastery over space.... Visually space is rendered the property of the individual detached observer, from whose divine location it is a dependent, appropriated object" (Cosgrove 1985, 48–49). Through such visual effects, landscape created a Cartesian separation between humans and the natural world, subject and object. These aspects of landscape—the composition of land according to the principles of geometry, the notion of a detached, controlling spectator, and the sense of control over land rendered as object—constitute, in Cosgrove's terms, a "visual ideology" that aligns landscape representation with material processes of possession and control (Cosgrove 1985, 55; and 1998, 1).

For these reasons, landscape has close historical connections to European expansion. Crucially, the emergence of the concept of land as property as encoded in landscape coincided with the so-called "age of discovery," when Europe staked its first imperial claims across the globe. These associations, suggests W. J. T. Mitchell, explain why landscape, labeled by art historian Kenneth Clark as the "chief creation" of the nineteenth century, accompanied the rise of European global domination including western expansion in the United States and Canada. The "semiotic features of landscape"—including the erasure of human activity in its own creation, its presentation as a "*natural* representation of a natural scene"—are, in Mitchell's words,

> tailor-made for the discourse of imperialism, which conceives itself precisely (and simultaneously) as an expansion of landscape understood as an inevitable, progressive development in history, an expansion of "culture" and "civilization" into a "natural" space in a progress that is itself narrated as "natural." Empires move outward in space as a way of moving forward in time; the "prospect" that opens up is not just a spatial scene but a projected future of "development" and exploitation. (1994a, 17)

Yet, even as realism facilitates the appropriation of land as property integral to capitalism and imperialism, it simultaneously effaces the social relationships of labor and empire that transform land into an object for possession. Thus, Mitchell continues, landscape constitutes "what Marx called a 'social hieroglyph,' an emblem of the social relations it conceals" that "must represent itself ... as the antithesis of 'land,' as an 'ideal estate' quite independent of 'real estate'" (W. J. T. Mitchell 1994a, 15). Landscape as a mode of cultural expression, in short, is the site where imperialism asserts and naturalizes its vision as "the real," obscuring other histories and meanings of land along with contending territorial claims.[8]

Bierstadt's *Mount Corcoran*, the inspiration for Monkman's *History Is Painted by the Victors*, exemplifies the entanglements of exploration, capitalism, and art in western expansion. A landscape painter renowned for his association with the Hudson River School, Bierstadt first traveled to the US West in 1859 with a US Army survey of the Rocky Mountains led by Colonel Frederick Lander. Lander was an instrumental figure in westward expansion, having previously undertaken surveys for the transcontinental railroad and built a segment of the first national wagon route to California. On this 1859 journey westward, surveyor and artist played complementary roles. In the nineteenth century, observes art historian Rachael Ziady DeLue, landscape painting constituted "a form of mapmaking" that was "shaped by the explosion of cartography" so that paintings themselves were "experienced cartographically." Landscapes often employed the visual perspective of the map, so that the "mapping gaze" from above joined with the "panoramic gaze, looking outwards" ("The Art Seminar" 2008, 129–30). The reality effect of such images created a sense of familiarity with the land that aligned with material projects of expansion and even military planning.[9] As Lander mapped the land to facilitate military conquest and colonial settlement, Bierstadt and other artists who accompanied him created cartographic landscape paintings that reshaped popular understandings of the West, encouraging migration by presenting the territory as desirable and habitable space (Cash 2012; Elston 2012; Snyder 1994). In 1863, Bierstadt returned to the West, this time to California, on a journey that coincided with mass migrations driven by the prospects of gold and free land. After spending time in the Yosemite Valley and the Sierra Nevada, he returned to New York and began painting the spectacular western landscapes, including *Mount Corcoran*, that came to define his career, works that Kent Monkman would later describe as "billboard[s] for the expansion of the West" (Monkman 2015).

Mount Corcoran exposes connections between artistic representation and territorial possession through the nature of the image and the conditions sur-

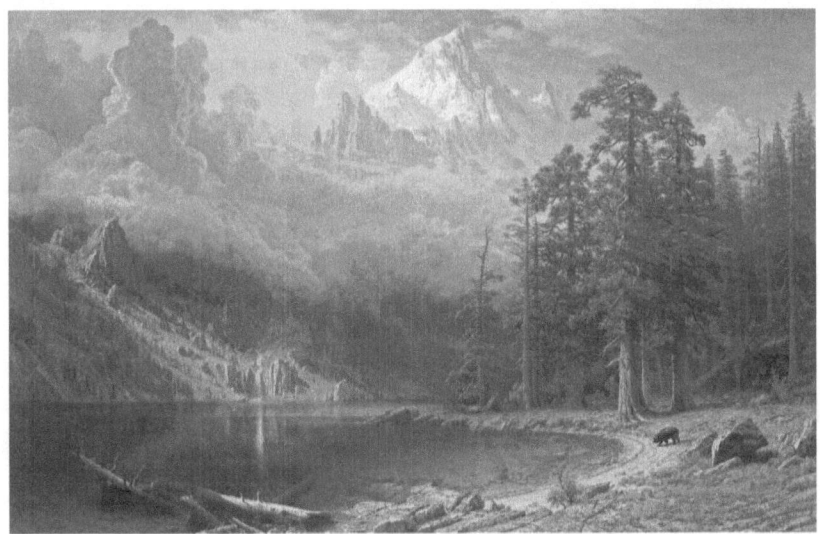

FIGURE 13. Albert Bierstadt, *Mount Corcoran*, c. 1876–77. Oil on canvas, 154 cm × 243 cm. Corcoran Collection. Courtesy of the National Gallery of Art, Washington, DC.

rounding its creation. The painting depicts a placid lake surrounded by forests against a backdrop of dramatic, snow-covered peaks and descending storm clouds (fig. 13). The image is at once lush and grand, its monumental dimensions contributing to its splendor.[10] Typical of the genre, the land in Bierstadt's rendering is unencumbered by human (Indigenous) presence. "A landscape that is absent inhabitants may seem to be more accommodating to potential settlement," explains art historian Kate Morris, and when Indigenous people do appear in conventional landscapes, artists tend to "diminish that presence by shrinking the figures to insignificant scale or, alternatively, to so romanticize the figures as to consign them to an ineffectual, premodern state" (Morris 2019, 115). As the painting depicts the land as empty, the formal qualities of *Mount Corcoran* augment the illusion of settler possession and control. Perspective creates a sense of realism, an experience of gazing at the land itself, so that the painting presents the viewer with an unobstructed view of the scene and a virtual entry point onto the clearing by the lake. The image, in short, invites the gaze—and, by implication, the presence—of the viewer. The history of the painting is tied to territorial appropriation in more material ways as well. Bierstadt had initially titled this work *Mountain Lake*, but in an effort to secure patronage, he renamed it after banker and gallery owner William Wilson Corcoran. To convince Corcoran to purchase the work, he provided a War Department map as proof that he had renamed the mountain peak in Corcoran's honor. But in this instance, too, art preceded possession, because the renaming of the peak followed the renaming of the painting.[11] Naming constitutes an assertion of settler ownership as well as an act of erasure, in this case of Indigenous histories on and claims to the territory.

In this story surrounding the painting's creation, the mention of the War Department map alludes to a history of conquest that is obscured by the empty space of the landscape as well as by Bierstadt's act of naming. Despite what Bierstadt might have reported to his patron, *Mount Corcoran* does not represent a particular place but is instead a composite of sites in the Sierra Nevada range that he visited in the 1860s and early 1870s (Cash 2012). In a sense, then, this is an abstract image, unmoored from a particular place and emptied of its histories. Yet, at the same time, this composite image calls up the multiple histories of the places that influenced its creation. This is the area of the California gold rush, a site of devastation for Native people. When the gold rush commenced in 1848, the population of Native California stood at approximately 150,000, a figure that already testified to drastic depopulation as the result of Spanish colonization. Within two years after the discovery of gold, the Native population had plummeted by two-thirds, to 50,000, and by the early 1870s, around the time of Bierstadt's journeys, only around 30,000 survivors remained. The US Cavalry, state-sponsored militias, and vigilante groups wantonly slaughtered entire communities, while other Native people fell prey to disease and malnutrition as their lands became a target for fortune seekers and the settlements that sprang up to support them. After 1850, statehood worsened the situation of California's Native peoples as the state government negotiated treaties that the US Senate ultimately refused to ratify, so that Native communities ceded most of their territories but did not receive even the small parcels of land promised to them in the agreements, and the state militia placed bounties on the scalps of Native men, women, and children. The mention of the War Department map in Bierstadt's story hints at the dependence of the entwined journeys of painter and surveyor on state violence. But in *Mount Corcoran*, the absence of human figures erases these histories of violence on the land to naturalize settler claims. Registering the importance of such visual narratives in the national imaginary, Bierstadt's painting is prominently displayed in the National Gallery of Art in Washington, DC.

Monkman's *History Is Painted by the Victors*, by contrast, populates Bierstadt's landscape to direct attention to the social dynamics that bear on land. Whereas *Mount Corcoran* offers an open vista that invites the colonial

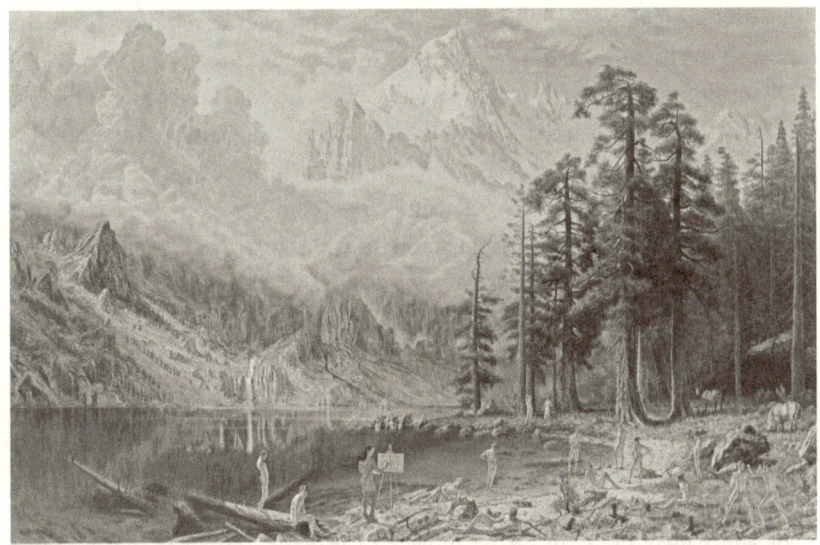

FIGURE 14. Kent Monkman (Fisher River Band Cree), *History Is Painted by the Victors*, 2013. Acrylic paint on canvas, 72 in. × 113 in. Denver Art Museum. Gift from Vicki and Kent Logan. 2016.288. © Kent Monkman. Photograph courtesy of the Denver Art Museum. Reprinted by permission of the artist.

gaze, Monkman's painting depicts a range of human figures, some drawn from iconic paintings and others that refer to historical events (fig. 14). At the center of the field of vision stands Miss Chief Eagle Testickle, Monkman's gender-fluid alter ego. Miss Chief appears in front of an easel, paintbrush in hand, glancing slyly over her shoulder at the viewer. Her most obvious significance is that she renders visible a Native presence on the land at the virtual entry point to the scene. In conventional landscape painting, writes art historian Ann Bermingham, "the vastness of nature suggests the freedom of the imagination guided by the eye to *take up* residence in the 'wide and undetermined' prospect" (1994, 84), a description that applies to *Mount Corcoran*. By contrast, in *History Is Painted by the Victors*, Miss Chief blocks visual access to the landscape. Miss Chief, explains Monkman, "was created to reverse the gaze," to counter the colonial spectator's visual appropriation of space as "she looks back at European settlers" (cited in Brooks 2014, n.p.). In Monkman's painting, Miss Chief's gaze is directed in part at the land—the position of her easel aligns her visual field with that of the spectator—so that the Native figure obstructs the imperial gaze and, by extension, access to the land. Her presence thus constitutes what art historian Kate Morris calls an "anti-invitational device" that redirects attention to Native presence on the land and the histories that presence calls up (Morris 2019, 63).

By undoing the socially empty space of conventional landscape and looking back at European settlers, Miss Chief redefines the land as a site of colonial encounter. In Indigenous colonial contexts, the gaze bears on colonized people as well as territory, associating Native people with passive land in a relationship codified in the savagism-civilization binary and thereby rendering them as naturally subordinate objects.[12] The act of looking, of seeing while remaining unseen, constitutes an act of social mastery that in turn constitutes the colonial subject. In Monkman's image, by contrast, Miss Chief paints the human figures within the frame and looks at the viewer, thus upending the colonial dynamics of the gaze. Only Miss Chief is the bearer of the look; none of the other figures in the painting meet her gaze, nor do they meet ours. Crucially, the other human figures in the painting are nude white men. Here the settler subject is the object (rather than subject) of the gaze. Further dismantling the savagism-civilization binary, Monkman's painting associates settler bodies, rather than Native bodies, with passive nature. The naked white bodies mimic and align with natural shapes (tree trunks, logs, boulders), while the backdrop features abundant phallic imagery such as the thrust of the mountain and trees. This phallic imagery verges on irony, undercutting the seriousness and authority of the settler figures in the painting. Taken together, the dynamics of the gaze and the depiction of the white men within the frame constitute a critique of white masculinity.

In colonial discourse, white masculinity signifies settler superiority in a logic that coheres around sexuality. This logic defines white and Native men in opposition to each other to justify colonial control. In contrast with colonial representations of Native women—which, as we have seen, foreground ostensible submissiveness and availability—images of Native men take contradictory forms. On one hand, Native men appear as irredeemably violent, as a hypermasculine threat to civilization embodied in white womanhood. (This figure takes center stage in the following section of this chapter.) On the other hand, as Scott Lauria Morgensen explains, settlers have feminized Native men by attributing queerness to Indigenous societies, thus marking their "primitive" difference from "the civilizational sex and sexuality of Europeans" (2011, 36–37). Both renderings call for white men to assert control, thus solidifying racial hierarchies that justify colonial rule. In the nineteenth century, the logic that equated civilization with heteropatriarchy motivated projects of colonial reform, such as boarding school education and land allotment, that sought to reorganize Native societies by centering the nuclear family (see chapter 1). Reformers endeavored at once to tame what they saw as hypermasculine Native men and to eradicate feminized two-spirit identities. Within many Indigenous societies, two-spirit people—often, those who adopted the social roles of the opposite gender or an alternative gender status—occupied prominent positions, including those of spiritual leadership. Beyond projects of reform, the elimination of two-spirit identities took place through violence enacted on queered Native bodies.[13] In this way, sexuality, in Morgensen's words, became "a method *to produce* settler colonialism, and settler subjects, by facilitating ongoing conquest and naturalizing its effects," thus "establishing the masculinist and heteropatriarchal terms of colonial power" (2011, 42, 37).

In *History Is Painted by the Victors*, Monkman unravels the colonial logic of sexuality by making visible a presence on the land that is not only Indigenous but also two-spirit. The most prominent two-spirit presence is Miss Chief herself, who appears clad only in thigh-high red stiletto boots, hair spilling over her shoulders, looking out provocatively from the frame and compelling the viewer to see her. Regarding his creation of Miss Chief, Monkman recounts, "I wanted a persona that could reflect empowered sexuality, empowered Indigenous sexuality," so he drew on two-spirit traditions from across Native America that were repressed through colonization (Canadian Broadcasting Corporation / Radio-Canada 2019; Scudeler 2015). As the painting thus defies the erasure of two-spirit sexuality, it emphasizes the queerness of settler society itself. The other figures in Monkman's landscape are settlers who enact queer eroticism. Nude male figures lounge on the beach, wrestle, wade in the water, and swim. Extending Monkman's scrutiny of Western art history, some of these individual scenes are drawn from classic Western paintings, such as Thomas Eakins's *The Swimming Hole* (1884–85) and *The Wrestlers* (1899) (see Bailey 2017, 692). By making legible the specter of queerness in high art, the penultimate signifier of white civilization, *History Is Painted by the Victors* dismantles the distinction between "savage" and "civilized" sexuality that grounds settler expansion.

Dismantling the savage-civilized distinction opens the possibility for an alternative visual narrative of historical encounter. In Monkman's painting, Miss Chief is the subject not only of the gaze but also of representation (a painter at her easel). This fact, along with the painting's title, foregrounds the act of representation and embeds it in social power relations. This conjunction of social power and representation further denaturalizes the colonial representations that Monkman takes to task, those of Native people and lands as objects. At the same time, it enacts a shift in authority in order to foreground Native perspectives. This holds true for the painting as a whole and for the image on Miss Chief's easel. This painting-within-a-painting has a historical referent: it is a pictograph from the ledger drawings compiled as *The Battle of the Little Bighorn: An Eyewitness Account by the Lakota Chief Red Horse* (1881) (Bailey 2017, 692). Chief Red Horse, a contemporary of Bierstadt, created a visual narrative of the West that centers on Native victory in one of the best-known events in the Plains Indian Wars. In 1876, as the United States celebrated the progress of civilization on its centennial anniversary, the Seventh US Cavalry met its demise at the hands of the Sioux and Cheyenne in the Battle of the Little Bighorn. The Native victory made headlines across the country and threw into question the national narrative about "progress" inevitably defeating Indian "savagery." In Monkman's painting, sexuality further unsettles this national narrative in that the nude white men who appear in the frame represent Custer's soldiers, identified by their blue and gold uniforms strewn across the ground. As nudes on the landscape engaged in homoerotic play, they stand in stark contrast to the ideals of civilizational sexuality and colonial mastery. As the painting undermines the colonial premise of white superiority, its invocation of the Battle of the Little Bighorn calls up the violent conquest of Indigenous lands. Significantly, the battle took place in the same year that Bierstadt began to paint *Mount Corcoran*. Not only does *History Is Painted by the Victors* populate Bierstadt's empty landscape, but it also renders visible brutal assaults on Indigenous people obscured by Bierstadt's painting, thus undermining the legitimacy of settler territorial claims.

The temporality of *History Is Painted by the Victors* further challenges the progressive historical logic of expansion. The imperial notion of progressive history underwrote the relegation of Native people to the historical past. "The artwork of the 19th century," in Monkman's words, "was really about freezing Aboriginal people in time and setting us backward" (cited in Timm 2007, 94–95). Monkman created Miss Chief to challenge these representations by making her a "a time traveller" who can "be in every time period" (J. Hughes 2017, n.p.). In *History Is Painted by the Victors*, she is an anachronistic figure. Her red boots are a multivalent symbol: red demands visibility as it signifies Indigeneity, violence, and sexuality (subjects of colonial erasure that the painting commands the viewer to see). The boots' design is also a marker of modernity, so that Miss Chief appears as contemporary in contrast with the time-bound settler figures who occupy the scene with her. Here it is the settlers, not the Natives, who are frozen in time. Rendering Miss Chief as a contemporary figure serves another purpose as well: it brings the dynamics of settler colonialism into the present and gestures to ongoing land conflicts such as the multiple modern treaty negotiations in Canada that provide a crucial context for Monkman's work.

In the nineteenth century, says Monkman, western landscape paintings presented "visual versions" of the "myths" that the United States and Canada created for themselves (Canadian Broadcasting Corporation / Radio-Canada 2019), the national origin stories that erased or demonized Indigenous people to naturalize settler territorial claims. In the twentieth century, as the popularity of landscape painting waned, such myths found new expression in the emergent Western genre (Cosgrove 1998, xxiii).[14] Since the 1902 appearance of Owen Wister's *The Virginian* (the first Western novel) and the release of *The Great Train Robbery* (the first Western film) in the following year, European settlement of the frontier, conflicts between savagism and civilization, and violent struggles for justice have defined the Western. For this reason, Native artists and writers have sometimes turned to the Western film genre to present their own perspectives on European settlement and assert their own territorial claims. In Canada, the land conflicts that unfolded following the 1973 *Calder* decision include the monumental 1993 Nunavut Land Claim Agreement. While the 1975 James Bay and Northern Québec agreement (discussed in chapter 2) was the first modern treaty, the Nunavut Land Claim Agreement represents the largest Indigenous claims settlement in Canadian history. Like the past of western expansion that Monkman's work calls up, the battles over land that led to the Nunavut settlement unfolded on a frontier space—in this case, that of the Arctic, a place that symbolizes Canadian national identity. Since the 1990s, the films of Zacharias Kunuk have revolved around Inuit territorial claims in the Arctic. But in the era of Canadian national reckoning with Indigenous issues that began around 2010, he turned to the Western genre to tell a frontier story that fractures settler national mythologies and envisions social and territorial restoration for Inuit communities.

REWRITING THE WESTERN: ZACHARIAS KUNUK'S *MALIGLUTIT (SEARCHERS)*

In 2016, directors Zacharias Kunuk and Natar Ungalaaq released *Maliglutit (Searchers)*, a remake of John Ford's classic Western film *The Searchers* (1956).

For Kunuk, whose career as director spans more than forty years, *Maliglutit* extends a lifelong endeavor to represent Canadian Inuit histories, culture, and perspectives on film. In 1990, he cofounded Igloolik Isuma Productions, the first independent Inuit film production company, with the goal of producing Inuit-language media "from the inside and through Inuit eyes," as its website states. Igloolik Isuma's early work focused on historical re-creations of life in the Igloolik region in the 1930s and 1940s, designed primarily for Inuit viewers. In 2001, Kunuk gained international acclaim for directing *Atanarjuat, the Fast Runner*, the first feature film in an Indigenous language (Inuktitut) and winner of prestigious prizes including the Cannes Film Festival's coveted Caméra d'Or for best first feature.[15] *Maliglutit* is his third feature film.[16] Written, produced, directed, and acted by Inuit peoples in the Inuktitut language, his work portrays traditional lifeways, critiques Canadian expansion in the Arctic and its effects on Inuit peoples, and gives voice to Inuit perspectives on historical events along with contemporary politics. Given these commitments to Inuit cultural and political revitalization, it may seem puzzling at first that Kunuk should choose to remake John Ford's *The Searchers*.[17] Critics have long implicated the Western film genre in European expansion and the creation of settler colonial mythologies (see, for example, Prats 2002 and Slotkin 1992). But even among the most anti-Indian Westerns, *The Searchers* stands out for its brutal treatment of Native people and representations of Native "savagery."[18] In obvious respects, the political aims of Kunuk's work starkly oppose those of conventional Western films.

Indeed, Kunuk himself has described Western films as exemplifying the problems he seeks to address in his own work. In an interview recalling the expansion of Canadian power in the far North during his childhood, Kunuk recounts a scene from *The Searchers* to show how dominant media have advanced the destruction of Inuit communities wrought by church and state:

> While my parents lived on the land I stayed in town and learned the English language. Most weeks they showed movies at the Community Hall.... I remember John Wayne in the West. He spearheads the U.S. cavalry and kills some Indians at the fort. One time the scouts didn't return, we go out where there's arrows sticking out of dead soldiers and horses and one soldier says, "What kind of Indians did this!" I was shocked too. That's what I learned in my education, to think like one of the soldiers.... Four thousand years of oral history silenced by fifty years of priests, schools, and cable TV? This death of history is happening in my lifetime. (Kunuk 2002, 17–18)

Here Kunuk points to the same problems addressed by Monkman: the role of Western narratives in erasing Native peoples and casting European expansion as a triumph of "civilization" over "savagism" so as to naturalize settler power and territorial claims.[19] So ubiquitous are these stories, Kunuk suggests in the interview, that they have completely obscured Native perspectives and taught even Native people to "think like one of the soldiers."

Paradoxically, though, concerns with territorial claims and national narratives align the Western genre with the political work of contemporary Inuit media.[20] In the late twentieth century, Inuit media in Canada emerged out of ongoing conflicts over land and sovereignty. After the 1973 *Calder* decision opened the possibility for Native land claims, Inuit political organizations advocated for the creation of an independent territory under their control, the official recognition of Inuktitut language, and significant participation in Canadian governmental forums. These struggles for political autonomy and land claims culminated in the 1993 Nunavut Land Claim Agreement, the largest Indigenous land settlement in Canadian history, and the establishment of Nunavut territory six years later. Media played a key role in these endeavors. From the beginning, cultural distinctiveness provided a rationale for political autonomy, and revitalizing traditions (language, subsistence practices, and spiritual beliefs) became an explicit goal of the Nunavut settlement.[21] The Inuit Broadcasting Corporation (IBC), which aired its first program in 1982, takes as its mandate to strengthen Inuit "language, culture and identity" (cited in M. Mitchell 1996, 416) with programming focused on historical, cultural, and entertainment programs in Inuktitut (Sørensen 2000, 173; see also M. Mitchell 1996, 416). Explicitly political goals consistent with the establishment of Nunavut also find a place in IBC's mission. In addition to its focus on language and culture, IBC aims to "integrate the different isolated communities in the Nunavut region" and to "accelerate the economic, cultural and political development process in the region" (Sørensen 2000, 171). Beyond promoting cultural knowledge and a sense of common history and collective identity among communities dispersed across a wide geographic area, IBC has also provided a forum for debating issues of governance. So strong has IBC's role been in the creation of an Inuit regional identity that some have speculated that "Nunavut would not have become a reality had IBC not existed" (Sørensen 2000, 176).[22]

Kunuk joined the IBC soon after its inception, first as a producer and later as a station manager. This experience launched his career as an independent filmmaker. From the beginning, Kunuk's films have extended IBC's goals of cultural and political revitalization along with its commitment to support Inuit territorial claims in the Far North. Creating works written, directed, and acted by Inuit people aligns with broader endeavors to achieve political autonomy. As Kunuk's films critique ongoing colonization in the Arctic, they also participate in language and cultural revitalization, or the cultivation of cultural distinctiveness that underlies arguments for political distinctiveness. His work focuses heavily, for example, on subsistence practices, the methods of fishing, hunting, and gathering that have structured Inuit life for thousands of years. As this focus conveys traditional knowledge to younger generations, it demonstrates deep ties between Inuit people and the land, ties central to the histories of use and occupancy that support territorial claims in the present. Inuit cultural and political distinctiveness in turn contravenes both the notion of a multicultural Canadian state and the containment of Inuit homelands within the nation-state boundaries (and, by extension, the very legitimacy of those national boundaries, because Inuit communities extend across the Arctic regions, well beyond the Canadian border). These aims shed light on Kunuk's choice to re-create *The Searchers*, which is similarly concerned with nation-building and territorial claims. Remaking one of the best-known Westerns of all time broadens the audiences for this film as it enables Kunuk and Ungalaaq to provide an alternative history of the Arctic "frontier" that supports contemporary Inuit political endeavors. In reflecting on settler expansion in the Far North, *Maliglutit* upends the racial and gendered logic of settler narratives while also providing an allegory of Inuit social restoration in the aftermath of colonial destruction. After briefly analyzing the ideological work of *The Searchers*, I turn to *Maliglutit* to consider how Kunuk reworks Ford's classic Western narrative for Inuit political purposes.

. . .

Lauded by critics as one of the most influential films ever made, John Ford's *The Searchers* takes up the politics of Indigenous-settler relations on contested land in a story about captivity and redemption. Set in 1868, the film opens when Ethan Edwards, a Civil War veteran played by John Wayne, returns to his brother's family ranch in West Texas. Shortly after his arrival, a group of Comanche warriors, led by a chief ominously named Scar, attacks the ranch and burns the family home. The story begins, then, with a symbolically laden scene. The image of "the family on the land," asserts film scholar Virginia

Wright Wexman, constitutes a foundational aspect of US national mythologies that finds a prominent place in Western films. The family home, according to the Jeffersonian ideal, anchors an egalitarian, democratic social system premised on individual property ownership (see Wexman 1993, 79; and 1996). But this connection between property and egalitarianism creates a tension in such narratives because acquiring land entails violent dispossession, a problem that is symbolically resolved by racializing the original occupants of the land as "savages." In *The Searchers*, the Comanche attack on the family home constitutes a symbolic attack on US national ideals and claims to property, thus inaugurating the paradigmatic conflict between savagism and civilization that unfolds through the film. Crucially, within and beyond the film, this conflict bears not only on race but also on gender. "What is most conspicuously at issue in Westerns," argues Wexman, is the intimate connection between "the right to possess women" and "the right to possess the land" (Wexman 1993, 75). This holds true because, in a system of private property ownership, women within the nuclear family bear children who become heirs to the land, thereby ensuring the transfer of property within the father's lineage.[23] In Ford's film, the Comanches kill Ethan's brother's family, sparing only daughters Lucy and Debbie to take them as captives. The remainder of the story centers on Ethan's search for his nieces. Soon he finds Lucy's body, mutilated and (the film insinuates) raped, then continues to look for Debbie. This quest to recover Debbie (or, in Wexman's terms, to possess the woman) stands in for broader contests over who holds a future on the land.

In Ford's film, then, the conflict between savagism and civilization takes shape as a captivity narrative, the quintessential American literary genre.[24] The genre emerged in the seventeenth century as, according to one literary critic, "a major vehicle for reflecting upon the meaning of the European occupation of the captured space of the New World" (Ebersole 1995, 3). Over time, it has provided a lens through which to understand settler territorial conflicts, including the Indian Wars. The prototypical narrative—wherein the white female captive, representing settler society, falls victim to Indian savages—exemplifies the ways that colonial discourse draws on the logic of gender as well as race to rationalize Indigenous dispossession. Following captivity-narrative conventions, the white women captives in *The Searchers* appear as defenseless and innocent in the face of Indian violence. Again and again, Ford's film stages scenes of Native brutality, particularly as they relate to white women. Beyond the murder of Ethan's sister-in-law and insinuations about her daughter Lucy's cruel fate, one notorious scene depicts a group of rescued women captives who have fallen into madness, evidence of the horrors they experienced at the hands of their Indian captors. Such scenes align the viewer's sympathies with the women as victims, if not with Ethan himself (who turns out to be a problematic hero). As the creation of private property at the center of settler expansion hinges on the subjugation of women, the logic of patriarchy rationalizes dispossession. Within and beyond *The Searchers*, the patriarchal notion of (white) female helplessness couples with the racist notion of Native brutality to invert the colonial power dynamic, recasting the violence of settler expansion as self-defense. *The Searchers* calls up multiple histories of settler expansion. Ford famously lingers on western landscapes in his films, and critics have labeled *The Searchers* in particular as a "visual masterpiece" because of its spectacular rendering of the desert landscape. The film's setting is Monument Valley (Diné territory), an iconic space synonymous with the US West (Engel 1994; L. Mitchell 2004). This location evokes the removal of Diné people in the "Long Walk" of 1864–66, just two years before Ford's story begins. In the film, Ethan's years-long quest to find Debbie draws him across territories that evoke other histories of Indigenous displacement and dispossession, though the film does not name them as such. The story unfolds in the time and place of the Texas-Indian wars, clashes that earned Comanche people the reputation of fierce defenders of their territory. Defense sometimes took the form of raids on Anglo settlers who, by the time period of the film, were rapidly building homesteads on Comanche land. This history is represented by Ethan's brother, giving cause for the Comanche attack on his home in the opening scene.

But, whereas conventional captivity narratives recast land conflicts as a paradigmatic struggle between good (settlers) and evil (Natives),[25] *The Searchers* complicates this paradigm when the actions of the white characters mimic those of the Comanche warriors in dynamics that take shape around gender. In conventional Westerns, the male hero epitomizes patriarchal power, a paradigm that emerges from the genre's origins in the "crisis in masculinity" at the turn of the twentieth century.[26] Ford cast John Wayne, an icon of mid-twentieth-century masculinity, in the role of Ethan, so that the character embodies the quintessential masculine Western hero. But Ethan, the viewer soon discovers, is a complicated figure. He searches for Debbie not to rescue her, as it initially seems, but rather to kill her because her contact with Scar, he says, has reduced her to "the leavings of a Comanche buck." This murderous plan upsets the notion of white (masculine) civilization as the defense of white womanhood by making Ethan as much of a danger to Debbie as Scar. Uncharacteristically for a Western, the film depicts violence not only against white women but against Indigenous women as well. After a transaction over a blanket, Martin, Ethan's accomplice in the search, learns that he has inadvertently acquired an Indian wife, whom the men call "Look." The film depicts this character as a joke and an object of derision, a stereotypical embodiment of the sexually available "squaw" (Ethan's demeaning term for her). When Look attempts to sleep near Martin, he kicks her, sending her body rolling down the hill. In one sense, the scene calls upon the viewer to "look" at settler violence, including gendered violence against Native women, that is suppressed in colonial narratives. But *The Searchers* undermines the potential critical dimensions of this scene by turning gendered violence into comedy, as registered by the humorous soundtrack to Look's fall. This pattern, wherein settlers engage in savage acts,[27] continues throughout the film in scenes that reprise events in the Indian Wars. One recalls the 1868 Battle of the Washita River, when the US Cavalry brutally attacked a group of peaceful Southern Cheyenne, slaying women and children. In the film's reenactment of this event, Look dies in this attack, her murder paralleling that of Lucy. Another scene shows Texas Rangers attacking Scar's band, killing him in the process. When Ethan scalps Scar, the scene asserts the dominance of the white male hero but in a way that questions his civility. Reiterating a paradigm of Western narratives that historian Richard Slotkin labels "regeneration through violence," the white masculine hero in Ford's film must paradoxically descend into savagery in order to defeat savagery (see Slotkin [1973] 2000). The film thus uses a gendered narrative to expose the savagery at the heart of civilization, eroding the boundaries between settlers and Native people on which the legitimacy of dispossession depends.[28]

The Searchers, however, unsettles the boundaries between savagery and civilization only to restore them. Near the film's end, Ethan partially redeems himself when, after a search that continues for five years, he finally finds Debbie. After a harrowing chase, he sweeps her up in his arms, but rather than shooting her, he promises to bring her home. He then returns her to the Jorgensen ranch, the home of her family's lifelong friends. This final scene mirrors that of the film's opening, so that the story takes shape as a narrative of restoration of the "family on the land" after a perilous encounter with Native savagery. In this final scene, the film symbolically resolves the problem of the savagery of civilization through a gendered colonial logic centered on domesticity. Importantly, Ethan does not enter the family home. Instead, the last image shows him returning to the land as the door of the Jorgensen

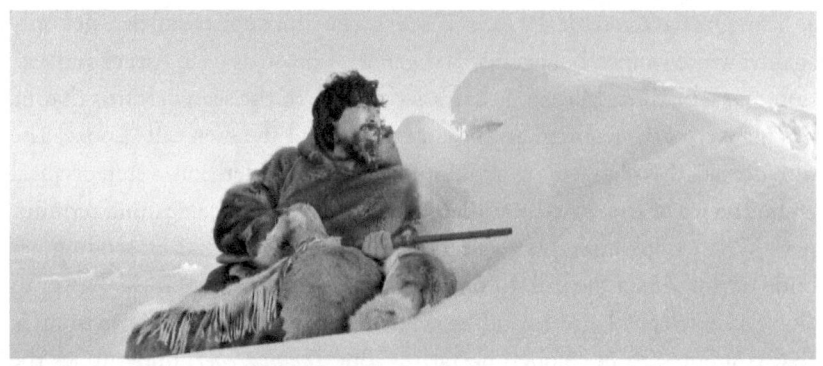

FIGURE 15. Benjamin Kunuk plays Kuanana in Zacharias Kunuk's *Maliglutit (Searchers)*, 2016. © Kingulliit Productions, Inc. Reprinted with permission.

family home closes behind him. This expulsion of savagery secures the innocence of the "family on the land" and hence the legitimacy of its territorial claims. *The Searchers*, then, advances a settler national narrative wherein gender solidifies distinctions between white civilization and Native savagery while also obscuring the violence of conquest, thus answering the question of who holds legitimate claims to the land.

Concerns with nation-building, territorial claims, and social restoration at the center of *The Searchers* also underlie the political project of *Maliglutit*. But this film—"a western genre movie made entirely the Inuit way," as Kunuk calls it (Kingulliit Productions 2016, 3)—upends the racial and gendered distinctions of Ford's film in order to undermine settler territorial claims and support contemporary Inuit nation-building projects in the contemporary Arctic. Like Ford's film, *Maliglutit* uses the captivity narrative to reflect on the "captured space" of the frontier (in this case, the Canadian Arctic) in a story that roughly follows that of *The Searchers*. Set in 1913, the film centers on small Inuit communities before Canadian expansion disrupted traditional lifeways in the Arctic (fig. 15). It opens on a scene of discord when elders banish Kupak and his three followers for murder, debauchery, and refusal to meet obligations such as providing food for the band. Exiled, the four offenders begin to wander. They happen upon a family igloo and decide to attack it in hopes of finding women to capture. Soon after, Kuanana returns from hunting with his eldest son, Siku, to find his home destroyed, his wife, Ailla, and daughter, Tagaq, kidnapped, and the rest of his family murdered. Like Ethan Edwards, Kuanana then embarks on a quest to return the captives home.

Maliglutit restages the encounter between "civilization" and "savagery" at the center of captivity narratives by casting the captors—who are murderers and rapists—as the film's "savages." But, whereas colonial narratives pivot on a racialized distinction between white civilization and Native savagery, Kunuk's film includes only Inuit characters. This fact transforms "savagery" from a racialized attribute to one that denotes behavior that departs from Inuit social norms. Beyond the obvious violent transgressions, these departures entail failing to care for the welfare of the band and disrespecting women. Like the oral narratives that Kunuk describes as a major influence on this work (see Kingulliit Productions 2016), *Maliglutit* thus takes shape in part as a cautionary tale about the consequences of disregarding traditional beliefs and practices. In this way, Kunuk upends the conventional savage-civilized dichotomy: here, savagery involves rejecting Indigenous lifeways (rather than, as colonial narratives hold, abiding by them), so that the film undercuts the idea of Native brutality at the center of colonial discourse. Overturning the savage-civilized dichotomy in turn carries implications for territorial claims.

Maliglutit, like *The Searchers*, takes land conflicts as a fundamental, though implicit, theme. Whereas Ford's film is set in the time and place of the Texas-Indian wars, the context for *Maliglutit* is Canadian expansion in the Arctic "frontier." According to Isuma's promotional materials, the story takes place in Nunavut in 1913. The place-name is anachronistic: the Inuit territory of Nunavut was established eight decades later, but the name positions the story as a prehistory of the land claims settlement and contemporary Inuit control of the region. Too, the meaning of the word "Nunavut"—"our land" in Inuktitut language—underscores Inuit claims to the territory. Importantly, the year 1913 marks the beginning of serious challenges to Inuit lifeways and territorial control through forced integration into the capitalist system and the Canadian nation-state. Beginning in 1912, the Hudson's Bay Company, a dominant force in the Canadian fur trade for more than two centuries, established its first permanent trading posts in the Arctic. Others soon followed, enabling the rapid development of the fur trade in the region (see Usher 1971). For Inuit communities, the shift from subsistence hunting to commercial trapping created economic dependence and undermined prohibitions on overexploitation of animals (Pauktuutit Inuit Women Canada and Comack 2020, 15). In the decades that followed, the Canadian government expanded its presence, which had previously been largely symbolic, throughout the region. During the 1950s, when Kunuk was a young child, officials forced Inuit families to relocate to permanent settlements, severing their traditional relationships to the land. Children attended federal day or boarding schools where they learned Western values—such as individualism, acquisitiveness, and exploitation of the natural world—that were at odds with traditional Inuit lifeways (Pauktuutit Inuit Women Canada and Comack 2020, 13).

In *Maliglutit*, the transgressions of Kupak's group—especially their disregard of community responsibilities—resonate with the colonial project of annihilating Inuit values and practices. But here, such disregard counts not as uplift but rather as "evil" that must be expelled. As the film condemns Kupak and his followers for violating Inuit social norms, it iterates the value and power of these and other traditional practices. At the beginning, Kuanana's father, Ituk, consults his divining stone to ascertain the location of caribou. (Kuanana is hunting caribou when Kupak attacks his home and, in a symbolically laden act, kills Kuanana's father, the holder of Inuit spiritual knowledge.) As Kuanana searches for his wife and daughter, he relies on his spirit guide Kallulik, the loon, whose cries alert him to the location of the captives. In the historical context of the emerging fur trade in the Arctic, representing the loon as powerful spirit guide contrasts with the notion of animals as objects to be exploited for profit. The relationship of humans to the rest of the natural world has multiple thematic registers throughout the film. Like Kunuk's other films, *Maliglutit* lingers on subsistence lifeways, so that the film itself provides a means of advancing traditional land-based practices and the values they represent. Laying out the connection between subsistence and cultural survival in another Arctic context, Yup'ik culture bearer John Active writes that the subsistence lifestyle teaches "to not waste, but share; to not steal, but provide for myself; to remember my elders, those living and dead and share with them; to be watchful at all times that I do not offend the spirits of the fish and animals; . . . to take from the land only what I can use; and to give to the needy if I have enough to share" (Active 1999, 186–87). Relationships that privilege the needs of the community and viability of animals contravene ideologies of individualism and capitalist accumulation at the center of colonial reform. At the same time, representing subsistence practices is a cartographic practice in itself that makes visible Indigenous sites and paths on the land, tracing the histories of use and occupancy that underlie Inuit territorial claims in the present.

Maliglutit raises the issue of Canadian power over the Far North by setting its story in 1913, the year that Vilhjalmur Stefansson commenced the

Canadian Arctic Expedition. More than thirty years after Britain had transferred title to the Arctic Archipelago to Canada in 1880, the new nation-state had little ability to enforce its sovereignty over the region. In the early twentieth century, the government sponsored a series of expeditions to secure its territorial claims (see Stern 1998). Among these, the Canadian Arctic Expedition proved the most significant. Beyond claiming thousands of miles on behalf of Canada and remapping the region, Stefansson transformed popular understandings of the Arctic in ways that remain influential today. In addition to becoming a source of wealth through the fur trade, the Arctic at the turn of the twentieth century gained symbolic importance in an emerging Canadian nationalism: like the US West, it figured as a frontier space offering opportunities for adventure, riches, and self-realization, and as a place to forge national ideals through the process of settlement. The notion of the Arctic as a "treasure house" holding "vast, untapped riches," writes anthropologist Robert G. Williamson, subsequently became "a powerful motivating force in the Canadianising of the north" (cited in Pauktuutit Inuit Women of Canada and Comack 2020, 16). The Arctic came to represent, in other words, the "nation's heartland" and the "embodiment of the national ideal" (Steinberg, Tasch, and Gerhardt 2018, 122). Stefansson was instrumental in this transition. Advancing the idea that the Arctic was central to Canadian national identity in books such as *The Friendly Arctic* and *The Northward Course of Empire*, he promoted the idea of the region as amenable to settlement and resource development. As his 1913 expedition literally redrew the map of the Arctic, it generated an unprecedented number of photographs that circulated widely among the public as well as government officials. The images created a sense of proximity to the region, the vicarious sense of being there, and thus encouraged a "public sense of ownership of the Arctic" (Stern 1998, 50). After Stefansson's expedition, the "trickle of outsiders" to the North "became a flood" (Stern 1998, 51). This growing settler population increased control over the Inuit by mid-century (the period of Kunuk's childhood) when the government forced communities into permanent settlements and launched assimilation programs. In colonial narratives, Stefansson's Canadian Arctic Expedition marks the beginning of the end for the Inuit, the time when loss of land and sovereignty, along with the inevitability of assimilation, transformed Native life forever.

Maliglutit takes 1913 as the starting point for a counternarrative of colonial transformations of Inuit life. In one sense, the film constitutes a colonial allegory that criticizes the social disruptions brought by the rise of Canadian power and the systematic undermining of traditional practices. This critique takes shape through the harm and suffering caused by Kupak and his followers as they reject Inuit social norms. Part of this critique centers on gender. Historically, the changes brought by colonial forces at mid-century—especially the loss of the land-based economy as Inuit people were relocated to permanent settlements and their children were sent to government schools—disrupted traditional gender roles that entailed mutual dependency. Diminishing Inuit women's social influence in turn made them more vulnerable to violence (Pauktuutit 2020, 4). Importantly, *Maliglutit* foregrounds the gendered dimensions of Kupak's transgressions. In the opening scene, he harasses another man's wife, and the attack on Kuanana's home is prompted by the desire to capture women. This reflects in part on an ancient practice of wife stealing, as the promotional materials state, so that the film subjects some traditional practices to criticism. But in the context of the film's scrutiny of Canadian expansion, this abuse also invokes the gendered violence that ensued from the loss of traditions (Pauktuutit 2020, 6). Whereas Ford's *The Searchers*, and conventional Western narratives more broadly, focus on the actions and perspectives of male characters, *Maliglutit* shifts the attention to women's experiences. The film endeavors to imagine "what it would feel like to live through or witness a kidnapping" and "to find the emotional truth of the situation" (Kingulliit Productions 2016, 3), and it opens with the female narrator's reminiscence: "Way back then, my world was torn apart. Men. When they want to get a wife, they become fearless and act without mercy." As the film literally gives voice to women's experiences, thereby countering the colonial silencing of Indigenous women, the story unfolds as a critique of male violence in a rape scene that lingers painfully on the victim's struggle. In contrast with the abuse of Look in *The Searchers*, this scene renders the violence as tragedy and solicits viewers' sympathies for the captured women. A musical score by Inuit celebrity performer Tanya Tagaq augments this critique by foregrounding a woman's voice in a traditional expressive form (throat singing). Shortly before the release of *Maliglutit*, Tagaq dedicated her prize-winning 2014 album, *Animism*, to missing and murdered Indigenous women, a fact that aligns the purpose of Kunuk's film with the gender critique of Tagaq's performances. Underscoring this association, Kuanana's daughter is named Tagaq. Whereas *The Searchers* uses the rape of Lucy to demonstrate Native brutality and justify settler aggression, the rape scene in *Maliglutit* instead demands attention to sexual violence against Indigenous women as an indictment of the colonial project.

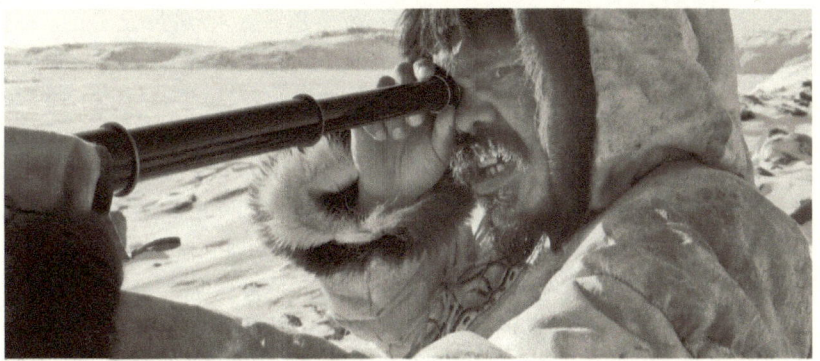

FIGURE 16. Joey Sarpinak plays Kupak in Zacharias Kunuk's *Maliglutit (Searchers)*, 2016. © Kingulliit Productions, Inc. Reprinted with permission.

As it subverts the racial and gendered logic of settler expansion, *Maliglutit* tells a story of restoration in the wake of social destruction. Restoration, in this context, necessarily entails affirming Inuit claims to land. Like Ford's film, *Maliglutit* features wide shots of sublime vistas, emphasizing the importance of land in the story. The film commences with a caribou hunt that calls up histories of use and occupancy at the center of contemporary Indigenous land claims. In the remainder of the film, Kuanana's search for the captives shows him traveling across the land in scenes that make visible Inuit presence in the Arctic. Like Monkman, Kunuk foregrounds the Native gaze on the land that contends with the colonial gaze and heightens the sense of Native possession (fig. 16). In the film, the Inuit gaze is embodied not only by the filmmaker but also by the character of Kuanana. Multiple scenes depict him looking through a spotting scope first for caribou and later for his wife and daughter. These filmic images of the Arctic constitute an alternative visual iconography to that created by Stefansson's 1913 voyage. If photographs from Stefansson's voyage represented the Arctic as Canadian national space, Kunuk's film depicts the land as Inuit territory.

Maliglutit creates a sense of uninterrupted Inuit presence on the land in other ways as well. The fact that the film includes only Inuit characters minimizes the significance of colonial disruptions by emphasizing community continuity. Although no *qallunaat* (non-Inuit people) appear among its characters, the film does invoke settler presence in the form of technology (spotting scopes, hunting rifles) typically acquired through trade in the time frame of the story. In colonial discourse, the "primitive" encounter with technology is a weighted trope that registers Indigenous backwardness and inevitable demise in the face of modernity.[29] But in *Maliglutit*, European technology and traditional practices exist alongside each other without contradiction—in fact, technology aids practices such as subsistence hunting—so that the film dismantles the temporal opposition between tradition and modernity. Like Kunuk's earlier work, *Maliglutit* re-creates historical lifeways with painstaking accuracy, with elders having advised the filmmakers on clothing, food preparation, and igloo building. Scenes linger on traditional cultural practices (hunting caribou, preparing skins, consulting spirit guides), and all dialogue is in Inuktitut, so that the film not only represents but also advances cultural survival. Dismantling the colonial logic that situates Indigenous people in the past enables a narrative of Indigenous survival in the present.

In the story, these traditional cultural practices ultimately enable the captives' rescue when the loon leads Kuanana to his wife and daughter. Finding his daughter alone, he frees her from bondage. He then sets out to rescue his wife, but Kupak attacks him. As the two men fight, Ailla stabs Kupak from behind, killing him. By having the female captive slay her captor and rescue her husband, the film upends patriarchal conventions of the captivity narrative. This is not the only instance of women's agency in the film. Unlike Lucy and Debbie in *The Searchers*, Ailla and her daughter, Tagaq, are not helpless victims. They repeatedly resist their captors, including in the emotionally fraught rape scene. One conflict significantly centers on domestic roles: when Kupak calls Ailla "dear" and instructs her to make him a cup of tea, she throws the scalding drink in his face. Such acts refute colonial representations of Indigenous women as passive and acquiescent and, by extension, the idea that Indigenous societies and lands are available for colonization (see chapter 1). At the same time, they accord Inuit women a powerful role in the emergent society, a meaning that resonates with debates surrounding gender parity in the Nunavut government (see, for example, Gombay 2000).

Like *The Searchers*, *Maliglutit* ends with a scene of restoration. After Ailla kills her captor, Kuanana and Ailla embrace and the family is reunited. In the historical context of colonial assaults on the Native family, argues Joanna Hearne, such scenes of family reunion carry political meanings, and the figure of the Native child in particular "acts as a symbolic embodiment of an Indigenous future" (Hearne 2012, 25). As in Ford's film, the defeat of savagery sets the stage for nation-building; here, though, nation-building entails addressing social disruptions by affirming the value of Inuit social and spiritual traditions (an explicit goal of Kunuk's work as a whole). This final scene departs in other vital respects from *The Searchers*. Whereas Ford's film concludes with the restoration of the family home—a symbol, as we have seen, of colonial national ideals that hinge on private property and the subjugation of women—the last scenes of *Maliglutit* take place on open land rather than in domestic space. This distinction signals social formations and relationships to land that distinguish Inuit practices from those of settlers. In Kunuk's film, domestic space (here, the igloo) differs from the home associated with the "family on the land" in part because of its inherent impermanence; that is, because the igloo is a temporary dwelling that enables subsistence practices across a wide geographical area, it does not represent property relations that entail the subjugation of women. Nevertheless, in *Maliglutit*, the igloo as domestic space becomes the location of violence against women, most starkly in the scenes of the captives' confinement and rape. Significantly, then, Ailla kills her captor on the open space of the land, and the women captives, unlike Debbie in *The Searchers*, are never returned to the home. The reversal of gender roles in the killing, along with the location of the action outside the containment of domestic space, signals the possibility of equitable roles for Inuit women in an Inuit nation-building project. At the same time, the wide shots on the land in the concluding scenes register a relationship to land contrary to the boundedness of private property, a relationship that inheres in the subsistence practices traced by the film, while also reiterating Inuit presence across the immense region. Fittingly, *Maliglutit* concludes with an image of an *inukshuk* (stone territorial marker) that claims the Arctic as Inuit territory.

By underscoring connections between gendered violence and colonial transformations of Inuit society, *Maliglutit* calls attention to an urgent contemporary issue in Indigenous communities in the Arctic. According to a 2020 report by Pauktuutit, the national organization of Inuit women in Canada, women in Nunavut experience the highest rate of police-reported domestic abuse of any group and are thirteen times more likely to become victims of violent crime than other women in the country. Their heightened vulnerability, Pauktuutit reports, stems in good measure from colonial disruptions of Inuit relationships to the land that accelerated in the mid-twentieth century, including the dismantling of interdependent roles of men and women in a subsistence economy. Severing ties to the land took away women's essential community roles, marginalizing them and eliminating their social protections. Beginning in this same period, the arrival of military employees and other government personnel in the Arctic further increased

Native women's vulnerability to sexual exploitation and violence (Pauktuutit Inuit Women of Canada and Comack 2020, 4, 21). Thus, according to the 2019 final report by the National Inquiry into Missing and Murdered Indigenous Women and Girls (2019), government intervention in the far north "is the root cause of a great deal of the violence Inuit women are exposed to today" (310). By invoking this history in an allegory of nation-building that hinges on the strength and agency of its women characters, *Maliglutit* calls for the restoration of the social power of women in contemporary Inuit society. Notably, Kunuk's film was released the same year as the launch of the National Inquiry (2016), timing that put the film in conversation with broader debates surrounding violence against Native women within and beyond the Arctic regions.

In the post-1960s United States and Canada, the Arctic regions have been the site of multiple land conflicts and Native claims that include the two largest Indigenous land settlements in those countries' histories (the 1971 Alaska Native Claims Settlement Act and the 1993 Nunavut Land Claim Agreement). The conclusion analyzes how two Native women artists, Erica Lord and Heather Campbell, use their work to dismantle the racial and gendered hierarchies that have historically enabled dispossession and underlie violence against Native women in the present. In so doing, they envision new relationships between Indigenous bodies and land that tie Native territorial claims to gender justice within and beyond the Arctic.

Conclusion

BODIES OF LAND, REDUX

Since the 1960s, no place has been the site of more Indigenous land conflicts than my home territory, the Arctic regions. An area with large, politically active Indigenous populations, the Arctic has been the location of major discoveries of natural resources, large-scale extractive industry, and consequent territorial conflicts among Native communities, settler governments, and multinational corporations. It is also the site of the two largest Indigenous land settlements in US and Canadian history: the 1971 Alaska Native Claims Settlement Act, which was prompted by the discovery of the massive oil field at Prudhoe Bay (Iñupiat land), and the 1993 Nunavut Land Claim Agreement, which established Nunavut as the first Indigenous territory in Canada. Despite the size of their Indigenous populations and the significance of these land settlements, the Arctic regions remain neglected and their politics little understood in Native American and Indigenous studies. Art and politics of the Arctic regions form a significant thematic thread throughout this book, from the work of Tlingit and Unangax̂ artist Nicholas Galanin (see the introduction), to the effects of the James Bay hydroelectric project on Cree and Inuit communities (the subject of Hogan's *Solar Storms*, discussed in chapter 2), to the productions of Inuit filmmaker Zacharias Kunuk (chapter 4). I return to the Arctic in this conclusion to underscore its importance in the Indigenous world and to emphasize the cultural and political vibrancy of its communities. Specifically, I focus on two works—Erica Lord's multimedia installation *Native American Land Reclamation Project* (2000) and Heather Campbell's painting *Methylmercury* (2017)—that engage territorial conflicts in the Arctic by reworking the connections between Native bodies and lands explored throughout this book.

Historically, the entanglements of dispossession, gendered violence, and the social marginalization of Indigenous women have hinged in part on the colonial association of Native women's bodies with land (see chapter 1). Throughout the era of expansion, imperial depictions of feminized lands naturalized European possession of the "New World," and conversely, representations of Native people as part of feminized nature have supported settler domination, with particular consequences for Native women. The social marginalization of Native women also manifested in colonial policies enacted to remove them from positions of influence as a means to bring Native communities and territories under control. The previous chapters analyze how contemporary Native artists, writers, and filmmakers contend with the enduring consequences of the gendered dimensions of dispossession as they engage with ongoing Indigenous territorial struggles. Here I revisit the connection between Native bodies and lands analyzed in chapter 1 by examining the ways that Native women artists alter this connection in the context of recent Indigenous land activism in the Arctic regions. Erica Lord (Athabascan and Iñupiat) and Heather Campbell (Inuit) compel viewers to see Native bodies and lands in ways that subvert the political work of colonial representations and envision new relationships that position gender justice as intrinsic to territorial claims.

Exemplifying deep ties between contemporary Native culture and land politics, Erica Lord created the multimedia installation *Native American Land Reclamation Project* (2000) in response to the 1998 US Supreme Court decision in the case *Alaska v. Native Village of Venetie Tribal Government.* In essence, the decision denied sovereignty rights to Alaska Native communities because of the status of lands conferred under the 1971 Alaska Native Claims Settlement Act (ANCSA). For the first time, the US Congress settled Native land claims by establishing for-profit Native corporations rather than reservations with tribal governments. The settlement was passed during the era when Congress unilaterally terminated the status and seized the lands of 109 tribes, so, predictably, it refused to recognize more than two hundred additional tribes in Alaska (federal recognition of these communities would come later, in a different political moment). Congress enacted the legislation to enable construction of an eight-hundred-mile pipeline to transport oil across tribal lands from Prudhoe Bay to the port of Valdez, so that resource exploitation became the condition for settling Alaska Native territorial claims.[1] In the *Venetie* case more than two decades later, the Supreme Court decided the implications of the land settlement for tribal sovereignty in Alaska. Land held by Alaska Native communities under the settlement, according to the Court, does not count as Native land because it is held in fee simple (as property) rather than in trust by the federal government (as are reservation lands). According to the decision's perverse logic, owning lands outright means that Native communities do not hold sovereign rights—or, in Lord's words, "Even though you are sovereign people, you have no land to be sovereign on" (Lord 2010, n.p.). The decision was more than ironic, as the Court held that traditional territories acknowledged as Native lands in the settlement were not Native lands at all, and it dealt a significant blow to tribal rights in Alaska. Lord's *Native American Land Reclamation Project* protests the *Venetie* decision by connecting it to the long history of broken treaties with Native nations, showing dispossession as a continuous process, from the origins of the United States to the present, that occurs in part by means of colonial law. As the installation compels viewers to confront the ongoing dispossession of Native communities throughout the continent, it conveys meanings of land alternative to those that inhere in settler laws, with implications for contemporary Indigenous political struggles.

Native American Land Reclamation Project is an enclosure with mirrored walls, and from its ceiling hang red prayer ties, each one holding soil from Alaska Native villages, Indian reservations, and other tribal lands (Lord 2000). There are 371 prayer ties in all, one for each treaty that the United States ratified and subsequently broke with Indigenous nations. The prayer ties, then, signify histories of dispossession that unite Native communities across cultural and geographical boundaries. Made from the red stripes of the US flag, the bundles bespeak the violence of dispossession—the blood shed trying to hold onto the land, explains Lord, and the blood-soaked earth, the Native lives and lands lost in the creation of the colonial nation-state (Lord 2010, n.p.). This invocation of violence and broken treaties undermines the moral authority and territorial claims of the settler state while calling up the political autonomy of Native communities enshrined in the nation's own laws and treaties. As the surrounding mirrors amplify the message of the bundles, forcing viewers to confront theft and violence, they also impel viewers to see the land in ways rooted in Indigenous epistemologies. As spiritual offerings, the prayer ties mark the land as sacred and as commanding respect (the color red denotes the sacred along with violence). Their position above eye level, so that viewers literally have to look up to them, augments this sense of sacredness as it undercuts notions of land as an object to be bought, sold, and exploited for profit.

Native American Land Reclamation Project further alters understandings of land through the dynamics of the gaze and the way it positions viewers in relation to the land. As discussed in previous chapters, visual perspective, in the words of geographer Denis Cosgrove, "directs the external world towards the individual located outside that space," so that "visually space is rendered the property of the individual detached observer, from whose divine location it is an independent, appropriated object" (Cosgrove 1985, 48–49). In numerous other works, Lord engages the ways that colonial images have objectified and subordinated Indigenous bodies, especially women's bodies, but in this installation, she unfixes the positions of observer and observed so as to make objectification impossible. In the installation, there is no "divine location" from which to view space from outside. Here the body that appears in the mirrors is the observer's own, so that the viewer becomes both spectator and object of the gaze. The mirrors disable visual separation between observer and observed, thereby disallowing the visual appropriation of space by a detached observer. Instead, visitors inevitably see themselves in relation to the prayer ties of land hanging from the ceiling. Visual proximity invokes a sense of relationality to (rather than separation from) the land while also raising questions about viewers' relationships to the histories of dispossession that the prayer ties call up. Because spatial hierarchies are also social hierarchies, disrupting the notion of land as object also disrupts the race, gender, and class relations that inhere in property relations and that rationalize settler appropriations of Native lands. By disabling the convention of the detached observer, Lord's installation also undermines the sense of social mastery that arises from it, thereby unsettling the social hierarchies on which settler expansion depends.

Ultimately, these meanings of land support Native political claims in the present, encompassing and extending beyond the Alaska Native contexts that prompted Lord to create *Native American Land Reclamation Project*. Lord describes the installation as an act of reclamation in itself because the prayer ties hold, and the floor is composed of, soil from Native territories, so that to create the work, she "reclaimed that tiny bit" of Native land (Lord 2010, n.p.). As the installation title suggests, the work also engages in a broader project of reclamation. The prayer ties denote not only sacredness but also futurity, the continuing struggle for Indigenous lands that the installation's title registers. By engaging in a prayerful act designed to bring about political change and invoking meanings of land that support Indigenous claims, the installation itself constitutes a Native American land reclamation project that joins with material political endeavors. By calling up a common history of dispossession (broken treaties) registered by the 371 prayer ties, *Native American Land Reclamation Project*, like other activist and artistic projects of the post-1960s era, defines land reclamation as a common political cause for Indigenous people across boundaries of culture, geography, and settler nation-state.

Like Erica Lord, Heather Campbell drew inspiration for her work *Methylmercury* (2017) from territorial upheavals in the Far North. She created this watercolor in response to two interrelated crises: the threats posed to Labrador Inuit communities by construction of the Muskrat Falls hydroelectric project and disappearances of Indigenous women and girls. Inuit resistance to the dam at Muskrat Falls commenced in the early 2010s, when the project was still in the planning phase, because of concerns about predicted effects on the land and animals on which Native communities depend. Protests reached their peak in 2016 after Harvard University researchers concluded that flooding caused by the dam would contaminate northern Labrador waterways with methylmercury, thereby poisoning fish, seals, and other food sources. The Inuit community of Rigolet, where Campbell grew up, was at particular risk. In an effort to stop the project, Inuit land and water protectors launched hunger strikes, organized marches, and, at one point, occupied part of the dam site. Campbell's own family members faced arrest for joining the protests. For her part, Campbell turned to art as a means of resistance. "I realized, as an artist," she later wrote, "I have a voice and I would try my best to use it" (Campbell 2021, n.p.). As the dam protests were being staged, the trial for the killers of Loretta Saunders, an Inuk woman from the region, occupied local headlines. In Campbell's mind, the two events became "inseparable" (cited in Croskery 2018, n.p.). *Methylmercury* took shape as an image that limns the interconnections of Indigenous dispossession and gendered violence as it advocates for alternative understandings of land and the social places of women that are rooted in Inuit epistemologies. Beyond calling attention to settler violence and protesting its logic, Campbell's art supported the Muskrat Falls dam protests in material ways as she sold prints of *Methylmercury* to provide funds to land and water protectors.

At the center of Campbell's painting is Nuliajuk, more commonly known as Sedna, a figure who appears in Inuit stories from across the Arctic.[2] In the version that Campbell remembers, the story begins when Nuliajuk, a beautiful young Inuk, marries a mysterious man and moves to his home in a high cave. Upon discovering that her new husband is actually a shapeshifting fish hawk, she flees in a boat with her father, but her husband pursues them. As the enraged bird flaps its wings, it creates perilous waves that threaten to

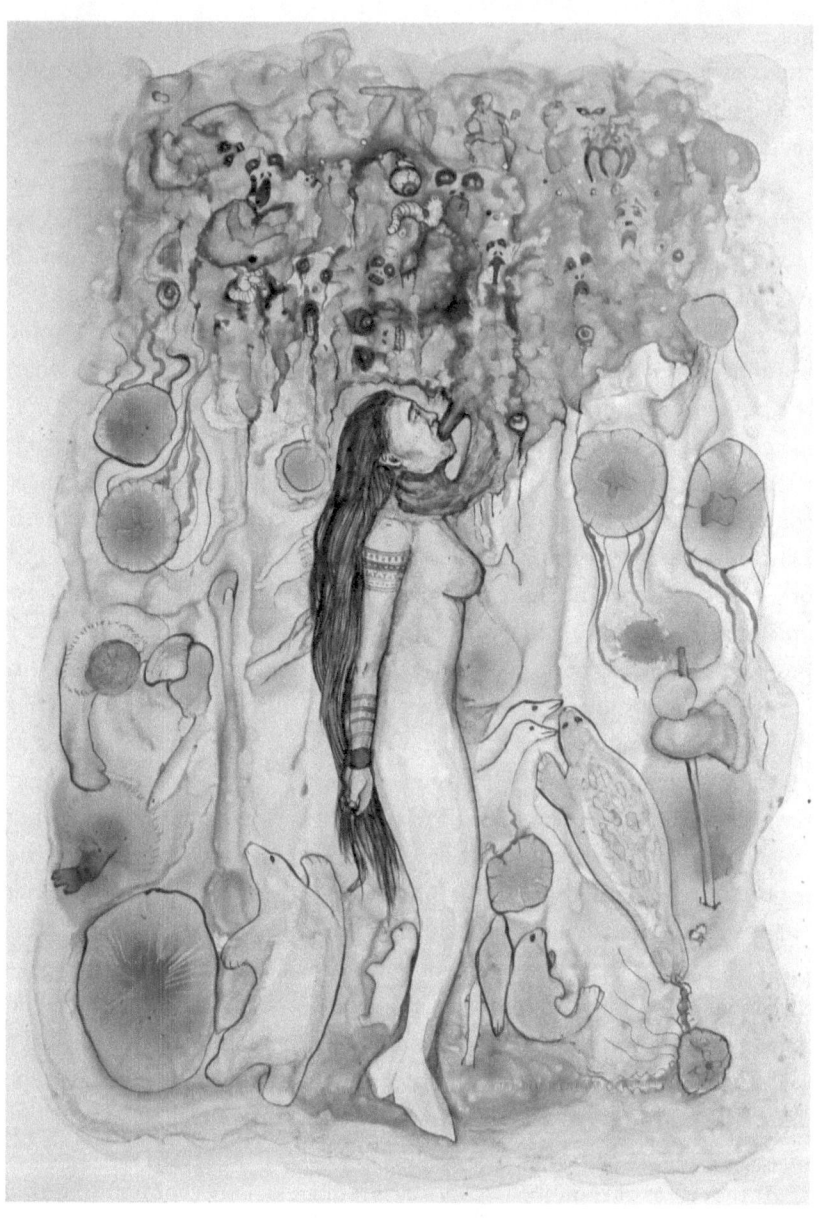

FIGURE 17. Heather Campbell, *Methylmercury*, 2017. Ink on mineral paper, 71 cm × 51 cm. Photo courtesy of the artist.

capsize the boat. To save himself, Nuliajuk's father throws his daughter overboard, and when she hangs onto the sides of the boat, he cuts off her fingers. As her severed fingers fall into the water, they transform into seals, whales, and other sea creatures. Nuliajuk then sinks to the bottom of the ocean and becomes a powerful being who controls sea creatures, deciding whether or not to release them to Inuit hunters who depend on them for food. In *Methylmercury*, Campbell paints Nuliajuk in watercolors, depicting her as half human, half beluga and surrounded by seals, a polar bear, and other sea animals. Whereas Lord's installation controverts representational conventions that associate Native women's bodies with land, Campbell's painting calls up an Inuit tradition in which a female figure, Nuliajuk, personifies the natural world (in this case, the sea). But unlike the imperial transcoding of woman and nature (exemplified by the images discussed in chapter 1) that naturalizes patriarchal power and territorial possession, *Methylmercury* recalls Inuit connections between bodies and lands to refute these settler colonial dynamics.

In *Methylmercury*, Nuliajuk is a multivalent figure, her body a site where conflicting Inuit and colonial meanings come to bear. Campbell rallies the power of the visual to convey multiple meanings that set Inuit and settler understandings against each other and draw out their implications. In Inuit tradition, Nuliajuk is a formidable being. She is, in Campbell's words, "the ultimate symbol of female power in Inuit culture across the Arctic" (Campbell 2017, 17). As the spiritual force who controls sea animals, she in turn controls Inuit survival. She is also associated with creation; not only did her severed fingers turn into the first sea animals, but in some versions of her story, she begets children who become the ancestors of human races across the world. Beyond her status as a powerful female figure who commands respect, her story carries meanings about appropriate relationships between human and nonhuman beings. When hunters are unable to find food, it means that people have failed to abide by rules for proper behavior, which encompass regard for other creatures. When this happens, only the most capable shamans possess the ability to intercede and appease Nuliajuk so that the animals reappear. Nuliajuk, says Campbell, thus "symbolizes the sacred respect we have for our ocean and its creatures" (Campbell 2017, 17). In the perspective captured by Nuliajuk's story, the natural world is powerful and agential, and humans disregard their obligations to it at their own peril.

But in *Methylmercury*, although Nuliajuk is a powerful being, she falls victim to violence at the hands of men. In some versions of her story, she suffers not only mutilation by her father but also mistreatment by her husband. Campbell's painting shows her experiencing other forms of harm as she is choked by a dark mass of poison with ominous death imagery, a symbol of the methylmercury that threatened to poison the waters as a result of dam construction at Muskrat Falls. A dark tendril constricts Nuliajuk's neck while a phallic extension is forced down her throat. A red tie binds her wrists, an allusion to the National Inquiry into Missing and Murdered Indigenous Women that commenced around the time of the Muskrat Falls protests (Campbell 2017, 17). In *Methylmercury*, representing environmental destruction as sexual violence is no mere metaphor ("rape of the land"). Instead, by representing both forms of violence in a single image, Campbell emphasizes material connections between violence against Indigenous women and violence against the land, the ways that Indigenous dispossession takes shape as brutality against Native women. In addition, depicting environmental destruction as rape heightens the poignancy of the image and prompts viewers to question the dam project. "I want them to have that feeling in their gut," Campbell explains, "that same feeling that we're feeling, that we're powerless against this giant project that's happening. We feel like we've got our hands tied behind our back. I want them to get an idea of how that might feel" (cited in Croskery 2018, n.p.). In this regard, too, Campbell rallies the power and immediacy of the visual, compelling viewers to confront the violence of ongoing dispossession (in this case, the dam project) and its effects on Indigenous communities. In contrast to the sexualized, feminized depictions of land analyzed in chapter 1, which obscure imperial violence and naturalize European territorial possession, Campbell's image of a Native woman's body condemns settler brutality and elicits spectator outrage and sympathy.

Despite her victimization, Nuliajuk does not represent defeat. Perhaps above all, she is a figure of transformation. In her story, acts of brutality (as when her father severs her fingers) change her into a being of immense power. By extension, as *Methylmercury* condemns the denigration of Native women and territories under settler colonialism, so too does it offer a vision of restoration premised on Inuit epistemologies. By calling up Nuliajuk's story, *Methylmercury* valorizes an Inuit worldview that joins together respect for women with respect for the natural world, a perspective that carries relevance for the entwined crises that inspired *Methylmercury* (the Muskrat Falls hydroelectric project and missing and murdered Indigenous women). By compelling viewers to understand these crises as inseparable, it insists that restoration of Native lands must entail restoration of the social places of Indigenous women. For Campbell, as for the other artists and writers discussed in this book, culture provides a necessary tool in these endeavors. "For so long Inuit art and culture were used as emblems of Canadiana," she says, "but we are now reclaiming our symbols and using them to resist colonization" (Campbell 2017, 17).

NOTES

INTRODUCTION

1. Under the original covenants, only white people could purchase land in the area, which was initially called Hollywoodland. They were also prohibited from selling land to nonwhite people.

2. Galanin quoted in Schulman (2021, n.p.).

3. In 2018, for example, the Eureka City Council completed its return of Duluwat Island to the Wiyot people, and the city of Vancouver, British Columbia, repatriated a Musqueum burial site to that community. In 2019, the United Methodist Church made headlines when it gave land back to the Wyandotte Nation of Oklahoma. In 2020, an environmental group leveraged the return of 1,200 acres of Big Sur in Northern California to the formerly landless Esselen tribe.

4. On the issue of resource exploitation on Native lands during this period, see LaDuke and Churchill (1985).

5. Miranda Johnson points out, for example, that "indigenous peoples had to forgo violence and assertions of full sovereignty and submit their claims to [and thereby validate] settler law" (2016, 11).

6. See, for example, the Land Back manifesto. Other organizations devoted to these causes include Land Is Life, Honor the Earth, and multiple local groups such as the Native Conservancy in Alaska, White Earth Land Recovery Project in Minnesota, Native American Land Conservancy in Los Angeles, the Sogorea Te' Land Trust in the San Francisco Bay Area, and Coast Protectors in British Columbia. Their activities encompass acquiring land for Native communities, protecting sacred sites, acting as stewards over traditional territories, and reinvigorating traditional practices on Native homelands.

7. Miranda Johnson's analysis focuses on activist strategies in Australia, Aotearoa / New Zealand, and Canada, but many of her arguments are relevant to political organizing in the United States as well.

8. The fact that Said scarcely mentions Native America in his seminal work reflects the way that postcolonial studies neglects this critically important aspect of

European imperialism. For an argument for greater attention to Native America in postcolonial studies, see Cheyfitz (1997).

9. Roy Harvey Pearce's *Savagism and Civilization: A Study of the Indian and the American Mind* (1988) is the classic study of the notion of Native people as "savage" counterparts to European "civilization" and the implications of this idea for US national identity. Later in the nineteenth century, this idea found scientific rationale in the emerging theory of human evolution. For an example of how social evolution reshaped understandings of Native people, see, most famously, Lewis Henry Morgan, *Ancient Society*.

10. Explaining the convergence of capitalism and settler colonialism in Indigenous dispossession, geographer Cole Harris writes: "The momentum to dispossess derived primarily from the interest of capital in profit and of settlers in getting somewhat ahead in the world, both interests, in a new colony where land was the principal resource, dependent on the acquisition of land" (Harris 2004, 179). On connections between capitalism and colonialism, see Harvey (2006); Lloyd and Wolfe (2016).

11. On the connections among perspectivism, emergent capitalism, and imperialism, see Jay (1993), especially chapter 1, "The Noblest of the Senses"; and Jay and Ramaswamy (2014).

12. A voluminous body of relevant contemporary works focus on what Nichols calls a "renaissance" of "Fourth World critiques of dispossession"; see Nichols (2020, 109–13). On the notions of reciprocity and relationality, see, especially, the writing of Leanne Betasamosake Simpson. "The opposite of dispossession is not possession," she writes in an influential work, but "deep, reciprocal, consensual *attachment*. Indigenous bodies don't relate to the land by possessing or owning it or having control over it. We relate to land through connection" (Simpson 2017, 43; see also Simpson 2014).

13. Classic sources include J. Rose (2006); Berger ([1972] 1990); and Mulvey (1975). In these and other analyses, sexualized images and the dynamics of the gaze relate directly to lived sexual relations.

14. These works also examine historical periods different from the one at the center of my analysis.

15. Important work on Native visualities also includes Rader (2011); Cummings (2011); and Hearne (2012).

16. I have discussed this issue in the case of Silko's *Almanac of the Dead*, a landmark novel of this era that narrates Indigenous revolution in the Americas. See S. Huhndorf (2009, ch. 4).

17. On the complexities of the Alaska Native Claims Settlement Act, see S. Huhndorf (2022) and R. Huhndorf and S. Huhndorf (2011).

18. To make sense of the apparent contradiction between Native traditional beliefs and resource exploitation by Native communities, Andrew Curley (2019) cautions against framing Indigenous resistance to extractive industry as an environmentalist project (manifested, for example, in the phrase "water is life" in the #NoDAPL movement). Instead, he advocates understanding Native activism surrounding resource exploitation as a critique of the ongoing colonial appropriation of Native lands.

19. I make an extended argument for this transnational approach and its implications for gender justice in S. Huhndorf (2009).

CHAPTER ONE. BODIES OF LAND

1. Europe, insisted prominent sixteenth-century Italian thinker Giovanni Botero, "was born to rule over Africa, Asia and America" (cited in Honour 1975, 92).
2. On images of America among the four continents, see also Honour (1975) and Fleming (1965).
3. "Imperialist literature," as geographers Alison Blunt and Gillian Rose explain, "often incorporated sexual imagery to create and sustain the heroic stature of male colonizers who conquered and penetrated dangerous, unknown continents.... The construction of a 'sexual space' paralleled the construction of space to be colonized, and the desire for colonial control was often expressed in terms of sexual control" (Blunt and Rose 1994, 10).
4. An account of Columbus's second voyage includes an infamous scene of captivity and rape of an Indigenous woman. See Michele de Cuneo, "Letter to a Friend," in Castillo and Schweitzer (2001).
5. On the ways the United States used Native images and narratives about Native Americans to create a national identity distinct from that of Europe, see S. Huhndorf (2001) and P. Deloria (1999).
6. Significantly, Barman begins her essay by describing the 1996 trial of Bishop Hubert O'Connor for having raped or assaulted four young Aboriginal women. The essay is an analysis of the histories that give rise to contemporary sexual violence against Aboriginal women in British Columbia.
7. The *Federal Indian Boarding School Initiative Investigative Report*, issued in 2022 by the US Department of the Interior, does not mention gender at all (Newland 2022). In Canada, the Truth and Reconciliation Committee's summary final report (2015b) mentions only in passing the disempowerment of Native women in the schools and its connection to ongoing violence.
8. The Truth and Reconciliation Commission (2015a) documented that between 1936 and 1944 alone, officials destroyed 200,000 Indian Affairs files.
9. In June 2021, the Department of the Interior announced the Federal Indian Boarding School Truth Initiative, created to assess the consequences of boarding school education and its intergenerational effects. The following year it released a preliminary report on the issue with the recommendation for further extensive research. Native people have long organized around the enduring legacies of boarding school education, creating such advocacy groups as the National Native American Boarding School Healing Coalition.
10. Decades later, a 1969 US congressional report explicitly acknowledged this connection: "From the beginning, Federal policy toward the Indian was based on the desire to dispossess him of his land. Education policy was a function of our land policy" (Committee on Labor and Public Welfare 1969, 142).

11. Foundational studies of boarding schools in the United States include Lomawaima (1994), Adams (1995), and Child (2000). A valuable purpose of scholarship such as that of Lomawaima, Child, and, more recently, Krupat (2018, 2020) has been to recover, to the extent possible, firsthand accounts by students at the schools and to convey the complex, sometimes contradictory nature of their experience there. My goal here is to highlight the colonial purposes of boarding school education, especially their gendered dimensions and connections to dispossession, but Native people who attended boarding schools have often had much to say about their experiences that defy generalizations. For accounts of residential school experiences that emerged as part of the Truth and Reconciliation Commission in Canada, see Truth and Reconciliation Commission (2015a).

12. An interactive map released in September 2023 by the National Native American Boarding School Healing Coalition places the total number of known Native boarding schools in the United States and Canada at 523.

13. In the United States, enthusiasm for boarding schools as a means of assimilation waned in the aftermath of World War I, and Carlisle Indian Industrial School, the flagship boarding school during the assimilation era, closed in 1918. A decade later, the Meriam Report (officially titled *The Problem of Indian Administration*; Meriam 1928) offered a scathing indictment of federal Indian policies, including mandatory boarding school education and Reel's *Uniform Course of Study* (discussed below).

14. For data on the number of schools at different points in time, see Truth and Reconciliation Commission (2015b).

15. Throughout most of the assimilation era, from 1883 until 1916, an influential group of reformers that called itself Friends of the Indian met annually to discuss federal Indian policy. They called the annual meeting the Lake Mohonk Conference. The group regularly made recommendations to the US government that profoundly affected policies.

16. See, for example, J. Brown (1970), Klein (1995), Fiske (1987), Bauer (2022), Pesantubbee (2005), and Fur (2009).

17. The boarding school policy, as described above, was fundamentally tied to dispossession. For an analysis of how Reel herself contributed materially to dispossession, in part by facilitating leases and transfers of Native lands, see Lomawaima (1996).

18. In 1893, for example, the World's Columbian Exposition in Chicago included a popular exhibition of an Indian boarding school classroom. Visitors to the exhibition could view actual Native students (taken from boarding schools in Pennsylvania and Kansas) in a model classroom.

19. The names are listed in a printed caption on the reverse side of the photograph. See "Four Pueblo Children from Zuni, New Mexico, c. 1880."

20. Under the original terms of the General Allotment Act, those Native people who were categorized as "mixed blood" were granted fee simple title to their lands, and they were forced to accept US citizenship and relinquish tribal status. Those categorized as "full blood" received trust patents to land over which the federal

government retained control for at least twenty-five years. At the end of the trust period, these allottees would receive full title to their land and US citizenship.

21. The political valences of citizenship count among the issues that mark crucial differences between Indigenous communities and other racialized peoples. The 1887 General Allotment Act and the 1924 Indian Citizenship Act compelled Native people to accept US citizenship as a means of forced assimilation. These policies constituted a means of undermining the distinct status of tribal nations.

22. When directed to select allotments, reports historian Emily Greenwald, Nez Perce people chose places as near as possible to their birthplace rather than those appropriate for farming. In this way, Greenwald writes, "the Nez Perces asserted spatial systems rooted in their longstanding cultural and subsistence practices" (Greenwald 2002, 39–40).

23. Under the original legislation, allotments were to remain inalienable and exempt from taxation for twenty-five years, though this policy was often not followed in practice. The Burke Act of 1906 amended the General Allotment Act to enable the Secretary of the Interior to force individuals to accept allotments and to issue those allotments in fee simple to Native people classified as "competent and capable" (often those identified as mixed blood). Fee simple title meant the removal of trust status so that lands could be sold and were subject to taxation.

24. On fraudulent sales in the Anishinaabe context, discussed in chapter 2, see Meyer (1994).

25. Initially, until 1891, married women had no property rights under the General Allotment Act.

26. Legal scholar Robert Williams Jr. argues that the legal framework for Indigenous possession was "the overarching principle of European racial and cultural superiority over the Indians of the New World. Because of their savage 'character and religion,' Indians were regarded as inferior peoples with lesser rights to land and territorial sovereignty" (2005, 53). Williams is specifically referring to the 1823 US Supreme Court case *Johnson v. McIntosh*, part of the "Marshall Trilogy" of decisions that still provide the foundation of federal Indian law.

27. A major reason for this distinction, according to the Truth and Reconciliation Commission, is that Canada simply did not have the budget for military campaigns (2015b, 52).

28. The Gradual Assimilation Act built on an 1839 statute, the Act for the Protection of the Indians in Upper Canada, and the first residential school, as previously noted, opened in 1831. These early dates indicate the extent to which the assimilation endeavor in Canada preceded similar laws in the United States.

29. For accounts of the effects of Canadian policies on women's social roles, see Lawrence (2003) and McGrath and Stevenson (1996). My own brief account is heavily indebted to these sources. See also McGillivray and Comaskey (1999).

30. The Gradual Enfranchisement Act presaged by more than fifty years the 1934 Indian Reorganization Act in the United States, which similarly mandated European-style governance in the form of elected tribal councils and a constitution, but it did not include the explicitly gendered provisions of the Gradual Enfranchisement

Act (though the social marginalization of Indigenous women recounted in this chapter favored male leadership in other ways).

CHAPTER TWO. "MAPPING BY WORDS"

1. I use the term "Anishinaabe," the community's name for itself, rather than "Chippewa" a term coined by outsiders. These differences are sometimes significant in Erdrich's work as the characters with tenuous ties to the community tend to use the latter terminology.

2. For a discussion of the turn-of-the-century collaboration of federal and state governments and lumber companies in the dispossession on the White Earth Anishinaabe Reservation, a key historical context for *Tracks*, see Meyer (1994).

3. I am not the first critic to interpret Native women's writing as a cartographic endeavor. In a 2007 essay titled "Writing Deeper Maps," Kelli Lyon Johnson contends that mapmaking has become a dominant theme in Native women's literature as part of a "remarkable turn to Indigenous knowledges in Native writing" (103), in particular by advancing Indigenous representations and understandings of land (see K. Johnson 2007). Similarly, in *Mark My Words* (2013), Mishuana Goeman argues that Native women's writing critically engages colonial policies and practices while also constituting "subversive or alternative geographies" to those of colonialism and capitalism (24). Goeman focuses in particular on works by E. Pauline Johnson, Esther Belin, Joy Harjo, and Leslie Marmon Silko. In *Mapping the Americas* (2009), I write about Silko's monumental novel *Almanac of the Dead* as a cartographic project. In this chapter, however, I am particularly concerned with the particular form that literary mapping takes in relation to post-1960s Indigenous land claims movements.

4. Here I am attending to Andrew Thacker's call for a "critical literary geography," which he defines as a means to "think geographically" about the interconnections among cultural texts, material locations, histories, and social power (2005, 60). For an important analysis of space in Chicana literature, see Brady (2002). Chicana literature, she argues, offers a critique of space that lays bare the significance of race, gender, and sexuality to the making of space and offers cartographies other than those of capital and US nationalism.

5. The reservation was established under the 1867 Treaty with the Chippewa of the Mississippi.

6. *State v. Zay Zah* contested the illegal taxation and subsequent sale of Zay Zah's trust allotment because of tax delinquency, and it raised questions about the legality of other allotments lost because of the contravention of trust protection. In the early 1980s, the Bureau of Indian Affairs began notifying the current "owners" of several hundred thousand acres of reservation land that their titles may be clouded (see Youngbear-Tibbetts 1991, 95, 117). The ensuing conflict resulted in the 1986 passage of the highly controversial White Earth Land Settlement Act (WELSA), which restored a small portion (about 10,000 acres) of the lost land and provided some

restitution to the heirs of the dispossessed (see www.welsa.org). Many Anishinaabe consider WELSA inadequate, and in 1989, the White Earth Land Recovery Project, led by Winona LaDuke, formed to raise money to repurchase lost reservation lands.

7. My argument that contemporary events on the White Earth Reservation in Minnesota bear relevance to *Tracks* requires a word of explanation. Although Erdrich doesn't identify the specific setting of *Tracks*, many readers assume that this story, along with her other works, takes place on the Turtle Mountain Reservation in North Dakota. Erdrich's family is from Turtle Mountain, and it is the only Anishinaabe reservation in North Dakota, which she does identify as the setting of the tetralogy. Further, critics have noted correspondences between the history of the Turtle Mountain Reservation and events recounted in the novels (see, for example, Maristuen-Rodakowski 1988). At the same time, it was White Earth, not Turtle Mountain, that was the site in the postallotment era of depredations by lumber companies such as those recounted by *Tracks*, and it seems significant that Erdrich chose to address contemporary events at White Earth in the essay cited above in the same month that *Tracks* appeared. In interviews, Erdrich has insisted that her novels address "pan-Indian" issues of broad relevance to Native communities (cited in Stripes 1991, 280), and the story in *Tracks* appears to draw on events that transpired beyond Turtle Mountain, including at White Earth (Stripes also makes this point). For histories of dispossession on the White Earth reservation and their contemporary effects, see Meyer (1994) and Youngbear-Tibbetts (1991).

8. The Burke Act of 1906 amended the General Allotment Act to enable the removal of trust status on lands of allottees deemed "competent," an often arbitrary determination frequently bestowed against the wishes of allottees. The removal of trust status caused the loss of substantial portions of Native land because of sales (many of them fraudulent) as well as tax forfeiture.

9. For a discussion of the role of trickster figures in the novel, see Gross (2005). These figures, he argues, "find ways to . . . adapt to changing realities" and "survive to build a new world on the ashes of the old" (Gross 2005, 64, 49). For an analysis of the trickster figure in Native American literature more broadly, see Krupat (2009).

10. The name underscores the novel's anticolonial critique as it recalls the historical figure King Leopold II, the nineteenth-century Belgian ruler notorious for his cruel exploitation of the Congo.

11. The irony here is striking: as the novel's invocation of oral tradition demonstrates the ways Native writers turn Western modes to support cultural continuity, it also demonstrates the limits of writing, which can recall but cannot reproduce the oral tradition and thus exemplifies the cultural losses it takes to task.

12. I am disagreeing with Catherine Rainwater's contention that in Erdrich's work the coexistence of Indigenous and Judeo-Christian codes "vexes the reader's effort to decide upon an unambiguous, epistemologically consistent interpretive framework. Encoded 'undecidability' leads to the marginalization of the reader by the text" (Rainwater 1990, 407). In my reading, *Tracks* draws traditional Indigenous and Christian epistemologies into conflict in order to affirm the former and criticize the latter.

13. This also holds true elsewhere in the novel. The places of violence in the novel further connect Indigenous bodies and land as intersecting sites of colonial power: Fleur's rape transpires in the "white town" of Argus; Margaret is kidnapped as she returns from church, and her attackers take her to the land owned by a family that supports the lumber company purchase agreement; cursed by Fleur for this attack, Boy Lazarre collapses and dies in the trading post, bringing down a cascade of traps that snap shut around him. All colonial spaces of violence, these sites draw together the forces of the state, church, and capital that collude in dispossession.

14. This narrative turn repeats a dominant paradigm of the Native American novel that signifies social and cultural regeneration after colonization. On the connections between the return narrative and Native cultural and social regeneration, see Bevis (1987) and Krupat (1996).

15. Nancy J. Peterson notes the stark contrast between *Tracks*, which she describes as "a novel entirely haunted by historical dispossession and tribal splintering, with only small hope for effective resistance," and *The Bingo Palace*, the final novel in Erdrich's tetralogy. The latter novel, she contends, is remarkable for its "comic plot," and its humor demands "that readers recognize Indians not as tragic victims but as comic actors and agents" (Peterson 1994, 161–62). This narrative trajectory, I would add—from tragedy in *Tracks* to comedy in *The Bingo Palace*—demonstrates that the tetralogy composes a narrative of survival and persistence rather than one of disappearance.

16. This happens in *Four Souls*, a later novel outside the tetralogy that takes up Fleur's story where *Tracks* leaves off. In this story Fleur exacts revenge on the lumber company executive and recovers Matchimanito.

17. Legal arguments in the James Bay conflict underscore these connections. The James Bay Development Corporation argued that their claim to Indigenous lands stemmed from the 1670 royal charter conferred by Charles II to the Hudson's Bay Company (see Hellegers 2015, 5).

18. For other analyses of cartography in *Solar Storms*, see K. Johnson (2007) and Stacks (2010).

19. See, for example, Smith and Fiori (2010).

CHAPTER THREE. SCENES FROM THE FRINGE

1. Jiwani and Young (2006) demonstrate that mainstream media accounts cast Aboriginal victims as drug-addicted sex workers and typically blamed the victims for their own fates. "In the realm of representations," they write, "prostitution and Aboriginality mark these women as missing, but naturally so" because their "irresponsible behavior" is seen as "naturally inviting victimization" (902).

2. As a result, 58 percent of Aboriginal migrants to cities are women (Government of Canada 2016, 431). The scholarly literature on these topics is voluminous. On the connections among the Indian Act, residential schools, and sexual violence, see Jacobs and Williams (2008).

3. The issue of missing and murdered women has recently prompted an outpouring of scholarly work that includes Anderson, Campbell, and Belcourt (2018); Hargreaves (2017); and Lavell-Harvard and Brant (2016).

4. The murders also became the subject of public memorials. See The Cultural Memory Group (2006), especially chapter 1, "Vancouver: Missing, Murdered, and Counting."

5. Scholarship on Indigenous feminism has tended to neglect culture (Huhndorf and Suzack 2010, 9), and those scholars who have analyzed culture as an Indigenous feminist practice have mostly focused on literature (see, for example, Suzack 2017 and Goeman 2013). For an inquiry into the possibilities of visual art as a form of Indigenous feminist engagement, see Mithlo (2009).

6. The 1991 CBC television miniseries *Conspiracy of Silence* provided one of the first mainstream news accounts of missing and murdered Indigenous women. The series focused on the brutal killing of nineteen-year-old Helen Betty Osborne in 1971, a case that went unsolved for nearly twenty years. In 2004, Amnesty International released its exposé "Stolen Sisters: A Human Rights Response to Discrimination and Violence against Indigenous Women in Canada"; Beverley Jacobs, an Aboriginal attorney and activist who later became president of the Native Women's Association of Canada, served as lead writer and researcher for the project. Three years later, Amnesty International released a parallel report for the United States, "Maze of Injustice: The Failure to Protect Indigenous Women from Sexual Violence in the USA," written by Native legal scholar Sarah Deer.

7. Some established national Native organizations have begun to attend to this problem; the Indian Law Resource Center, for example, created the Safe Women, Strong Nations project to end violence against Native women and children. Other national organizations, such as the National Indigenous Women's Resource Center (NIWRC), were founded specifically to address this issue. The NIWRC website includes a list of tribal organizations and coalitions dedicated to addressing violence against Indigenous women (see https://www.niwrc.org/tribal-coalitions).

8. On the history of activism in the neighborhood and the emergence of the march, see Culhane (2003).

9. See, for example, Institute for the Advancement of Aboriginal Women, "Written Submission to the National Inquiry into Missing and Murdered Indigenous Women and Girls," National Inquiry into Missing and Murdered Indigenous Women and Girls, December 14, 2018, https://www.mmiwg-ffada.ca/wp-content/uploads/2019/02/IAAW-Final-Written-Submission.pdf. The presentation includes news clippings that should have prompted governmental awareness and action.

10. May 5 is the birthday of Hanna Harris, a twenty-one-year-old Northern Cheyenne woman who went missing in 2013.

11. In a related development, the 2013 reauthorization of the Violence Against Women Act included a provision acknowledging the authority of tribal governments to exercise criminal jurisdiction over non-Native perpetrators of domestic or dating violence against Native people on tribal lands.

12. Later, *Fringe* appeared in museum contexts as a light box display. There it calls up histories that identify the museum as a space of Indigenous dispossession.

13. Here Tagg is describing nineteenth-century project of representation, but his arguments in some ways extend to contemporary discourses surrounding Indigenous people.

14. See, for example, Vicente Rafael's argument that photography serves as a "technology of subjugation" as well as of "disavowal" (Rafael 2000, 77). Mary Louise Pratt similarly argues, with regard to colonial rhetorical strategies, that the "seeing man," or "he whose imperial eyes passively look out and possess," is the "main protagonist of the anti-conquest," or the means by which "European bourgeois subjects seek to secure their innocence in the same moment as they assert European hegemony" (Pratt 1992, 7).

15. The vigil is a strategy used by Native women's organizations to call attention to and honor missing and murdered Indigenous women. The Native Women's Association of Canada, for example, holds "Sisters in Spirit Vigils" annually.

16. See Jaime Black's REDress Project (http://www.theredressproject.org/), as well as wearing of red dresses in protests (Jasper 2018).

17. Welsh places the number of missing women at more than five hundred, but since the film's release in 2006, the estimates have risen dramatically into the thousands.

18. For a critique of this strategy, see Hargreaves (2015).

19. For an astute analysis of the poster, see Dean (2015), especially chapter 3.

20. On the connection between domestic photography and domestic ideologies, see Sekula (1986), Hirsch (1997), and G. Rose (2010).

21. See, for example, G. Rose's (2010) discussion of British journalists' coverage of the 2005 London Bombings (esp. 100–104).

22. Some critics, however, convincingly argue that family photographs can at once challenge and perpetuate domestic ideologies. Rose, for example, contends that family albums frequently "negotiate" rather than "naively reproduc[e] dominant ideologies of domestic femininity" (G. Rose 2010, 8). Similarly, Marianne Hirsch writes that family photographs, especially when placed in narrative contexts (in her terms, "image-texts"), can "expose and resist the conventions of family photography and hegemonic familial ideologies" (1997, 8).

23. The term is Judith Butler's (2006).

CHAPTER FOUR. CONTESTED LANDSCAPES

1. At the time of the exhibit, the museum was called the National Museum of American Art, but in 2000 its name changed to Smithsonian American Art Museum.

2. In his 1893 address, Turner proclaimed that the nation's history had been "in a large degree the history of the colonization of the Great West," a process that drove

"American development," "the growth of nationalism," and the "evolution of American political institutions" (Turner [1893] 1994, 31, 49).

3. "We thought we were doing a show on images in history," commented curator Treuttner, "but the public was more concerned that we had challenged a sacred premise" (cited in Gulliford 1992, 205).

4. Western history is not a new subject of Native cultural production. It has long been the subject of the Native American novel, beginning with John Rollin Ridge's *The Life and Adventures of Joaquin Murieta* (1854), the first Native novel in English. D'Arcy McNickle's *The Surrounded* (1936), which is generally regarded as laying the foundation for twentieth-century Native fiction, sets conventional Western narratives against a story that condemns the effects of expansion on Native communities. Later in the century, novels by N. Scott Momaday (including his Pulitzer Prize–winning *House Made of Dawn*), Leslie Marmon Silko, James Welch, and others told historical stories that reflected critically on western expansion. As film critic Joanna Hearne (2012) demonstrates, Native filmmakers have also focused heavily on western history.

5. This is art historian Elizabeth Kalbfleisch's term, cited in Yogaretnam (2019).

6. In Canada, where Monkman works, the landscape genre came to prominence in the early twentieth century (later than in the United States) when the Group of Seven created the first major national art movement with landscapes that came to be associated with Canadian identity. These works are the subjects of other Monkman paintings.

7. With the phrase "way of seeing," Cosgrove reprises John Berger's classic 1972 book of the same name, an analysis of the ways that ideologies shape understandings of aesthetic images.

8. For an influential analysis of western landscapes and their differences from Laguna Pueblo understandings of land, see Silko (1999).

9. In the words of art historian Michael Newman, "The whole idea of the panorama is tied to the military domination of the landscape, which is conceived as a battlefield" (cited in DeLue and Elkins 2008, 130).

10. Bierstadt is known for creating monumental landscapes, and this one is no exception. According to the National Gallery of Art, it measures about 61 by 96 inches.

11. The naming of the painting and the peak, as well as the circumstances under which Bierstadt persuaded William Corcoran to purchase the painting, are matters of some controversy. See Cash (2012, 140).

12. See E. Ann Kaplan's discussion (1997) of the imperial gaze, as well as Beardsell (2000).

13. Morgensen describes some of these acts of violence (2011, 38–39), and this is also the subject of recent Native writers. See, for example, Miranda (2013).

14. On the continuities between western landscape painting and the Western film genre, see Gunning (2017) and Buscombe (1984).

15. Kunuk and Ungalaaq partnered on *Atanarjuat* as well, with Kunuk as director and Ungalaaq in the starring role. I have written more extensively about

Atanarjuat and Isuma's work more broadly, including the connection to land claims, in *Mapping the Americas* (2009), chapter 2.

16. In addition to feature films, Kunuk continues to direct documentaries and short films. He also executive produces films as part of the Isuma film collective. In 2010, Igloolik Isuma Productions reopened as Kingulliit Productions, part of the Isuma collective.

17. In *Native Recognition: Indigenous Cinema and the Western* (2012), film scholar Joanna Hearne argues that Native filmmakers have long turned to the Western film genre for inspiration. Her focus, though, is on the "sympathetic" or "pro-Indian" Western. Ford's *The Searchers* cannot be considered in that category.

18. See, for example, Angela Aleiss's essay (1994) on the role of Native people in John Ford's movies. *The Searchers*, she argues, is "a study in modern savagery" that is "undeniably racist" (178, 180).

19. For an astute analysis of the racial and gender dimension of Western narratives in the context of shifts in US politics, see Bold (2013).

20. In fact, argues film critic Joanna Hearne, Native filmmakers have frequently turned to the Western film genre precisely because it has been influential in shaping popular understandings of Native people. "The generic arena of the Western," Hearne writes, "informs the constellation of popular representations from which a range of Native filmmakers have drawn a counterdiscourse advocating tribal autonomy" along with renewed connections to land (Hearne 2012, 5).

21. The Nunavut Implementation Commission explicitly mandated that "the Government of Nunavut will undertake to protect and preserve the distinct society which has existed in Nunavut for thousands of years" (Légaré 1997, 411).

22. Although the IBC has contributed substantially to the creation of a collective Inuit identity that enabled the Nunavut settlement, the relationship between the two is somewhat more complicated than my cursory account suggests, in part because the Nunavut government has provided little support for IBC (Sørensen 2000, 176).

23. Here Wexman is citing Friedrich Engels's classic 1884 study *The Origin of the Family, Private Property, and the State* ([1884] 2010).

24. The captivity narrative was also a visual genre that includes US painting. On Monkman's engagement with this genre, see Monkman (2015).

25. Indeed, from the origins of the genre, captivity narratives relied heavily on a Christian framing that demonized Native people. The classic example is *Narrative of the Captivity and Restoration of Mrs. Mary Rowlandson; or, The Sovereignty and Goodness of God* (1682).

26. See, for example, Lee Clark Mitchell, *Westerns: Making the Man in Fiction and Film* (1998) and Jane Tompkins, *West of Everything: The Inner Life of Westerns* (1993). Tompkins argues that the Western emerged as a response to the increasing prominence of women's novels and women's presence in the public sphere.

27. Notably, Ethan's suggestion that Martin has Native ancestry contributes to the erosion of boundaries between savage and civilized.

28. For this reason, some critics have likened *The Searchers* to Joseph Conrad's *Heart of Darkness*.

29. I have discussed this paradigm in the context of Arctic colonization in Huhndorf (2000). See also Stam and Shohat (1994).

CONCLUSION

1. As in other instances, such as the imposition of Western governance structures on tribal communities under the Indian Reorganization Act, Native people have transformed these organizations to the extent possible to serve community purposes. See R. Huhndorf and S. Huhndorf (2011) and S. Huhndorf (2022).

2. On the various versions of the Sedna story, see Swinton 1985. Florence (2019) includes astute analyses of the figure of Sedna in contemporary Inuit art, including Campbell's work. For a discussion of contemporary political uses of the story, see K. Martin (2011).

WORKS CITED

Active, John. 1999. "Why Subsistence Is a Matter of Cultural Survival: A Yup'ik Point of View." In *Alaska Native Writers, Storytellers, and Orators: The Expanded Edition*, edited by Ronald Spatz, Patricia H. Partnow, and Jeane Breinig, 182–87. Anchorage: University of Alaska Press.

Adams, David Wallace. 1988. "Fundamental Considerations: The Deep Meaning of Native American Schooling, 1880–1900." *Harvard Educational Review* 58, no. 1 (February): 1–28.

———. 1995. *Education for Extinction: American Indians and the Boarding School Experience, 1875–1928*. Lawrence: University Press of Kansas.

Aleiss, Angela. 1994. "A Race Divided: The Indian Westerns of John Ford." *American Indian Culture and Research Journal* 18, no. 3: 167–86.

Allen, Ann Taylor. 1999. "Feminism, Social Science, and the Meanings of Modernity: The Debate on the Origin of the Family in Europe and the United States, 1860–1914." *American Historical Review* 104, no. 4 (October): 1084–113.

Amnesty International. 2004. "Stolen Sisters: A Human Rights Response to Discrimination and Violence against Indigenous Women in Canada." London: Amnesty International Publications. https://www.amnesty.ca/sites/default/files/amr200032004enstolensisters.pdf.

———. 2007. "Maze of Injustice: The Failure to Protect Indigenous Women from Sexual Violence in the USA." London: Amnesty International Publications. https://www.amnestyusa.org/pdfs/mazeofinjustice.pdf.

———. 2022. "Submission to the Study on Violence against Indigenous Women and Girls." United Nations Office of the High Commissioner on Human Rights. https://www.ohchr.org/sites/default/files/2022-03/Amnesty.pdf.

Anderson, Kim, Maria Campbell, and Christi Belcourt, eds. 2018. *Keetsahnak: Our Missing and Murdered Indigenous Sisters*. Edmonton: University of Alberta Press.

Anderson, Nancy K. 1991. "'The Kiss of Enterprise': The Western Landscape as Symbol and Resource." In Truettner, *The West as America*, 237–84.

Architect of the Capitol. N.d. "Baptism of Pocahontas." Accessed December 28, 2023. https://www.aoc.gov/explore-capitol-campus/art/baptism-pocahontas.

"The Art Seminar." 2008. In DeLue and Elkins, *Landscape Theory*, 87–156.

Atleo, E. R. (Umeek). 2017. "A Nuu-chah-nulth Perspective on Kent Monkman's Reply to Giambattista Tiepolo's *Apollo and the Four Continents*." In Monkman, *The Four Continents*, 54–67.

Bailey, Doug. 2017. "Disarticulate-Repurpose-Disrupt: Art/Archaeology." *Cambridge Archaeological Journal* 27, no. 4 (November): 691–701.

Banner, Stuart. 2007. *How the Indians Lost Their Land: Law and Power on the Frontier*. Cambridge, MA: Belknap Press of Harvard University Press.

Barker, Joanne. 2017. Introduction to *Critically Sovereign: Indigenous Gender, Sexuality, and Feminist Studies*, edited by Joanne Barker, 1–44. Durham, NC: Duke University Press.

Barman, Jean. 1997–98. "Taming Aboriginal Sexuality: Gender, Power, and Race in British Columbia, 1850–1900." *BC Studies*, nos. 115–16: 237–66.

———. 2011. "Indigenous Women and Feminism on the Cusp of Contact." In *Indigenous Women and Feminism: Politics, Activism, Culture*, edited by Cheryl Suzack, Shari M. Huhndorf, Jeanne Perreault, and Jean Barman, 92–108. Vancouver: University of British Columbia Press.

Barrows, Isabel C., ed. 1897. *Proceedings of the Fourteenth Annual Meeting of the Lake Mohonk Conference of Friends of the Indian, 1896*. Lake Mohonk, NY: Lake Mohonk Conference.

Barthes, Roland. (1980) 2010. *Camera Lucida: Reflections on Photography*. New York: Hill and Wang.

Bauer, Brooke. 2022. *Becoming Catawba: Catawba Indian Women and Nation-Building, 1540–1840*. Tuscaloosa: University of Alabama Press.

Bear Robe, Amber-Dawn. 2013. "Rebecca Belmore's Performance of Photography." Aboriginal Curatorial Collective / Collectif des commissaires autochtones, January 29. Archived at I-Portal: Indigenous Studies Portal at the University of Saskatchewan. Accessed February 18, 2024. https://iportal.usask.ca/record/23579.

Beardsell, Peter. 2000. *Europe and Latin America: Returning the Gaze*. Manchester: Manchester University Press.

Beattie, Sara, Jean-Denis David, and Joel Roy. 2018. "Homicide in Canada, 2017." Statistics Canada, November 21. https://www150.statcan.gc.ca/n1/pub/85-002-x/2018001/article/54980-eng.htm

Bell, Shannon. 2009. "Rebecca Belmore: Fiercely Political, Politically Fierce." *Canadian Dimension* 43, no. 1: 35–39.

Belmore, Rebecca. 2002. *Vigil*. Performance. Vancouver, British Columbia.

———. 2007. *Fringe*. Photograph, color. National Gallery of Canada, Ottawa.

Berger, John. (1972) 1990. *Ways of Seeing*. London: Penguin Books.

Bermingham, Ann. 1994. "System, Order, and Abstraction: The Politics of English Landscape Drawing around 1795." In Mitchell, *Landscape and Power*, 77–102.

Bevis, William. 1987. "Native American Novels: Homing In." In *Recovering the Word: Essays on Native American Literature*, edited by Brian Swann and Arnold Krupat, 580–620. Berkeley: University of California Press.

Bhandar, Brenna. 2018. *Colonial Lives of Property: Law, Land, and Racial Regimes of Ownership*. Durham, NC: Duke University Press.

Bierstadt, Albert. *Mount Corcoran*. Oil on canvas, 1876–77, National Gallery of Art, Washington, DC. https://www.nga.gov/collection/art-object-page.166428.html.

Blunt, Alison, and Gillian Rose. 1994. "Introduction: Women's Colonial and Postcolonial Geographies." In *Writing Women and Space: Colonial and Postcolonial Geographies*, edited by Alison Blunt and Gillian Rose, 1–25. New York: Guilford Press.

Bobroff, Kenneth H. 2001. "Retelling Allotment: Indian Property Rights and the Myth of Common Ownership." *Vanderbilt Law Review* 54, no. 4 (May): 1560–1623.

Bold, Christine. 2013. *The Frontier Club: Popular Westerns and Cultural Power, 1880–1924*. Oxford: Oxford University Press.

Brady, Mary Pat. 2002. *Extinct Lands, Temporal Geographies: Chicana Literature and the Urgency of Space*. Durham, NC: Duke University Press.

Braund, Kathryn E. Holland. 1990. "Guardians of Tradition and Handmaidens to Change: Women's Roles in Creek Economic and Social Life during the Eighteenth Century." *American Indian Quarterly* 14, no. 3 (Summer): 239–58.

Bromley, Neil. 2003. "Law, Property, and the Geography of Violence: The Frontier, the Survey, and the Grid." *Annals of the Association of American Geographers* 93, no. 1: 121–41.

Brooks, Katherine. 2014. "Kent Monkman, Aka Miss Chief Eagle Testickle, Confronts Native American Myths." *Huffington Post*, May 21. Online.

Brotherston, Gordon. *Book of the Fourth World: Reading the Native Americas through Their Literature*. Cambridge: Cambridge University Press, 1992.

Brown, DeNeen. 2004. "On Willy's Pig Farm, Sifting for Clues." *Washington Post*, September 5, D01.

Brown, Judith. 1970. "Economic Organization and the Position of Women among the Iroquois." *Ethnohistory* 17: 151–67.

Buscombe, Edward. 1984. "Painting the Legend: Frederic Remington and the Western." *Cinema Journal* 23, no. 4 (Summer): 12–27.

Butler, Judith. 2006. *Precarious Life: The Powers of Mourning and Violence*. London: Verso.

Campbell, Heather. 2017. "Insurgence/Resurgence: Winnipeg Art Gallery." *Inuit Art Quarterly*, September 15, 17.

———. 2017. *Methylmercury*. Ink on mineral paper.

———. 2021. "How Nunatsiavut Artists Use Their Work to Fight Climate Change." *Arctic Arts Summit*, November 26. https://arcticartssummit.ca/articles/how-nunatsiavut-artists-use-their-work-to-fight-climate-change/.

Canadian Broadcasting Corporation / Radio-Canada. 2019. "Kent Monkman: Decolonizing Art History," interview with Paul Kennedy. February 12.

Carter, Paul. 2010. *The Road to Botany Bay: An Exploration of Landscape and History*. Minneapolis: University of Minnesota Press.

Cash, Sarah, ed. 2012. *Corcoran Gallery of Art: American Paintings to 1945*. Washington, DC: Corcoran Gallery of Art. Online at National Gallery of Art, https://www.nga.gov/content/dam/ngaweb/research/publications/pdfs/corcoran-american-art.pdf.

Castillo, Susan and Ivy Schweitzer. 2001. *The Literatures of Colonial America: An Anthology*. Hoboken, NJ: Wiley-Blackwell.

Chapin, Mac, Zachary Lamb, and Bill Threlkeld. 2005. "Mapping Indigenous Lands." *Annual Review of Anthropology* 34: 619–38.

Chapman, John Gadsby. 1840. *Baptism of Pocahontas*. Oil on canvas. U.S. Capitol Rotunda.

Cheyfitz, Eric. 1997. *The Poetics of Imperialism: Translation and Colonization from "The Tempest" to "Tarzan."* Philadelphia: University of Pennsylvania Press.

———. 2004. "The (Post)Colonial Construction of Indian Country: U.S. American Indian Literatures and Federal Indian Law." In *The Columbia Guide to American Indian Literatures of the United States Since 1945*, edited by Eric Cheyfitz, 1–126. New York: Columbia University Press.

———. 2019. *The Disinformation Age: The Collapse of Liberal Democracy in the United States*. Updated edition. Durham, NC: PaperBoat Press.

Child, Brenda J. 2000. *Boarding School Seasons: American Indian Families, 1900–1940*. Lincoln: University of Nebraska Press.

Cohen, Felix. 1960. *The Legal Conscience: Selected Papers*. New Haven, CT: Yale University Press.

Collaert, Adriaen. N.d. *America*, from the *Four Continents*. Engraving. After Maerten de Vos. The Metropolitan Museum of Art, New York. https://www.metmuseum.org/art/collection/search/385674.

Committee on Labor and Public Welfare. 1969. *Indian Education: A National Tragedy—A National Challenge*. S. Rep. 91-501. https://www.bia.gov/sites/default/files/dup/inline-files/bsi_investigative_report_may_2022_508.pdf.

Conrad, Joseph. 2008. *Heart of Darkness and Other Tales*. Oxford: Oxford University Press.

Cosgrove, Denis E. 1985. "Prospect, Perspective, and the Evolution of the Landscape Idea." *Transactions of the Institute of British Geographers* 10, no. 1: 45–62.

———. 1998. *Social Formation and Symbolic Landscape*. Madison: University of Wisconsin Press.

Coulthard, Glen Sean. 2014. *Red Skin, White Masks: Rejecting the Colonial Politics of Recognition*. Minneapolis: University of Minnesota Press.

Croskery, Charlie. 2018. "With Droplets of Water and Ink, Inuit Artist Heather Campbell Calls for Justice for Indigenous Women." *CBC Arts*, March 20. https://www.cbc.ca/arts/exhibitionists/with-droplets-of-water-and-ink-inuit-artist-heather-campbell-calls-for-justice-for-indigenous-women-1.4584446.

Culhane, Dara. 2003. "Their Spirits Live within Us: Aboriginal Women in Downtown Eastside Vancouver Emerging into Visibility." *American Indian Quarterly* 27, nos. 3–4 (Summer): 593–606.

Cummings, Denise K. 2011. *Visualities: Perspectives on Contemporary American Indian Film and Art*. East Lansing: Michigan State University Press.
Curley, Andrew. 2019. "Beyond Environmentalism: #NoDAPL as Assertion of Tribal Sovereignty." In *Standing with Standing Rock: Voices from the #NoDAPL Movement*, edited by Nick Estes and Jaskiran Dhillon, 158–68. Minneapolis: University of Minnesota Press.
The Cultural Memory Group. 2006. *Remembering Women Murdered by Men*. Toronto: Sumach Press.
Day, Iyko. 2015. "Being or Nothingness: Indigeneity, Antiblackness, and Settler Colonial Critique." *Critical Ethnic Studies* 1, no. 2 (Fall): 102–21.
Dean, Amber. 2015. *Remembering Vancouver's Disappeared Women: Settler Colonialism and the Difficulty of Inheritance*. Toronto: University of Toronto Press.
De Certeau, Michel. 1988. *The Writing of History*. Translated by Tom Conley. New York: Columbia University Press.
Deer, Sarah. 2015. *The Beginning and End of Rape: Confronting Sexual Violence in Native America*. Minneapolis: University of Minnesota Press.
Deloria, Philip J. 1999. *Playing Indian*. New Haven, CT: Yale University Press.
Deloria, Vine, Jr. (1969) 1988. *Custer Died for Your Sins: An Indian Manifesto*. Norman: University of Oklahoma Press.
Deloria, Vine, Jr., and Daniel R. Wildcat. 2001. *Power and Place: Indian Education in America*. Golden, CO: Fulcrum.
DeLue, Rachael Ziady, and James Elkins, eds. 2008. *Landscape Theory*. New York: Routledge.
De Vos, Laura, and Michele R. Willman. 2021. "Settler Colonial Praxis and Gender in Contemporary Times." *Settler Colonial Studies* 11, no. 2: 103–17.
Diamond, Elin, ed. 1996. *Performance and Cultural Politics*. London: Routledge.
Duthu, N. Bruce. 2008. "Broken Justice in Indian Country." *New York Times*, August 10, A17.
———. 2009. *American Indians and the Law*. New York: Penguin.
Ebersole, Gary L. 1995. *Captured by Texts: Puritan to Postmodern Images of Indian Captivity*. Charlottesville: University Press of Virginia.
Edwards, Kyle. 2018. "The Stunning Number of First Nations Kids in Foster Care— And the Activists Fighting Back." *Maclean's*, January 10. https://www.chatelaine.com/living/first-nations-fighting-foster-care/.
Elston, M. Melissa. 2012. "Subverting Visual Discourses of Gender and Geography: Monkman's Revised Iconography of the American West." *Journal of American Culture* 35, no. 2 (June): 181–90.
Engel, Leonard. 1994. "Mythic Space and Monument Valley: Another Look at John Ford's *Stagecoach*." *Literature / Film Quarterly* 22, no. 3: 174–80.
Engels, Friedrich. (1884) 2010. *The Origin of the Family, Private Property, and the State*. London: Penguin.
Erdrich, Louise. 1988. *Tracks: A Novel*. New York: Henry Holt.
———. 2012. *The Round House: A Novel*. New York: Harper.

Erdrich, Louise, and Michael Dorris. 1988. "Who Owns the Land?" *New York Times Magazine*, September 4, 32+.

Fabian, Johannes. 1983. *Time and the Other: How Anthropology Makes Its Object*. New York: Columbia University Press.

Faris, James C. 2003. *Navajo and Photography*. Salt Lake City: University of Utah Press.

Finding Dawn. 2006. Directed by Christine Welsh. Montreal: National Film Board of Canada.

Fiske, Jo-Anne. 1987. "Fishing Is Women's Business: Changing Economic Roles of Carrier Women and Men." In *Native Peoples, Native Lands: Canadian Indians, Inuit, and Metis*, edited by Bruce Cox, 186–98. Ottawa: Carleton University Press.

Fleming, E. McClung. 1965. "The American Image as Indian Princess, 1765–1783." *Winterthur Portfolio* 2: 65–81.

Florence, Kathryn. 2019. "Tail/Tale/Tell: The Transformation of Sedna into an Icon of Survivance in the Visual Arts through the Eyes of Four Contemporary Urban Inuit Artists." Master of Arts thesis, Concordia University, Montreal.

Foster, Hal. 1988. Preface to *Vision and Visuality*, ed. Hal Foster, ix–xiv. Seattle: Bay Press.

"Four Pueblo Children from Zuni, New Mexico, c. 1880." Photographic print, black and white. Carlisle Indian School Digital Resource Center.

"Frank Cushing, Taylor Ealy, Mary Ealy, and Jennie Hammaker [version 2], c. 1880." Photographic print, black and white. Carlisle Indian School Digital Resource Center.

Fur, Gunlög Maria. 2009. *A Nation of Women: Gender and Colonial Encounters among the Delaware Indians*. Early American Studies. Philadelphia: University of Pennsylvania Press.

Galanin, Nicholas. 2021. *Never Forget*. C-print on Dibond with walnut frame. Peter Blum Gallery, New York.

Garroutte, Eva. 2003. *Real Indians: Identity and the Survival of Native America*. Berkeley: University of California Press.

Goeman, Mishuana. 2013. *Mark My Words: Native Women Mapping Our Nations*. Minneapolis: University of Minnesota Press.

Gombay, Nicole. 2000. "The Politics of Culture: Gender Parity in the Legislative Assembly of Nunavut." *Etudes/Inuit/Studies* 24, no. 1: 125–48.

González, Jennifer A. 2011. *Subject to Display: Reframing Race in Contemporary Installation Art*. Cambridge, MA: MIT Press.

Goulet, Keith. 2017. "Nituskeenan: Our Land." In Monkman, *The Four Continents*, 32–37.

Government of Canada. 2016. *Report of the Royal Commission on Aboriginal Peoples: Perspectives and Realities*. Library and Archives Canada, updated February 11. https://www.bac-lac.gc.ca/eng/discover/aboriginal-heritage/royal-commission-aboriginal-peoples/Pages/final-report.aspx.

Grand Council of the Crees (Eeyou Istchee) and Cree Nation Government. N.d. "Timeline: The Crees of Yesterday and Today." Accessed January 6, 2024. https://www.cngov.ca/community-culture/timeline/.

Green, Rayna. 1975. "The Pocahontas Perplex: The Image of Indian Women in American Culture." *Massachusetts Review* 16, no. 4 (Autumn): 698–714.

Greenwald, Emily. 2002. *Reconfiguring the Reservation: The Nez Perces, Jicarilla Apaches, and the Dawes Act*. Albuquerque: University of New Mexico Press.

Greer, Allan. 2018. *Property and Dispossession: Natives, Empires, and Land in Early Modern North America*. Cambridge: Cambridge University Press.

Gross, Lawrence W. 2005. "The Trickster and World Maintenance: An Anishinaabe Reading of Louise Erdrich's *Tracks*." *SAIL (Studies in American Indian Literature)* 17, no. 3: 48–66.

Gulliford, Andrew. 1992. "Review: The West as America: Reinterpreting Images of the Frontier." *Journal of American History* 79, no. 1 (June): 199–208.

Gunning, Tom. 2017. "The Moving Image of the Frontier: The Western Landscape before the Movies." In *Once Upon a Time... The Western: A New Frontier in Art and Film*, edited by Mary-Daily Desmarais and Thomas Brent Smith, 35–41. Denver: Denver Art Museum.

Hargreaves, Allison. 2015. "Finding Dawn and Missing Women in Canada: Story-Based Methods in Antiviolence Research and Remembrance." *Studies in American Indian Literatures* 27, no. 3: 82–111.

———. 2017. *Violence against Indigenous Women: Literature, Activism, Resistance*. Waterloo, Ontario: Wilfred Laurier University Press.

Harley, J. Brian. 1992. "Rereading the Maps of the Columbian Encounter." *Annals of the Association of American Geographers* 82, no. 3 (September): 522–36.

———. 2002. *The New Nature of Maps: Essays in the History of Cartography*, edited by Paul Laxton. Baltimore: Johns Hopkins University Press.

Harris, Cole. 2004. "How Did Colonialism Dispossess: Comments from an Edge of Empire." *Annals of the Association of American Geographers* 94, no. 1: 165–82.

Harvey, David. 2006. *Spaces of Global Capitalism: A Theory of Uneven Geographical Development*. London: Verso.

Hearne, Joanna. 2012. *Native Recognition: Indigenous Cinema and the Western*. Albany: State University of New York Press.

Hellegers, Desiree. 2015. "From Poisson Road to Poison Road: Mapping the Toxic Trail of Windigo Capitalism in Linda Hogan's *Solar Storms*." *SAIL (Studies in American Indian Literature)* 27, no. 2 (Summer): 1–28.

Herman, R. D. K. 2008. "Reflections on the Importance of Indigenous Geography." *American Indian Culture and Research Journal* 32, no. 3: 73–88.

Higham, John. 1991. "Indian Princess and Roman Goddess: The First Female Symbols of America." *Proceedings of the American Antiquarian Society* 100 (January 1): 45–79.

Hirsch, Marianne. 1997. *Family Frames: Photography, Narrative, and Postmemory*. Cambridge, MA: Harvard University Press.

Hogan, Linda. 1994. *Solar Storms*. New York: Scribner.

Honour, Hugh. 1975. *The New Golden Land: European Images of America from the Discoveries to the Present Time*. New York: Pantheon Books.

Hoxie, Frederick E. 2001. *A Final Promise: The Campaign to Assimilate the Indians, 1880–1920*. Lincoln: University of Nebraska Press.

Hubbard, Phil, Rob Kitchin, and Gill Valentine. 2004. Introduction to *Key Thinkers on Space and Place*, edited by Phil Hubbard, Rob Kitchin, and Gill Valentine, 1–15. London: Sage.

Hughes, Josiah. 2017. "Kent Monkman Talks Shame and Prejudice: A Story of Resilience—His New Exhibition at the Glenbow." *Calgary Herald*, June 14. https://calgaryherald.com/life/swerve/kent-monkman-talks-shame-and-prejudice-a-story-of-resilience-his-new-exhibition-at-the-glenbow.

Huhndorf, Roy M., and Shari M. Huhndorf. 2011. "Alaska Native Politics since the Alaska Native Claims Settlement Act." *South Atlantic Quarterly* 110, no. 2 (Spring): 385–401.

Huhndorf, Shari M. 2000. "Nanook and His Contemporaries: Imagining Eskimos in American Culture, 1897–1922." *Critical Inquiry* 27, no. 1: 122–48.

———. 2001. *Going Native: Indians in the American Cultural Imagination*. Ithaca, NY: Cornell University Press.

———. 2009. *Mapping the Americas: The Transnational Politics of Contemporary Native Culture*. Ithaca, NY: Cornell University Press.

———. 2022. "Native, Inc." *Washington Monthly*, April 3, 17–23.

Huhndorf, Shari M., and Cheryl Suzack. 2010. "Indigenous/Feminism: Theorizing the Issues." In *Indigenous Women and Feminism: Politics, Activism, Culture*, edited by Cheryl Suzack, Shari M. Huhndorf, Jeanne Perreault, and Jean Barman, 1–17. Vancouver: University of British Columbia Press.

Hulme, Peter. 1985. "Polytropic Man: Tropes of Sexuality and Mobility in Early Colonial Discourse." In *Europe and Its Others: Proceedings of the Essex Conference on the Sociology of Literature, July 1984*, volume 2, edited by Francis Barker, Peter Hulme, Margaret Iversen, and Diana Loxley, 17–32. Colchester, UK: University of Essex.

Institute for the Advancement of Aboriginal Women. 2018. "Written Submission to the National Inquiry into Missing and Murdered Indigenous Women and Girls." National Inquiry into Missing and Murdered Indigenous Women and Girls, December 14, 2018. https://www.mmiwg-ffada.ca/wp-content/uploads/2019/02/IAAW-Final-Written-Submission.pdf.

Jacobs, Beverley, and Andrea J. Williams. 2008. "Legacy of Residential Schools: Missing and Murdered Aboriginal Women." In *From Truth to Reconciliation: Transforming the Legacy of Residential Schools*, edited by Marlene Brant Castellano, Linda Archibald, and Mike DeGagné, 121–40. Ottawa: Aboriginal Healing Foundation.

Jaimes, M. Annette. 1992. "Federal Identification Policy: A Usurpation of Indigenous Sovereignty in North America." In *The State of Native America: Genocide, Colonization, and Resistance*, edited by M. Annette Jaimes, 123–38. Boston: South End Press.

Jaimes Guerrero, M. A. 2003. "'Patriarchal Colonialism' and Indigenism: Implications for Native Feminist Spirituality and Native Womanism." *Hypatia* 18, no. 2: 58–69.

Jasper, Marykate. 2018. "Why Marchers Wore Red for Missing and Murdered Indigenous Women at the 2018 Women's March." *The Mary Sue*, January 21. https://www.themarysue.com/Indigenous-mmiw-womens-march-2018/.

Jay, Martin. 1988. "Scopic Regimes of Modernity." In Foster, *Vision and Visuality*, 3–28.

———. 1993. *Downcast Eyes: The Denigration of Vision in Twentieth-Century French Thought*. Berkeley: University of California Press.

Jay, Martin, and Sumathi Ramaswamy, eds. 2014. *Empires of Vision: A Reader*. Durham, NC: Duke University Press.

Jiwani, Yasmin, and Mary Lynn Young. 2006. "Missing and Murdered Women: Reproducing Marginality in News Discourse." *Canadian Journal of Communication*, no. 31: 895–917.

Johnson, Kelli Lyon. 2007. "Writing Deeper Maps: Mapmaking, Local Indigenous Knowledges, and Literary Nationalism in Native Women's Writing." *SAIL (Studies in American Indian Literature)* 19, no. 4 (Winter): 103–20.

Johnson, Miranda. 2016. *This Land Is Our History: Indigeneity, Law, and the Settler State*. Oxford: Oxford University Press.

Kaplan, E. Ann. 1997. *Looking for the Other: Feminism, Film, and the Imperial Gaze*. London: Routledge.

Kappo, Tanya. 2014. "Stephen Harper's Comments on Missing, Murdered Aboriginal Women Show 'Lack of Respect.'" *CBC News*, December 19. https://www.cbc.ca/news/indigenous/stephen-harper-s-comments-on-missing-murdered-aboriginal-women-show-lack-of-respect-1.2879154.

Keliiaa, Caitlin. 2019. "Unsettling Domesticity: Native Women and US Indian Policy in the San Francisco Bay Area." PhD dissertation, University of California, Berkeley.

Kingulliit Productions. 2016. *Maliglutit (Searchers)* Press Notes. http://s3.amazonaws.com/isuma.attachments/maliglutitsearchers-notes-final_160825.pdf.

Klein, Laura. 1995. "Mother as Clanswoman: Rank and Gender in Tlingit Society." In *Women and Power in Native North America*, edited by Laura Klein and Lillian Ackerman, 28–45. Norman: University of Oklahoma Press.

Knott, Helen. 2018. "Violence and Extraction: Stories from the Oil Fields." In *Keetsahnak: Our Missing and Murdered Indigenous Sisters*, edited by Kim Anderson, Maria Campbell, and Christi Belcourt, 147–60. Edmonton: University of Alberta Press.

Kolodny, Annette. 1975. *The Lay of the Land: Metaphor as Experience in American Life and Letters*. Chapel Hill: University of North Carolina Press.

Krupat, Arnold. 1996. *The Turn to the Native: Studies in Criticism and Culture*. Lincoln: University of Nebraska Press.

———. 2009. "Trickster Tales Revisited." In *All That Remains: Varieties of Indigenous Expression*, 1–26. Lincoln: University of Nebraska Press.

———. 2018. *Changed Forever*. Volume 1 of *American Indian Boarding School Literature*. Albany: State University of New York Press.

———. 2020. *Changed Forever,* Volume 2 of *American Indian Boarding School Literature.* Albany: State University of New York Press.

Kunuk, Zacharias. 2002. "I First Heard the Story of Atanarjuat from My Mother." *Brick* 70 (Winter): 17–20.

Kuokkanen, Rauna. 2019. *Restructuring Relations: Indigenous Self-Determination, Governance, and Gender.* New York: Oxford University Press.

LaDuke, Winona, and Ward Churchill. 1985. "Native America: The Political Economy of Radioactive Colonialism." *Journal of Ethnic Studies* 13, no. 3 (Fall): 107–32.

Landback manifesto. N.d. LANDBACK. Accessed September 30, 2022. https://landback.org/manifesto/.

Langston, Donna Hightower. 2003. "American Indian Women's Activism in the 1960s and 1970s." *Hypatia* 18, no. 2 (May): 114–32.

LaRocque, Emma. 1996. "The Colonization of a Native Woman Scholar." In *Women of the First Nations: Power, Wisdom, and Strength,* edited by Christine Miller and Patricia Chuckryk, 11–18. Winnipeg: University of Manitoba Press.

Lauzon, Claudette. 2008. "What the Body Remembers: Rebecca Belmore's Memorial to Missing Women." In *Precarious Visualities: New Perspectives on Identification in Contemporary Art and Visual Culture,* edited by Olivier Asselin, Johanne Lamoureux, and Christine Ross, 155–79. Montreal: McGill-Queens University Press.

Lavell-Harvard, D. Memee, and Jennifer Brant, eds. 2016. *Forever Loved: Exposing the Hidden Crises of Missing and Murdered Indigenous Women and Girls in Canada.* Bradford, Ontario: Demeter Press.

Lawrence, Bonita. 2003. "Gender, Race, and the Regulation of Native Identity in Canada and the United States." *Hypatia* 18, no. 2 (Spring): 3–31.

———. 2004. *"Real Indians" and Others: Mixed-Blood Urban Native Peoples and Indigenous Nationhood.* Lincoln: University of Nebraska Press.

Le Corbeiller, Clare. 1961. "Miss America and Her Sisters: Personifications of the Four Parts of the World." *Metropolitan Museum of Art Bulletin* 19, no. 8 (April): 209–23.

Lefebvre, Henri. 1991. *The Production of Space.* Translated by Donald Nicholson-Smith. Oxford: Blackwell.

Légaré, André. 1997. "The Government of Nunavut (1999): A Prospective Analysis." In *First Nations in Canada: Perspectives on Opportunity, Empowerment, and Self-Determination,* edited by J. Rick Ponting, 404–31. Toronto: McGraw-Hill Ryerson.

LeMaster, Michelle. 2014. "Pocahontas Doesn't Live Here Anymore: Women and Gender in the Native South before Removal." *Native South* 7: 1–32.

Leo, Debra, Beatrice Starr, and Stella August and Downtown Eastside Power of Women Group. 2018. "Voices from the Downtown Eastside." In *Keetsahnak: Our Missing and Murdered Indigenous Sisters,* edited by Kim Anderson, Maria Campbell, and Christi Belcourt. Edmonton: University of Alberta Press.

Limerick, Patricia Nelson. 1987. *The Legacy of Conquest: The Unbroken Past of the American West.* New York: W. W. Norton.

Lloyd, David, and Patrick Wolfe. 2015. "Settler Colonial Logics and the Neoliberal Regime." *Settler Colonial Studies* 6, no. 2: 109–18.

Lomawaima, K. Tsianina. 1993. "Domesticity in the Federal Indian Schools: The Power of Authority over Mind and Body." *American Ethnologist* 20, no. 2 (May): 227–40.

———. 1994. *They Called It Prairie Light: The Story of the Chilocco Indian School.* Lincoln: University of Nebraska Press.

———. 1996. "Estelle Reel, Superintendent of Indian Schools, 1898–1910: Politics, Curriculum, and Land." *Journal of American Indian Education* 35, no. 3 (Spring): 5–31.

Lord, Erica. 2000. *Native American Land Reclamation Project.* Installation, mixed media. Photos online at Erica Lord. Accessed January 14, 2024. https://ericalord.com/artwork/160740-Native%20American%20Land%20Reclamation%20Project.html.

———. 2010. "Artist Lecture by Erica Lord." Northern Michigan University. http://mediasite.nmu.edu/NMUMediasite/Play/f516b02f556b400f9d3e047fff8035fb1d?catalog=29838ab43e4747818e5c175684cd523b21.

Lowman, John. 2000. "Violence and the Outlaw Status of (Street) Prostitution in Canada." *Violence Against Women* 6, no. 9 (September): 987–1011.

MacQueen, Ken. 2002. "Streets of Fear." *Maclean's,* March 25. https://archive.macleans.ca/article/2002/3/25/streets-of-fear.

Maliglutit (Searchers). 2016. Directed by Zacharias Kunuk. Igloolik Isuma Productions.

Manuel, George, and Michael Posluns. (1974) 2019. *The Fourth World: An Indian Reality.* Foreword by Vine Deloria Jr. Minneapolis: University of Minnesota Press.

Margolis, Eric. 2004. "Looking at Discipline, Looking at Labour: Photographic Representations of Indian Boarding Schools." *Visual Studies* 19, no. 1: 72–96.

Maristuen-Rodakowski, Julie. 1988. "The Turtle Mountain Reservation in North Dakota: Its History as Depicted in Louise Erdrich's *Love Medicine* and *Beet Queen.*" *American Indian Culture and Research Journal* 12, no. 3: 33–48.

Markey, Lia. 2012. "Stradano's Allegorical Invention of the Americas in Late Sixteenth-Century Florence." *Renaissance Quarterly* 65, no. 2 (Summer): 385–442.

Martin, Carol, and Walia Harsha. 2019. *Red Women Rising: Indigenous Women Survivors in Vancouver's Downtown Eastside.* Vancouver: Downtown Eastside Women's Center. https://dewc.ca/dewc-news/red-women-rising/.

Martin, Keavy. 2011. "Rescuing Sedna: Doorslamming, Fingerslicing, and the Moral of the Story." *Canadian Review of Comparative Literature* 38, no. 2: 186–200.

Massip, Nathalie. 2011. "Staging the American West: 'The West as America'; National Museum of American Art, March–July 1991." *South Atlantic Review* 76, no. 2 (Spring): 5–18.

Mauro, Hayes Peter. 2011. *The Art of Americanization at the Carlisle Indian School.* Albuquerque: University of New Mexico Press.

McClintock, Anne. 1995. *Imperial Leather: Race, Gender, and Sexuality in the Colonial Contest*. London: Routledge.

McGillivray, Anne, and Brenda Comaskey. 1999. *Black Eyes All of the Time: Intimate Violence, Aboriginal Women, and the Justice System*. Toronto: University of Toronto Press.

McGrath, Ann, and Winona Stevenson. 1996. "Gender, Race, and Policy: Aboriginal Women and the State in Canada and Australia." *Labour/Le Travail* 38 (Fall) / *Labour History* 71 (November): 37–53.

Meriam, Lewis. 1928. *The Meriam Report: The Problem of Indian Administration*. Washington, DC: Brookings Institution.

Meyer, Melissa L. 1994. *The White Earth Tragedy: Ethnicity and Dispossession at a Minnesota Anishinaabe Reservation, 1889–1920*. Lincoln: University of Nebraska Press.

Miranda, Deborah. 2013. *Bad Indians: A Tribal Memoir*. Berkeley, CA: Heyday Books.

Mitchell, Lee Clark. 1998. *Westerns: Making the Man in Fiction and Film*. Chicago: University of Chicago Press.

———. 2004. "Why Monument Valley? (And Why Again and Again?)." *Paradoxa* 19: 116–46.

Mitchell, Marybelle. 1996. *From Talking Chiefs to a Native Corporate Élite: The Birth of Class and Nationalism among Canadian Inuit*. Montreal: McGill-Queen's University Press.

Mitchell, W. J. T. 1994a. "Imperial Landscape." In W. J.T. Mitchell, *Landscape and Power*, 5–34.

———. 1994b. Introduction to W.J.T. Mitchell, *Landscape and Power*, 1–4.

Mitchell, W. J. T., ed. 1994c. *Landscape and Power*. Chicago: University of Chicago Press.

Mithlo, Nancy. 2009. "'A Real Feminine Journey': Locating Indigenous Feminisms in the Arts." *Meridians: Feminism, Race, Transnationalism* 9, no. 2: 1–30.

Monkman, Kent. 2012. *Miss America*. Acrylic on canvas, Montreal Museum of Fine Arts.

———. 2013. *History Is Painted by the Victors*. Acrylic on canvas, Denver Art Museum. https://denverartmuseum.org/object/2016.288.

———. 2015. "Casualties of Modernity." Lecture, University of Michigan Stamps School of Art and Design, Ann Arbor, April 2. Online, YouTube, https://www.youtube.com/watch?v=VW3amUsP-50.

———. 2017. *The Four Continents*. London: Black Dog Press.

Montrose, Louis. 1991. "The Work of Gender in the Discourse of Discovery." *Representations* 33 (Winter): 1–41.

Morgan, Lewis Henry. (1877) 1964. *Ancient Society; Or, Researches in the Lines of Progress from Savagery through Barbarism to Civilization*. Cambridge, MA: Harvard University Press.

Morgensen, Scott Lauria. 2011. *Spaces between Us: Queer Settler Colonialism and Indigenous Decolonization*. Minneapolis: University of Minnesota Press.

Morrell, Vivienne. 2014. "'The Four Parts of the World'—Representations of the Continents." Vivienne Morrell (blog), November 12. https://viviennemorrell.wordpress.com/2014/11/12/the-four-parts-of-the-world-representations-of-the-continents/.

Morris, Kate. 2019. *Shifting Grounds: Landscape in Contemporary Native American Art*. Seattle: University of Washington Press.

Mulvey, Laura. 1975. "Visual Pleasure and Narrative Cinema." *Screen* 16, no. 4: 6–18.

Mundy, Barbara. 1996. *The Mapping of New Spain: Indigenous Cartography and the Maps of the Relaciones Geográficas*. Chicago: University of Chicago Press.

National Inquiry into Missing and Murdered Indigenous Women and Girls. 2019. *Reclaiming Power and Place: The Final Report of the National Inquiry into Missing and Murdered Indigenous Women and Girls*, Volume 1a. https://www.mmiwg-ffada.ca/wp-content/uploads/2019/06/Final_Report_Vol_1a.pdf.

National Sexual Violence Resource Center. 2000. "Sexual Assault in Indian Country: Confronting Sexual Violence." https://www.nsvrc.org/sites/default/files/Publications_NSVRC_Booklets_Sexual-Assault-in-Indian-Country_Confronting-Sexual-Violence.pdf.

Native Council of Canada. 1992. "Decision 1992: Background and Discussion Points for the First Peoples Forums." Ottawa, Ontario: Congress of Aboriginal Peoples.

Native Women's Association of Canada. 2015. "Fact Sheet: Root Causes of Violence against Aboriginal Women and the Impact of Colonization." https://www.nwac.ca/wp-content/uploads/2015/05/Fact_Sheet_Root_Causes_of_Violence_Against_Aboriginal_Women.pdf.

NCAI Policy Research Center. 2013. "Statistics on Violence against Native Women." National Congress of American Indians. https://archive.ncai.org/resources/ncai_publications/policy-insights-brief-statistics-on-violence-against-native-women.

Nead, Lynda. 1990. "The Female Nude: Pornography, Art, and Sexuality." *Signs: Journal of Women in Culture and Society* 15, no. 2 (Winter): 323–35.

Newland, Brian. 2022. *Federal Indian Boarding School Initiative Investigative Report*. Office of the Assistant Secretary–Indian Affairs, US Department of the Interior. https://www.bia.gov/sites/default/files/dup/inline-files/bsi_investigative_report_may_2022_508.pdf.

Nichols, Robert. 2020. *Theft Is Property! Dispossession and Critical Theory*. Durham, NC: Duke University Press.

Niezen, Ronald. 2003. *The Origins of Indigenism: Human Rights and the Politics of Identity*. Berkeley: University of California Press.

O'Brien, Jean. 2003. *Dispossession by Degrees: Land and Identity in Natick, Massachusetts*. Lincoln: University of Nebraska Press.

Olund, Eric. 2002a. "From Savage Space to Governable Space: The Extension of United States Judicial Sovereignty over Indian Country." *Cultural Geographies* 9: 129–57.

———. 2002b. "Public Domesticity during the Indian Reform Era; or, Mrs. Jackson Is Induced to Go to Washington." *Gender, Place, and Culture* 9, no. 2: 153–66.

Ortner, Sherry B. 1974. "Is Female to Male as Nature Is to Culture?" In *Woman, Culture, and Society*, edited by Michelle Zimbalist Rosaldo and Louise Lamphere, 68–87. Stanford, CA: Stanford University Press.

Park, K-Sue. 2016. "Money, Mortgages, and the Conquest of America." *Law and Social Inquiry* 41, no. 4 (Fall): 1006–35.

Pauktuutit Inuit Women of Canada and Elizabeth Comack. 2020. *Addressing Gendered Violence Against Inuit Women: A Review of Police Policies and Practices in Inuit Nunangat*. Pauktuutit Inuit Women of Canada. Accessed October 16, 2022. https://pauktuutit.ca/wp-content/uploads/Pauktuutit_Addressing-Gendered-Violence_English_Full-Report-1.pdf.

Pearce, Margaret Wickens. 1988. "Native Mapping in Southern New England Indian Deeds." In *Cartographic Encounters: Perspectives on Native American Mapmaking and Map Use*, edited by G. W. Lewis, 157–86. Chicago: University of Chicago Press.

Pearce, Maryanne. 2013. "An Awkward Silence: Missing and Murdered Vulnerable Women and the Canadian Justice System." PhD dissertation, University of Ottawa.

Pearce, Roy Harvey. 1988. *Savagism and Civilization: A Study of the Indian and the American Mind*. Berkeley: University of California Press.

Perdue, Theda. 1998. *Cherokee Women: Gender and Culture Change, 1700–1835*. Lincoln: University of Nebraska Press.

Pesantubbee, Michelene E. 2005. *Choctaw Women in a Chaotic World: The Clash of Cultures in the Colonial Southeast*. Albuquerque: University of New Mexico Press.

Peterson, Nancy J. 1994. "History, Postmodernism, and Louise Erdrich's *Tracks*." *PMLA* 109, no. 5 (October): 982–94.

Pictou, Sherry. 2020. "Decolonizing Decolonization: An Indigenous Feminist Perspective on the Recognition and Rights Framework." *South Atlantic Quarterly* 119, no. 2 (April): 371–91.

Pollock, Griselda. 2003. "The Grace of Time: Narrativity, Sexuality, and a Visual Encounter in the Virtual Feminist Museum." *Art History* 26, no. 2: 174–213.

Poole, Deborah. 2005. "An Excess of Description: Ethnography, Race, and Visual Technologies." *Annual Review of Anthropology* 34: 159–79.

Prats, José Armando. 2002. *Invisible Natives: Myth and Identity in the American Western*. Ithaca, NY: Cornell University Press.

Pratt, Mary Louise. 1992. *Imperial Eyes: Travel Writing and Transculturation*. London: Routledge.

Rader, Dean. 2011. *Engaged Resistance: American Indian Art, Literature, and Film from Alcatraz to the NMAI*. Austin: University of Texas Press.

Rafael, Vicente L. 2000. *White Love and Other Events in Filipino History*. Durham, NC: Duke University Press.

Raheja, Michelle H. 2013. *Reservation Reelism: Redfacing, Visual Sovereignty, and Representations of Native Americans in Film*. Lincoln: University of Nebraska Press.

Rainwater, Catherine. 1990. "Reading between Worlds: Narrativity in the Fiction of Louise Erdrich." *American Literature* 62, no. 3 (September): 405–22.

Razack, Sherene H. 2002. "Gendered Racial Violence and Spatialized Justice: The Murder of Pamela George." In *Race, Space, and the Law: Unmapping a White Settler Society*, edited by Sherene H. Razack, 121–56. Toronto: Between the Lines.

RedBird, Elsie B. 1995. "Honoring Native Women: The Backbone of Native Sovereignty." In *Popular Justice and Community Regeneration: Pathways of Indigenous Reform*, edited by Kayleen M. Hazelhurst, 121–42. Westport, CT: Praeger.

Reel, Estelle. 1901. *Course of Study for the Indian Schools of the United States: Industrial and Literary*. Washington, DC: Government Printing Office.

Rickard, Jolene. 2005. "Rebecca Belmore: Performing Power." In *Rebecca Belmore: Fountain*, edited by Jessica Bradley and Jolene Rickard, 68–76. Vancouver: Kamloops Art Gallery and Morris and Helen Belkin Art Gallery.

———. 2011. "Visualizing Sovereignty in the Time of Biometric Sensors." *South Atlantic Quarterly* 110, no. 2 (Spring): 465–82.

Ritter, Kathleen. 2008. "The Reclining Figure and Other Provocations." In *Rebecca Belmore: Rising to the Occasion*, edited by Daina Augaitis and Kathleen Ritter, 53–68. Vancouver: Vancouver Art Gallery.

Rocheleau D., B. Thomas-Slayter, and D. Edmunds. 1995. "Gendered Resource Mapping: Focusing on Women's Spaces in the Landscape." *Cultural Survival Quarterly* 18: 62–68.

Roosevelt, Theodore. 1901. "First Annual Message." Speech to the Senate and House of Representatives, Washington, DC, December 3. American Presidency Project https://www.presidency.ucsb.edu/documents/first-annual-message-16.

Rosay, André B. 2016. *Violence against American Indian and Alaska Native Women and Men*. Washington, DC: National Institute of Justice, Office of Justice Programs, US Department of Justice. https://www.ncjrs.gov/pdffiles1/nij/249736.pdf.

Rose, Deborah Bird. 1996. "Land Rights and Deep Colonising: The Erasure of Women." *Aboriginal Law Bulletin* 85, no. 3 (October): 6–13.

Rose, Gillian. 1993. *Feminism and Geography: The Limits of Geographical Knowledge*. Minneapolis: University of Minnesota Press.

———. 2010. *Doing Family Photography: The Domestic, the Public, and the Politics of Sentiment*. Abingdon, UK: Ashgate.

Rose, Jacqueline. 2006. *Sexuality in the Field of Vision*. London: Verso.

Said, Edward. 1993. *Culture and Imperialism*. New York: Vintage Books.

Sandals, Leah. 2013. "Q&A: Kent Monkman on the Calgary Stampede, Castors, and More." *Canadian Art,* August 12. https://canadianart.ca/interviews/kent-monkman-the-big-four/.

Sasse, Julie. 2004. "Postmodern Messenger." In *Jaune Quick-to-See Smith: Postmodern Messenger*, edited by Mary Sasse, 1–21. Tucson: Tucson Museum of Art.

Schulman, Sandra Hale. 2021. "Art Installation Calls for Return of Native Lands." *Indian Country Today*, May 24. https://indiancountrytoday.com/news/art-installation-calls-for-return-of-cahuilla-land.

Schurz, Carl. (1881) 1973. "Present Aspects of the Indian Problem (1881)." *North American Review* (Winter): 45–54.

Scudeler, June. 2015. "'Indians on Top': Kent Monkman's Sovereign Erotics." *American Indian Culture and Research Journal* 39, no. 4: 19–32.

Scully, Pamela. 2005. "Malintzin, Pocahontas, and Krotoa: Indigenous Women and Myth Models of the Atlantic World." *Journal of Colonialism and Colonial History* 6, no. 3 (Winter): 1–28.

The Searchers. 1956. Dir. John Ford. Warner Bros.

Sekula, Allan. 1986. "The Body and the Archive." *October* 39 (Winter): 3–64.

Seznec, Jean. 1953. *The Survival of the Pagan Gods: The Mythological Tradition and Its Place in Renaissance Humanism and Art*. Princeton, NJ: Princeton University Press.

Silko, Leslie Marmon. 1996. "Language and Literature from a Pueblo Indian Perspective." In *Yellow Woman and a Beauty of the Spirit: Essays on Native American Life Today*, 48–59. New York: Simon and Schuster.

———. 1999. "Landscape, History, and the Pueblo Imagination." In *At Home on the Earth: Becoming Native to Our Place*, edited by David Landis Barnhill, 30–42. Berkeley: University of California Press.

Simonsen, Jane E. 2006. *Making Home Work: Domesticity and Native American Assimilation in the American West, 1860–1919*. Chapel Hill: University of North Carolina Press.

Simpson, Leanne Betasamosake. 2014. "Land as Pedagogy: Nishnaabeg Intelligence and Rebellious Transformation." *Decolonization: Indigeneity, Education and Society* 3, no. 3: 1–25.

———. 2017. *As We Have Always Done: Indigenous Freedom through Radical Resistance*. Minneapolis: University of Minnesota Press.

Slotkin, Richard. 1992. *Gunfighter Nation: The Myth of the Frontier in Twentieth-Century America*. New York: Atheneum.

———. (1973) 2000. *Regeneration through Violence: The Mythology of the American Frontier, 1600–1860*. Norman: University of Oklahoma Press.

Smith, Paul Chaat, and Robert Allen Warrior. 1996. *Like a Hurricane: The Indian Movement from Alcatraz to Wounded Knee*. New York: The New Press.

Smith, Theresa S., and Jill M. Fiori. 2010. "Landscape as Narrative, Narrative as Landscape." *SAIL (Studies in American Indian Literature)* 22, no. 4: 58–80.

Snyder, Joel. 1994. "Territorial Photography." In W.J.T. Mitchell, *Landscape and Power*, 175–202.

Sørenson, Laila. 2000. "The Inuit Broadcasting Corporation and Nunavut." In *Nunavut: Inuit Regain Control of Their Lands and Their Lives*, edited by Jens Dahl, Jack Hicks, and Peter Jull, 170–79. Copenhagen: International Work Group for Indigenous Affairs.

Stacks, Geoffrey. 2010. "A Defiant Cartography: Linda Hogan's *Solar Storms*." *Mosaic* 43, no. 1 (March): 161–76.

Stam, Robert, and Ella Shohat. 1994. *Unthinking Eurocentrism: Multiculturalism and the Media*. Abingdon, UK: Routledge.

Steinberg, Philip E., Jeremy Tasch, and Hannes Gerhardt. 2018. *Contesting the Arctic: Politics and Imaginaries in the Circumpolar North*. London: I. B. Tauris.

Stern, Pamela. 1998. "The History of Canadian Arctic Photography: Issues of Territorial and Cultural Sovereignty." In *Imaging the Arctic*, edited by J. C. H. King and Henrietta Lidchi, 46–52. Seattle: University of Washington Press.

Stripes, James. 1991. "The Problem(s) of (Anishinaabe) History in the Fiction of Louise Erdrich." *Wicazo sa Review* 7, no. 2: 26–33.

Suzack, Cheryl. 2015. "Indigenous Feminisms in Canada." *NORA—Nordic Journal of Feminist and Gender Research* 23, no. 4: 261–74.

———. 2017. *Indigenous Women's Writing and the Cultural Study of Law*. Toronto: University of Toronto Press.

Swinton, Nelda. 1985. "The Inuit Sea Goddess." Master of Arts thesis, Concordia University, Montreal. https://spectrum.library.concordia.ca/id/eprint/5705/1/MK68085.pdf.

Tagg, John. 1993. *The Burden of Representation: Essays on Photographies and Histories*. Minneapolis: University of Minnesota Press.

Taylor, Diana. 2003. *The Archive and the Repertoire: Performing Cultural Memory in the Americas*. Durham, NC: Duke University Press.

Thacker, Andrew. 2005. "The Idea of a Critical Literary Geography." *New Formations* 57: 56–73.

Tilton, Robert S. 1995. *Pocahontas: The Evolution of an American Narrative*. Cambridge: Cambridge University Press.

Timm, Jordan. 2007. "Landscape with Sexy Transvestite: Kent Monkman's Playful Subversions of an Old Form Tell a Different Story of the Frontier." *Maclean's*, December 31, 94–95.

Tompkins, Jane. 1993. *West of Everything: The Inner Life of Westerns*. New York: Oxford University Press.

Trennert, Robert A. 1987. "Selling Indian Education at World's Fairs and Expositions, 1893–1904." *American Indian Quarterly* 11, no. 3 (Summer): 203–20.

Truettner, William H. 1991. "Ideology and Image: Justifying Westward Expansion." In *The West as America: Reinterpreting Images of the Frontier*, 27–54. Washington, DC: Smithsonian Institution.

Truettner, William H., and Alex Nemerov. 1992. "What You See Is Not Necessarily What You Get: New Meaning in Images of the Old West." *Montana: The Magazine of Western History* 42, no. 3 (Summer): 70–76.

Truth and Reconciliation Commission. 2015a. *A Knock on the Door: The Essential History of Residential Schools from the Truth and Reconciliation Commission of Canada*. Winnipeg: University of Manitoba Press.

———. 2015b. *Honouring the Truth, Reconciling for the Future: Summary of the Final Report of the Truth and Reconciliation Commission of Canada*. Accessed September 29, 2022. https://publications.gc.ca/site/eng/9.800288/publication.html.

Tsosie, Rebecca. 2010. "Native Women and Leadership: An Ethics of Culture and Relationship." In *Indigenous Women and Feminism: Politics, Activism, Culture*, edited by Cheryl Suzack, Shari M. Huhndorf, Jeanne Perreault, and Jean Barman, 29–42. Vancouver: University of British Columbia Press.

Turner, Frederick Jackson. (1893) 1994. "The Significance of the Frontier in American History (1893)." In *Rereading Frederick Jackson Turner: "The Significance of the Frontier in American History" and Other Essays*, edited by John Mack Faragher, 31–60. New York: Henry Holt.

TVO Current Affairs. 2017. "Challenging Canada's History through Art." TVO Today, July 5. https://www.tvo.org/article/challenging-canadas-history-through-art.

Urban Indian Health Institute. 2018. *Missing and Murdered Indigenous Women and Girls*. http://www.uihi.org/wp-content/uploads/2018/11/Missing-and-Murdered-Indigenous-Women-and-Girls-Report.pdf.

Usher, Peter J. 1971. "Fur Trade Posts of the Northwest Territories, 1870–1970." Northern Science Research Group, Department of Indian Affairs and Northern Development. Online, Internet Archive. Accessed January 10, 2024. https://archive.org/details/furtradepostsofnoooushe/mode/2up.

Van der Straet, Jan, called Stradanus. 1587–89. *Allegory of America*. Drawing, pen and brown ink. Metropolitan Museum of Art, New York.

Vespucci, Amerigo. (1502–4) 2011. *The Letters of Amerigo Vespucci and Other Documents Illustrative of His Career*. Translated by Clements B. Markham. Issued by the Hakluyt Society. New York: Burt Franklin.

Wall Street Journal. 1991. "Pilgrims and Other Imperialists." May 17, A14.

Watson, Scott. 2003. Foreword to *Rebecca Belmore: The Named and the Unnamed*, edited by Charlotte Townsend-Gault and James Luna, 7–8. Vancouver: Morris and Helen Belkin Art Gallery.

———. 2005. "Interview: Scott Watson and Rebecca Belmore." In *Rebecca Belmore: Fountain*, edited by Jessica Bradley and Jolene Rickard, 23–28. Vancouver: Kamloops Art Gallery and Morris and Helen Belkin Art Gallery.

Westling, Louise H. 1996. *The Green Breast of the New World: Landscape, Gender, and American Fiction*. Athens: University of Georgia Press.

Wexman, Virginia Wright. 1993. *Star and Genre: John Wayne, the Western, and the American Dream of the Family on the Land*. Princeton, NJ: Princeton University Press.

———. 1996. "The Family on the Land: Race and Nationhood in Silent Westerns." In *The Birth of Whiteness: Race and the Emergence of U.S. Cinema*, edited by Daniel Bernardi, 129–69. New Brunswick, NJ: Rutgers University Press.

Whalen, Kevin. 2016. *Native Students at Work: American Indian Labor and Sherman Institute's Outing Program, 1900–1945*. Seattle: University of Washington Press.

Whitt, Sarah. 2020. "False Promises: Race, Power, and the Chimera of Indian Assimilation, 1879–1934." PhD dissertation, University of California, Berkeley.

Williams, Robert A., Jr. 2005. *Like a Loaded Weapon: The Rehnquist Court, Indian Rights, and the Legal History of Racism in America*. Minneapolis: University of Minnesota Press.

Wolfe, Patrick. 2001. "Land, Labor, and Difference: Elementary Structures of Race." *American Historical Review* 106, no. 3 (June): 866–905.

———. 2006. "Settler Colonialism and the Elimination of the Native." *Journal of Genocide Research* 8, no. 4 (December): 387–409.

Yogaretnam, Shaamini. 2012. "Portrait of John Ralston Saul Unveiled at Rideau Hall by Artist Kent Monkman." *Ottawa Citizen*, December 17. Online.

Youngbear-Tibbetts, Holly. 1991. "Without Due Process: The Alienation of Individual Trust Allotments of the White Earth Anishinaabeg." *American Indian Culture and Research Journal* 15, no. 2: 93–138.

INDEX

Aboriginal, use of term, xvii
Aboriginal title, 3–4, 62, 81
Acoose, Janice, 113–14
Act for the Protection of the Indians in Upper Canada of 1839, 161n28
Active, John, 140
activism, Native: novel aspects of modern, 3–5; women's role in, 92. *See also* resistance; *specific issues*
Adams, David Wallace, 41, 42
Africa, in hierarchy of continents, 24–25
agent system, 53–55
agriculture: at boarding schools, 43–44; in General Allotment Act, 49–51; in human development, 47
Alaska Native Claims Settlement Act (ANCSA) of 1971 (US), 4, 17, 146, 147–49
Alaska v. Native Village of Venetie Tribal Government, 148–49
Alcatraz Island, 4
Aleiss, Angela, 168n18
Allegory of America (Collaert), 25, 25*fig.*
Allegory of America (Stradanus), 26–32, 28*fig.*; cannibalism in, 29–31, 73; vs. Chapman's *Baptism of Pocahontas*, 35–38; imagery of Native women's bodies in, 19, 26–32
Allegory of America (Vos), 25–26, 25*fig.*
Allegory of the Planets and Continents (Tiepolo), 25, 56–57
allotment. *See* General Allotment Act
Almanac of the Dead (Silko), 158n16, 162n3

alternative cartographies, 62–64
America, Native women in imagery of: in age of exploration, 23–32; in era of nation-building, 33–40; in four-continents iconography, 24–25, 27, 33, 56–58; in Native art, 56–58
American Indian Women's Chemical Health Project, 88
American Revolution, 33–34
Amnesty International, 21, 89, 165n6
Amnesty International Film Festival, 108
anachronisms, 130, 139
Ancient Society (Morgan), 47–48
ANCSA. *See* Alaska Native Claims Settlement Act
Anglo-Powhatan Wars, 36–37
animal exploitation, 139, 140
Animism (Tagaq), 142
Anishinaabe: use of term, 162n1; White Earth reservation of, 64–65, 162n5, 163n7. *See also Tracks* (Erdrich)
Arctic, 147–55; in Campbell's *Methylmercury*, 22, 146–47, 151–55; Canadian expedition to, 141, 143; in Canadian national identity, 22, 141; fur trade in, 139, 140, 141; gaps in literature on, 22, 147; gendered violence in, 145–46; in Lord's *Native American Land Reclamation Project*, 22, 146–51. *See also Maliglutit* (film); *Solar Storms* (Hogan)
Army, US, 124. *See also* Cavalry
art history, Western, Monkman's critique of, 121–22, 129

artworks. *See* cultural works; visual art; specific works
Asia, in hierarchy of continents, 24–25
assimilation, 19, 26, 38–56; boarding schools in, 40–47; Canadian Gradual Enfranchisement Act in, 52–53; Canadian Indian Act in, 40, 53–56; citizenship in, 48; dispossession as goal of, 38–39, 41, 46, 55; in Erdrich's *Tracks*, 63–74; miscegenation's role in, 38; patriarchal nuclear families in, 19, 23, 39–40; rise of, in government policy, 38–39; US General Allotment Act in, 40, 47–51; in women's vulnerability to violence, 39–40
astrolabes, 27–29
Atanarjuat, the Fast Runner (film), 132, 167n15
attachment, to land, 3, 15, 158n12
Australia, European exploration of, 63

Baptism of Pocahontas (Chapman), 35–38, 36*fig*.; vs. boarding school photos, 45, 46; imagery of Native women's bodies in, 19, 26, 35–38; settler benevolence in, 37, 41
Barker, Joanne, 14
Barman, Jean, 39, 159n6
Barthes, Roland, 97, 98
Bear Robe, Amber-Rose, 99
Beet Queen, The (Erdrich), 65
Belcourt, Christi, 95
Belin, Esther, 162n3
Belkin Gallery, 102
Belmore, Rebecca, common themes in art of, 96. *See also* Fringe; *Vigil*
benevolence, settler, 37, 41
Berger, John, 167n7
Bermingham, Ann, 127
Bhandar, Brenna, 54
Bierstadt, Albert: national identity associated with, 118; travels in US West, 124, 126. *See also Mount Corcoran*
Big Sur, 157n3
Bill C-31 (Canada), 55
Bingo Palace, The (Erdrich), 65, 164n15
Black, Jaime, 94
Black people, assimilation of, 38

Blaney, Fay, 114
blood quantum, 51, 52
Blue Lake, 4
Blunt, Alison, 159n3
boarding (residential) schools, 40–47; assimilation through, 40–47; closure of, 42, 160n13; death of children at, 40–41; gender roles at, 43–46; General Allotment Act and, 51; goals of, 41–42, 159n10; legacy of, 47; location of, 41, 160n12; mandatory enrollment at, 41–42, 52; number of, 160n12; photos taken at, 44–46, 46*fig*.; in social marginalization of women, 43–47, 88–89
bodies of Native women, 19, 23–39; as allegorical figures, 19, 23; as anti-allegory, 95; in Belmore's *Fringe*, 96–103; in Belmore's *Vigil*, 102–7; in Campbell's *Methylmercury*, 146–48, 153–54; changes in political meaning of, 26, 32, 39; in Chapman's *Baptism of Pocahontas*, 19, 26, 35–38; in imagery of America, 23–26; land conflated with, 9–10, 24, 95, 100; in Lord's *Native American Land Reclamation Project*, 146–48, 150, 153; in Stradanus's *Allegory of America*, 19, 26–32, 35–38; visibility of race in, 11–12, 100–101. *See also* sexual violence
Bosse, Daleen, 111–12
Botero, Giovanni, 159n1
Brady, Mary Pat, 162n4
Britain: Canadian independence from, 52; in imagery of America, 34; Native people as subjects of, 51; transfer of Arctic to Canada by, 141; in War of 1812, 33
British Columbia: in *Calder v. British Columbia*, 4, 121, 131, 133; oil production in, 2–3; residential schools in, 40. *See also* Vancouver
Bromley, Neil, 8
Brotherston, Gordon, 62
Brown, James, 107
Bryce, Peter, 40–41
Burke Act of 1906 (US), 161n23, 163n8
Butler, Judith, 166n23

Calder v. British Columbia, 4, 121, 131, 133
California, gold rush in, 126. *See also specific locations*
Caméra d'Or, 132
Campbell, Heather, *Methylmercury*, 22, 146–47, 151–55, 152*fig.*
Canada: British transfer of Arctic to, 141; independence from Britain, 52. *See also specific laws, locations, and policies*
Canadian Arctic Expedition, 141, 143
Cannes Film Festival, 132
cannibalism, 25–26, 29–31, 34, 73
capitalism: in boarding schools, 42, 44; land as property in, 7–11; maps in origins of, 60–61; patriarchy and, 48; situating Native people outside, 16–17
Capitol, US, 33, 35, 118
captivity narratives: Christianity in, 168n25; in literary works, 135; in *Maliglutit* (film), 138–40, 143–45; in paintings, 168n24; in *The Searchers* (film), 135–36, 144
caribou, 140, 143
Carlisle Indian Industrial School, 41, 44–46, 46*fig.*, 160n13
Carter, Paul, 63, 66
cartography, colonial: in Arctic, 141; in Erdrich's *Tracks*, 20, 59–60, 64, 70–71; in Hogan's *Solar Storms*, 20, 64, 75, 77–81; as instrument of dispossession, 60–61; landscape paintings as form of, 124; pictorial vs. drawn to scale, 8–9
cartography, Native, 20, 59–86; alternative histories of land in, 62–64; in establishment of land rights, 62–63, 81; literature as form of, 61–64, 162n3; as "mapping by words," 20, 61, 64, 74; toponyms in, 79; unrecognized forms of, 61, 62; women's use of land in, 81. *See also Solar Storms* (Hogan); *Tracks* (Erdrich)
Catlin, George, 121
Cavalry, US, 126, 130, 137
Census Bureau, US, 118
Chapman, John Gadsby. *See Baptism of Pocahontas*
Charles II (king of England), 164n17
charters, royal, 164n17

Cherokee, 43
Cheyenne, 130, 137
Cheyfitz, Eric, 16–17, 84
Chicana literature, 162n4
children, Native: in foster care, 108, 111–13; patrilineage in identity of, 52–53. *See also* boarding schools
Chippewa, 162n1. *See also* Anishinaabe
Christianity: in boarding schools, 42; in captivity narratives, 168n25; in Erdrich's *Tracks*, 67–70, 163n12; in Hogan's *Solar Storms*, 79
Church, Frederic E., 118
cities, Native women's migration to: in Erdrich's *Tracks*, 72; vs. Native men, 56, 164n2; role of dispossession in, 88; social invisibility in, 89, 98
citizenship, Canadian, 53
citizenship, tribal. *See* tribal membership
citizenship, US, 48, 160n20, 161n21
civilization-savagism binary. *See* savages, Native people depicted as
civil rights movements of 1960s, 3
Clark, Kenneth, 123
Coast Protectors, 157n6
Cole, Thomas, 118
Collaert, Adriaen, 25, 25*fig.*
colonialism: central role of cultural depictions in, 6–13, 26; central role of gender hierarchies in, 10, 23, 27; maps as weapons of, 60–61; as progress, Native challenges to, 20, 56–57, 64. *See also specific issues and strategies*
Columbus, Christopher, 23, 32, 33, 117, 120, 159n4
Comanche, 134–35, 136
Congress, US: on elimination of land claims, 159n10; House Committee on Indian Affairs, 35; on missing and murdered Indigenous women and girls, 94; on Native treaties in California, 126; on Smithsonian, 118. *See also specific laws*
Conrad, Joseph, 76–77, 169n28
Conspiracy of Silence (television miniseries), 165n6
continents, iconography of four, 24–25, 27, 33, 56–58

Coon Come, Matthew, 75
Corcoran, William Wilson, 125–26, 167n11
corporations, for-profit Native, 148
Cosgrove, Denis, 9, 123, 150, 167n7
Coulthard, Glen, 11
countermaps, 81
Course of Study for the Indian Schools of the United States (Reel), 44
covenants, restrictive, 157n1
creation myth, American, 118–19, 131
Cree, 98. See also *Solar Storms* (Hogan)
Creek, 43
Crey, Dawn, 108–15. See also *Finding Dawn* (film)
Crey, Ernie, 110, 115
criminalization, of sex workers, 109
Culhane, Dara, 93
cultural works: central role in colonialism, 6–13, 26; politics of contemporary Native, 13–18. See also *specific genres and works*
culture, vs. nature, association of men with, 27–28
Culture and Imperialism (Said), 6, 157n8
Curley, Andrew, 158n18
Custer, George Armstrong, 130
cyanide, 80

Dakota Access Pipeline (DAPL), 2, 5
dams. See James Bay; Muskrat Falls
DAPL. See Dakota Access Pipeline
Dawes Act of 1887. See General Allotment Act
Day, Iyko, 16
deaths, Native: at boarding schools, 40–41; in removals, 37
Deer, Sarah, 88, 165n6
Deloria, Vine, Jr., 15, 38
DeLue, Rachael Ziady, 124
Desert X biennial exhibition, 1
Diamond, Elin, 103
Diné, 136
disease: in Erdrich's *Tracks*, 66, 68, 70, 71; in gold rush, 126
dispossession: attachment as opposite of, 158n12; gaps in scholarship on gendered dimensions of, 13–14. See also *specific strategies*
divorce, 54
domestic labor by Native women: in assimilation policies, 40, 44, 45, 50, 89; in Belmore's *Vigil*, 103–4
domestic spaces, in Welsh's *Finding Dawn*, 110–15. See also homes
Dorris, Michael, 64–65
Duluwat Island, 157n3
Duthu, N. Bruce, 7, 84–85

Eakins, Thomas, 129
education, dispossession as goal of, 41, 159n10. See also boarding schools
Engels, Friedrich, 48, 168n23
Enlightenment, 24, 28–29, 78
epidemics. See disease
Erdrich, Louise: *Four Souls*, 164n16; *The Round House*, 84–85, 94–95; tetralogy of novels by, 65–66, 164n15; "Who Owns the Land?," 64–65. See also *Tracks*
eroticism, 24, 28, 129
Esselen, 157n3
ethnographic photography, 99–102
Eureka (California), 157n3
Europe, in hierarchy of continents, 24–25, 56
European expansion. See colonialism; nation-building; westward expansion
European exploration and discovery: of Australia, 63; imagery of Native women's bodies in, 19, 26–32; Native women leading resistance to, 30–31
evidence, photographs as, 97, 98

Fabian, Johannes, 12, 101
family homes. See homes
family photographs, 110–13, 166n22
family structures. See kinship structures; patriarchal nuclear families
Faris, James, 99
farming. See agriculture
Federal Indian Boarding School Initiative Investigative Report, 159nn7,9
Federal Indian Boarding School Truth Initiative (US), 159n9

federal recognition of tribes, 148
fee simple title, 148–49, 161n23
feminism, Indigenous: backlash against, 14; role of artists in, 90–91, 165n5
films. *See* Western films; *specific films*
Finding Dawn (film), 21, 95, 107–16, 111*fig.*, 115*fig.*
First Nations, definition and use of term, xvii
flag, American, 34, 45, 149
flag, Canadian, 107
Fontaine, Tina, 93
Ford, John. *See Searchers, The*
forensic photography, 99–100
for-profit Native corporations, 148
foster care, 108, 111–13
foundation myth, 38
Four Continents, The (Monkman), 56–58
four-continents iconography, 24–25, 27, 33, 56–58
Four Souls (Erdrich), 164n16
"fourth world," 3, 15
Fourth World, The (Manuel), 15
Friendly Arctic, The (Stefansson), 141
Friends of the Indian, 42, 160n15
Fringe (Belmore), 21, 88*fig.*, 95–103; connotations of title, 90; display in museums, 166n12; display on billboards, 87, 97–99; meanings of body in, 96–103; photographic genres in, 99–102; red in imagery of, 90, 106
frontier myth, 118–19, 131
frontier thesis, 118, 166n2
fur trade: in Arctic, 139, 140, 141; in Hogan's *Solar Storms*, 20, 64, 75, 79

Gabrielino Tongva, 1
Galanin, Nicholas, 1–2, 2*fig.*, 4, 6, 147
gaze, the: in Belmore's *Fringe*, 100–103; in Bierstadt's *Mount Corcoran*, 125–27; in Lord's *Native American Land Reclamation Project*, 149–50; in *Maliglutit* (film), 22, 120, 143; in Monkman's *History Is Painted by the Victors*, 127–30; visibility of race in, 11–12
gender binaries, challenges to, 57
gender discrimination, in Indian Act, 53–56

gendered dimensions of dispossession, gaps in scholarship on, 13–14
gendered violence against Native women, 19–21, 87–116; assimilation in vulnerability to, 39–40; in Campbell's *Methyl-mercury*, 151–54; dispossession in vulnerability to, 20–21, 88–89; in Erdrich's *Tracks*, 20, 64, 71–74, 164n13; history of activism on, 91–96; in Hogan's *Solar Storms*, 20, 64, 75–80; in *Maliglutit* (film), 22, 120, 142, 144–46; vs. other groups of women, 87–88; in *The Searchers* (film), 137, 142; social invisibility in, 89, 95–97, 105; victim blaming in, 87, 90, 104, 164n1. *See also* missing and murdered Indigenous women and girls; Pickton murders; sexual violence
gender hierarchies: in assimilation, 39; association of women with nature in, 27; essential role in colonialism, 10, 23, 27; in marriage of Native women to colonial men, 37–38
gender justice: as central to Native land claims, 13–15, 19–20, 58, 60, 146, 148; as goal of Indigenous feminism, 91
gender roles: in Belmore's *Vigil*, 103; at boarding schools, 43–46; in Canadian laws, 52; in *Maliglutit* (film), 142, 144–45; precolonial, 43; in US laws, 50
General Allotment Act of 1887 (US), 47–51; allotment sales and taxes under, 49, 65, 66, 161n23, 162n6; assimilation through, 40, 47–51; citizenship in, 48, 160n20, 161n21; decline of Native acreage under, 49, 50–51, 65; eligibility of women under, 50, 161n25; in Erdrich's *The Round House*, 84; in Erdrich's *Tracks*, 20, 49, 65–67, 84; "mixed blood" vs. "full blood" people under, 50, 160n20
genocide, 52, 94, 95
Goeman, Mishuana, 162n3
gold rush, 126
González, Jennifer, 100
Gradual Civilization Act of 1857 (Canada), 51–52, 161n28
Gradual Enfranchisement Act of 1869 (Canada), 52–53, 161n30

Grand Council of the Crees, 98
Great Train Robbery, The (film), 131
Great Uprising of 1622, 36–37
greed, 42
Greenwald, Emily, 49, 161n22
Greer, Allan, 29
Gross, Lawrence W., 163n9
Group of Seven, 121, 167n6

Harjo, Joy, 162n3
Harley, J. B., 60, 61, 62, 63, 64, 77
Harper, Stephen, 93
Harris, Cole, 158n10
Harris, Hanna, 165n10
Harvard University, 151
Haudenosaunee, 43
Hearne, Joanna, 144, 167n4, 168nn17,20
Heart of Darkness (Conrad), 76–77, 169n28
Herman, R. D. K., 78
heroes, 136–37
hierarchy: of continents, 24–25, 56; of humanity, 26, 101. *See also* gender hierarchies
Highway of Tears, 115–16
Hirsch, Marianne, 112, 166n22
History Is Painted by the Victors (Monkman), 21–22, 120–31, 127*fig.*; the gaze in, 127–30; Native histories added to *Mount Corcoran* in, 21, 120, 126–31, 133; overview of themes in, 21–22, 120–21; queerness in, 21–22, 120, 128–29
Hogan, Linda. See *Solar Storms*
Hollywood sign, 1, 6, 157n1
Holocaust Memorial Museum, US, 95
homes, family: transition from big houses to single-family, 39–40; in Western films, 134–35, 137–38, 145
Honor the Earth, 157n6
House Committee on Indian Affairs, US, 35. *See also* Congress
House Made of Dawn (Momaday), 167n4
Hoxie, Frederick, 48
Hudson River School, 121, 122, 124
Hudson's Bay Company, 139, 164n17
humanity, hierarchy of, 26, 101
hydroelectric projects. *See* James Bay; Muskrat Falls
Hydro-Québec utility corporation, 75

hypervisibility of Native people, 12, 95–97, 99

IBC. *See* Inuit Broadcasting Corporation
identities, national. *See* national identity
identities, Native: Canadian laws on, 52–56; of children, patrilineage in, 52–53; Inuit, 133; in miscegenation, 38; place-based nature of, 3, 15; shared global, 3, 15–16; two-spirit, 57, 129
Igloolik Isuma Productions, 132, 168n16
imperialism. *See* colonialism
Indian, use of term, xvii
Indian Act of 1876 (Canada), 40, 53–56, 88
Indian Affairs, Canadian Department of, 38–39, 40–41, 159n8
Indian Affairs, US Bureau of, 45, 162n6
Indian Affairs, US House Committee on, 35
Indian Child Welfare Act of 1978 (US), 42
Indian Citizenship Act of 1924 (US), 48
Indian Law Resource Center, 165n7
"Indian problem," 32, 38–39
Indian Reorganization Act of 1934 (US), 17, 49, 161n30
Indian Wars, 130, 135, 137
Indigenous, use of term, xvii
Indigenous people. *See* Native people
industrial training, 42–43, 44
inheritance of land, by women, 54
Interior, US Department of, 49, 159nn7,9, 161n23
Inuit: Canadian relocation of, 139–40, 141–42; media of, 133–34; Nuliajuk in stories of, 151–54; rates of violence against, 145–46; regional identity of, 133. *See also* Nunavut; *specific artists and writers*
Inuit Broadcasting Corporation (IBC), 133–34, 168n22
Inuktitut language, 132, 133, 139, 144
invisibility, social. *See* social invisibility

Jacobs, Beverly, 165n6
James Bay and Northern Québec agreement (1975), 83, 131
James Bay Development Corporation, 164n17

James Bay Hydroelectric Project: in Hogan's *Solar Storms*, 20, 64, 75–83, 147; legal arguments for, 164n17; Native opposition to, 75, 98
Jamestown, 35–36
Jiwani, Yasmin, 164n1
Johnson, E. Pauline, 162n3
Johnson, Kelli Lyon, 162n3
Johnson, Miranda, 5, 157nn5,7
Johnson v. McIntosh, 161n26
jurisdiction, in gendered violence cases, 84–85, 94–95, 165n11

Kalbfleisch, Elizabeth, 167n5
Kamloops Indian Residential School, 40
"kill the Indian, save the man," 41
Kingulliit Productions, 168n16
kinship structures, end of: assimilation policies in, 19, 23, 39–40, 43, 49; role in dispossession, 13–14
Kunuk, Benjamin, 138*fig.*
Kunuk, Zacharias: career of, 132–34, 147, 167–68nn15,16; on Native depictions in Western films, 132–33. See also *Maliglutit* (film)

Labrador, 22, 151
LaDuke, Winona, 163n6
LaFontaine-Greywind, Savanna, 94
Lake Mohonk Conference, 160n15
land, European understandings of, 7–11; as abstract and empty space, 8–10, 28–29, 61; as female, 9–10, 24, 100, 148; as property, 7–11, 29, 123; quantification and measurement in, 8–9, 28–29, 60–61
land, Native understandings of, 1–5; attachment to land in, 3, 15, 158n12; in literature of cartography, 61–62; sacredness in, 5, 10, 15, 149
land, rape of the, 73, 154
land allotments. See General Allotment Act
Land Back movement, 1, 3, 157n6
land claims, Native: Canadian prohibition on legal pursuit of, 54; decline of acreage in Canada, 55; decline of acreage in US, 49, 50–51, 65; elimination of (*See* dispossession; *specific strategies*);

gender justice as central to, 13–15, 19–20, 58, 60, 146, 148; royal charters and, 164n17
land claims settlements: in Canada, 4, 22, 131, 133, 147; in United States, 4, 17, 147, 162n6. See also *specific settlements*
Lander, Frederick, 124
land inheritance, by women, 54
Land Is Life, 157n6
land reclamation: in Galanin's *Never Forget*, 1–2; in Lord's *Native American Land Reclamation Project*, 150–51; in reterritorialization, 60; role of cultural works in activism on, 1–2, 10; unity of activism on, 4, 15–16, 151
land returns, examples of, 3, 4, 157n3
land rights: in Aboriginal title, 3–4, 62, 81; colonial, through marriage to Native women, 38; Native maps in establishment of, 62–63, 81
landscape paintings: as dominant art genre, 122, 131, 167n6; as form of mapmaking, 124; perspective in, 122–23, 125; realism in, 123–25; westward expansion in, 21, 118–20, 122–24. See also *specific works*
land surveys, 8–9, 124
land title, Native: cartographies in reestablishment of, 62; under General Allotment Act, 50–51, 65, 66; restricted to men, 50
Lauzon, Claudette, 97
Lawrence, Bonita, 54, 55–56
Lefebvre, Henri, 7, 59
legal jurisdiction, in gendered violence cases, 84–85, 94–95, 165n11
Leopold II (king of Belgium), 163n10
Life and Adventures of Joaquin Murieta, The (Ridge), 167n4
Limerick, Patricia Nelson, 119
linear perspective. *See* perspective
literary works: captivity narratives in, 135; depictions of colonialism in, 6–7; as form of Native cartography, 61–64, 162n3; Native, western history as subject of, 167n4; origins of Western genre of, 131. See also *specific works and writers*

Little Bighorn, Battle of the, 130
Locke, John, 16
Lomawaima, K. Tsianina, 43, 44
Lone Wolf v. Hitchcock, 85
Long Walk of 1864–66, 136
loons, 140
Lord, Erica, *Native American Land Reclamation Project*, 22, 146–51
Los Angeles, 1, 157n1
Love Medicine (Erdrich), 65
Lowman, John, 109

Maliglutit (Searchers) (film), 21–22, 131–46, 138*fig.*, 143*fig.*; alternative history of the Arctic in, 22, 120, 131, 134, 141–42; Canadian national identity in, 22, 120; European technology in, 143–44; gendered violence in, 22, 120, 142, 144–46; setting and time frame of, 139, 140–41; social restoration in, 22, 120, 134, 138, 143–46; synopsis of, 21–22, 120–21, 138–39; traditional Inuit practices in, 138–44
Manuel, George, 3, 15
"mapping by words," 20, 61, 64, 74
Mapping the Americas (Huhndorf), 162n3
maps. *See* cartography
Mark My Words (Goeman), 162n3
marriage, of Native women: to colonial men, 37–38; to Native men in Canada, 52; to non-Native men in Canada, 52, 54, 88; wife stealing and, 142. *See also* patriarchal nuclear families
Marshall Trilogy, 85, 161n26
Marx, Karl, 124
masculinity, white, 128–30, 136
matriarchy, 23, 47
matrilineal societies, 43, 52–53, 55
"Maze of Injustice" (Amnesty International), 165n6
McClintock, Anne, 24, 27–28
McNickle, D'Arcy, 167n4
media, Inuit, 133–34
media coverage of gendered violence: earliest examples of, 165n6; gaps in, 92; in Pickton murders, 87, 90, 100, 104–5; victim blaming in, 87, 90, 164n1

men: association with culture, 27–28; imagery of white vs. Native, 128–30; masculinity, 128–30, 136; Native land title restricted to, 50
Meriam Report, 160n13
Methylmercury (Campbell), 22, 146–47, 151–55, 152*fig.*
#MeToo movement, 87
migration to cities. *See* cities
military, US: Cavalry, 126, 130, 137; Native service in, 55; use of landscape paintings in, 124, 167n9
militias, in California, 126
Minnesota Supreme Court, 65
mirrors, 149–50
miscegenation. *See* marriage
Miss America (Monkman), 56–58, 57*fig.*
Miss Chief Eagle Testickle, 57, 127–31
missing and murdered Indigenous women and girls (MMIWG): in Campbell's *Methylmercury*, 151, 154–55; data collection on, 92, 93, 94; earliest media coverage of, 165n6; government responses to, 93–95; history of activism on, 91–96; number of, in Canada, 166n17; origins and rise of movement, 19, 21, 86, 91. *See also* Pickton murders
Mitchell, W. J. T., 123–24
#MMIW Act, 94
MMIWG. *See* missing and murdered Indigenous women and girls
Mohawk Institute, 42
Momaday, N. Scott, 167n4
Monkman, Kent, 56–58; common themes in art of, 121–22; *The Four Continents* series, 56–58; *Miss America*, 56–58, 57*fig.*; reworking of historical landscape paintings by, 21–22, 120–22. *See also History Is Painted by the Victors*
Montreal, 98
Montrose, Louis, 30, 31
Monument Valley, 136
Morgan, Lewis Henry, 47–48, 49
Morgensen, Scott Lauria, 128, 129
Morris, Kate, 125, 127–28
Mount Corcoran (Bierstadt), 21, 120–30, 125*fig.*; as composite of sites, 126; creation of, 124–26, 130; Native

histories added by Monkman to, 21, 120, 126–31; size of, 125, 167n10; title of, 125–26, 167n11
mugshots, 109, 110
Mundy, Barbara, 62
Muskrat Falls, 22, 151–55
Musqueum, 157n3

Named and the Unnamed, The (Belmore), 102, 105, 105*fig.*, 106*fig.*
National Congress of American Indians (NCAI), 88
National Day of Awareness for Missing and Murdered Native Women and Girls, 94, 165n10
National Film Board of Canada, 108
National Gallery of Art, 126
national identity, Canadian, 22, 120, 141
national identity, US, 33, 38, 118–19, 122, 158n9
National Indigenous Women's Resource Center (NIWRC), 165n7
National Inquiry into Missing and Murdered Indigenous Women and Girls, 93–95, 120, 146, 154
National Museum of American Art, 117–19, 166n1
National Native American Boarding School Healing Coalition, 159n9, 160n12
nation-building, Native, in *Maliglutit* (film), 21–22, 121, 134, 138, 144–46
nation-building, settler: imagery of Native women's bodies in, 19, 26, 32–40; role of gender in, 9
Native, use of term, xvii
Native American Land Conservancy, 157n6
Native American Land Reclamation Project (Lord), 22, 146–51
Native Conservancy, 157n6
Native Council of Canada, 89
Native people: in hierarchy of humanity, 26, 101; origins of new global concept of, 3–4; as unified entity, problems with concept of, 15–16
Native resistance. *See* resistance
Native women. *See* women
Native Women's Association of Canada (NWAC), 92, 93, 166n15

nature, association of women with, 24, 27–29, 153
NCAI. *See* National Congress of American Indians
Nead, Lynda, 99
Never Forget (Galanin), 1–2, 2*fig.*, 4, 6
Newman, Michael, 167n9
New Western History, 117
Nez Perce, 48–49, 161n22
Nichols, Robert, 8, 158n12
NIWRC. *See* National Indigenous Women's Resource Center
#NoDAPL movement, 2, 5
nonstatus Indians, 52–53, 55
North Dakota, 2, 5, 163n7
Northward Course of Empire, The (Stefansson), 141
Nova Reperta, 27
novels. *See* literary works; *specific works and writers*
nuclear families. *See* patriarchal nuclear families
nude photography, 99–100
Nuliajuk, 151–54
Nunavut (territory), 133, 139, 147, 168nn21,22
Nunavut Implementation Commission, 168n21
Nunavut Land Claim Agreement (1993), 4, 22, 120, 131, 133, 146, 147
NWAC. *See* Native Women's Association of Canada

O'Connor, Hubert, 159n6
oil production, 2–3, 5, 17, 147, 148
Olund, Eric, 40, 49, 50, 51
Opechankanaugh, 36–37
oral tradition, 68, 163n11
organizing. *See* activism
Origin of the Family, Private Property, and the State, The (Engels), 48
Ortner, Sherry B., 27, 28, 29
Osborne, Helen Betty, 165n6
otherness, 101, 109–10

paintings: captivity narratives in, 168n24; depictions of land in, 9. *See also* landscape paintings; *specific works*

Palm Springs, 1
Pantheon, 33
Park, K. Sue, 8
patriarchal nuclear families: and boarding schools, 43; in Canadian Gradual Enfranchisement Act, 52–53; central role in dispossession, 13–14; and property, 26, 47–48, 135; transition from big houses to single-family homes in, 39–40; in US General Allotment Act, 49–50
patriarchy: in Belmore's *Fringe*, 99–100; in Belmore's *Vigil*, 103–4; in gendered violence, 89, 90–91; within Native communities, 13–14; Native women leading resistance as challenge to, 31; in nude photography, 99; in *The Searchers* (film), 136; in stages of human development, 47; in Welsh's *Finding Dawn*, 112–14
patrilineage, 52–53
Pauktuutit, 92, 145
Pearce, Margaret Wickens, 20, 61, 79
Pearce, Roy Harvey, 158n9
perspective: in cartography, 9; in landscape painting, 122–23, 125
Peterson, Nancy J., 164n15
phallic imagery, 128, 154
photographs: of Arctic, 141, 143; of boarding school students, 44–46, 46*fig.*; domestic, 110–13, 166n22; ethnographic, 99–102; forensic, 99–100; nude, 99–100; the other in, 109–10; police, 109–10, 112; reality effect of, 97–99; in Welsh's *Finding Dawn*, 108–12. *See also specific works*
Pickton, Robert: arrest of, 21, 85, 87, 102; trial of, 85, 108
Pickton murders, 21, 85–116; Belmore's *Fringe* on, 21, 87, 90, 95–103; Belmore's *Vigil* on, 21, 95, 102–7; disposal of bodies in, 108; lack of attention to racial dimensions of, 87, 89, 90; location of, 87–88, 90, 92; media coverage of, 87, 90, 100, 104–5; police responses to, 87, 90, 93, 97, 109–10; proportion of Native victims, 21, 87; significance of artistic responses to, 21, 95; victim blaming in, 87, 90, 104; Welsh's *Finding Dawn* on, 21, 95, 107–16
Pictou, Sherry, 13, 14, 56
pipeline construction. *See* oil production
place-based nature of Native identities, 3, 15
place-names, 79, 126
plant knowledge, 81
Pocahontas, 35–40. See also *Baptism of Pocahontas* (Chapman)
police photographs, 109–10, 112
police responses, to Pickton murders, 87, 90, 93, 97, 109–10
Pollock, Griselda, 99
Poole, Deborah, 100–101
Posluns, Michael, 3
poverty, and Pickton murders, 87, 93, 110
Powhatan, 36
Powhatan Confederacy, 36–37
Pratt, Mary Louise, 166n14
Pratt, Richard Henry, 41, 44–45
prayer ties, 149–51
private property. *See* property
Production of Space, The (Lefebvre), 7
progress: colonialism as, 20, 56–57, 64; westward expansion as, 117–19
property: boarding schools on value of, 42; and patriarchal nuclear families, 26, 47–48, 135; transformation of land into, 7–11, 29, 123; in Western films, 134–35
property taxes. *See* taxation
prostitution. *See* sex workers
Protestantism. *See* Christianity
Prudhoe Bay, 17, 147, 148

Qikiqtani Truth Commission, 120
"Qiksaaktuq" (Tagaq), 95
queerness, in Monkman's *History Is Painted by the Victors*, 21–22, 120, 128–29

race: in tribal membership in Canada, 52; visibility of, 11–12, 100–101
racial segregation, 1
racial uplift, 10, 44, 45
Rafael, Vicente, 166n14
Rainwater, Catherine, 163n12

rape. *See* sexual violence
rape of the land, 73, 154
Razack, Sherene, 90, 104
realism: in landscape painting, 123–25; in photography, 97–99
reclamation. *See* land reclamation
red: in Belmore's *Fringe*, 90, 106; in Belmore's *Vigil*, 106–7; in Campbell's *Methylmercury*, 154; in Lord's *Native American Land Reclamation Project*, 149; in Monkman's *History Is Painted by the Victors*, 130; in REDress Project, 94
RedBird, Elsie B., 83
red dresses, 94, 106–7
Red Horse, 130
REDress Project, 94
Reel, Estelle, 44
religion. *See* Christianity
Rematriation, 3
removal, 37, 38–39
republicanism, 42
reservations: checkerboard pattern of land of, 51, 84; conversion into allotments, 48–49; decline of acreage in Canada, 55; decline of acreage in US, 49, 50–51, 65; vs. for-profit Native corporations, 148; jurisdiction on, 84–85, 94–95, 165n11. *See also specific locations*
residential schools. *See* boarding schools
resistance, by Native women, 30–31; in Campbell's *Methylmercury*, 151; in Chapman's *Baptism of Pocahontas*, 36; in Erdrich's *Tracks*, 60; in Hogan's *Solar Storms*, 82–83; in Stradanus's *Allegory of America*, 30–31, 36
resource exploitation: in capitalism, 60–61; links between sovereignty and, 17; motivations for Native opposition to, 15–16, 158n18; vulnerability of Native women in areas of, 10
reterritorialization, 60
Rickard, Jolene, 99
Ridge, John Rollin, 167n4
Rigolet, 151
Rolfe, John, 35–37
Roosevelt, Theodore, 48
Rose, Gillian, 29, 45, 110–13, 159n3, 166n22

Round House, The (Erdrich), 84–85, 94–95
royal charters, 164n17

sacredness of land, 5, 10, 15, 149
Safe Women, Strong Nations project, 165n7
Said, Edward, 6–7, 77, 157n8
Sarpinak, Joey, 143*fig.*
Saunders, Loretta, 151
savages, Native people depicted as: central role in dispossession, 7, 9; in Chapman's *Baptism of Pocahontas*, 37; in imagery of America, 25–26, 30; in *Maliglutit* (film), 139, 144; in Monkman's *History Is Painted by the Victors*, 128–31, 133; in *The Searchers* (film), 132, 135–38, 168n18; in stages of human development, 47; in Stradanus's *Allegory of America*, 30; in US national identity, 118, 119, 158n9
Savagism and Civilization (Pearce), 158n9
Savanna's Act of 2018 (US), 94
scalps, Native, 126, 137
Schurz, Carl, 49
Scott, Duncan Campbell, 38–39
Scully, Pamela, 9, 38
Searchers, The (film), 132–38; depiction of Native people in, 132–36, 168n18; gendered violence against Native women in, 137, 142; remake of (See *Maliglutit*); setting of, 136, 139; social restoration in, 137–38, 144–45; synopsis of, 134–36
Sedna. *See* Nuliajuk
seeing, ways of: Native disruption of colonial, 6, 12, 22, 58, 102, 119–20; origins of phrase, 167n7
segregation, racial, 1
Sekula, Allan, 109–10
self-determination, 42, 53, 55–56
self-government, 4, 17, 53, 55–56
self-representation, 5, 12
Senate, US. *See* Congress
settler colonialism. *See* colonialism; nation-building

sexual imagery: in colonial literature, 159n3; in depictions of America, 25–26, 28; in Monkman's *History Is Painted by the Victors*, 128–30

sexualization of Native women: in assimilation, 39; in Belmore's *Fringe*, 99–100; in Belmore's *Vigil*, 106–7; Vespucci on, 32. *See also* bodies of Native women

sexual violence against Native women, 20–21, 87–116; assimilation in vulnerability of, 39–40; central role in dispossession, 13, 72; in Columbus's voyages, 32, 159n4; in Erdrich's *The Round House*, 84–85; in Erdrich's *Tracks*, 20, 64, 71–74; history of activism on, 91–96; interracial vs. intraracial, 85, 88; jurisdiction in, 84–85, 94–95, 165n11; as legacy of history, 21, 89; in *Maliglutit* (film), 142, 144–45; vs. other groups of women, 21, 87–88. *See also* Pickton murders

sex workers: and assimilation, 39; conflation of Native women with, 106, 109; in Hogan's *Solar Storms*, 80; Pickton's murder of, 87, 90, 97, 99, 109

Seznec, Jean, 35

silencing of Native women: in Erdrich's *Tracks*, 71, 73; in Hogan's *Solar Storms*, 82; in *Maliglutit* (film), 142; in Stradanus's *Allegory of America*, 31–32

Silko, Leslie Marmon, 10, 158n16, 162n3, 167n4

Simonsen, Jane E., 40

Simpson, Leanne Betasamosake, 158n12

Sioux, 130

"Sisters in Spirit" initiative, 92

"Sisters in Spirit Vigils," 166n15

Slotkin, Richard, 118, 137

Smith, John, 35

Smithsonian, 117–19, 166n1

social invisibility of Native people: in cities, 89, 98; in gendered violence, 89, 95–97, 105; hierarchy of humanity in, 101; of sex workers, 97; visual art countering, 12, 16, 95–96, 105, 107, 116

social marginalization of Native women: through boarding schools, 43–47, 88–89; in Canadian Gradual Enfranchisement Act, 52–53; in Canadian Indian Act, 53–56; centrality in dispossession, 13–14, 55, 147–48; earliest examples of, 39; in *Maliglutit* (film), 142, 145–46; as sovereignty issue, 55–56, 83; in US General Allotment Act, 49–50; in vulnerability to violence, 39–40. *See also* assimilation; patriarchal nuclear families; silencing

social restoration: in Campbell's *Methylmercury*, 154–55; in *Maliglutit* (film), 22, 120, 134, 138, 143–46; in *The Searchers* (film), 137–38, 144–45

Sogorea Te' Land Trust, 157n6

Solar Storms (Hogan), 20, 74–83; colonial maps in, 20, 64, 75, 77–81; Conrad's *Heart of Darkness* compared to, 76–77; Erdrich's *Tracks* compared to, 74–75; gendered violence in, 20, 64, 75–80; James Bay Hydroelectric Project in, 20, 64, 75–83, 147; Native maps in, 20, 81; place-names in, 79; synopsis of, 20, 63–64, 75

Soto, Hernando de, 33

sovereignty: allotment as assault on, 51; links between resource exploitation and, 17; Native women's rights as issue of, 55–56, 83; US Supreme Court on, 22, 148–49; visual, 12

spatial histories, 62–64

spectatorship, 101–4

Standing Rock Sioux Reservation, 2, 5

State v. Zay Zah, 65, 162n6

status Indians, 52–55

Stefansson, Vilhjalmur, 140–41, 143

"Stolen Sisters" (Amnesty International), 165n6

Sto:lo Nation, 113–15

Stradanus, Johannes. *See Allegory of America*

subsistence practices, 134, 139–40, 144–45

Supreme Court, Canadian, 4. *See also Calder v. British Columbia*

Supreme Court, Minnesota, 65

Supreme Court, US, 22, 148–49, 161n26

Surrounded, The (McNickle), 167n4

surveys, land, 8–9, 124

Suzack, Cheryl, 14, 90–91

Swimming Hole, The (Eakins), 129

Tagaq, Tanya, 95, 142
Tagg, John, 98, 166n13
Talking Stick Festival, 102
Taos Pueblo, 4
taxation, of allotments, 49, 65, 66, 161n23, 162n6
Taylor, Diana, 103
Tee-Hit-Ton Indians v. United States, 85
Teller, Henry, 49, 50
teoaxoxtli, 62
Terbasket, Lynn, 114
terminology, xvii
territorial claims. *See* dispossession; land claims
Texas-Indian wars, 136, 139
Thacker, Andrew, 162n4
Third World, 91
throat singing, 95, 142
Tiepolo, Giovanni Battista, 24–25, 56–57
title. *See* Aboriginal title; fee simple title; land title
tobacco, 34
Tompkins, Jane, 168n26
toponyms, 79
Tracks (Erdrich), 20, 63–75; allotment sales and taxes in, 49, 66; assimilation in, 63–74; colonial maps in, 20, 59–60, 64, 70–71; complicity with colonialism in, 18, 67–69, 71; gendered violence in, 20, 64, 71–74, 164n13; General Allotment Act in, 20, 49, 65–67, 84; resistance by Native women in, 60; *The Round House* compared to, 84; setting of, 163n7; synopsis of, 20, 63–64; terms for Anishinaabe in, 162n1; in tetralogy of novels, 65–66; time frame of, 20, 59, 66; trickster figures in, 67, 163n9
Trail of Tears, 37
treaties, 3–5; boarding schools in, 52; in California, 126; in Lord's *Native American Land Reclamation Project*, 149–50; modern, 3–5, 83
Treuttner, William H., 167n3
tribal governments: European style of governance in, 53, 161n30; Native women excluded from, 53, 54; self-government in, 4, 17, 53, 55–56
tribal jurisdiction, 84–85, 94–95, 165n11

tribal membership: Canadian government control over, 52–56; reinstatement of lost, 55–56; US government control over, 51
tribal names, use of, xvii
tribal recognition, 148
tribal sovereignty. *See* sovereignty
trickster figures, 67, 163n9
Trump, Donald, 94
Truth and Reconciliation Commission (Canada), 41, 47, 120, 159nn7,8, 161n27
Tsosie, Rebecca, 43
tuberculosis, 41
Turner, Frederick Jackson, 118, 166n2
Turtle Mountain Reservation, 163n7
two-spirit identities, 57, 129

Uncle Sam, 34
Ungalaaq, Natar, 131, 134, 167n15. *See also Maliglutit* (film)
United Methodist Church, 157n3
United Nations Commission on the Status of Women, 108
United States. *See specific laws, locations, and policies*
universalist narratives, 63, 74
University of British Columbia, 102
urban spaces. *See* cities
use and occupancy studies, 81

vacant land, depictions of, 8–9, 78
Vancouver: activism in, 92–93; Belmore's *Vigil* performance in, 102; Native lands occupied by, 104; repatriation of Native sites in, 157n3; Women's Memorial March in, 93. *See also* Pickton murders
Vespucci, Amerigo, 27–32
victim blaming, 87, 90, 104, 164n1
Vigil (Belmore), 21, 95, 102–7, 105*fig.*, 106*fig.*
vigils, 104, 166n15
Violence Against Women Act (US), 165n11
Virginian, The (Wister), 131
visibility: hyper-, of Native people, 12, 95–97, 99; of race, 11–12, 100–101. *See also* social invisibility

visual art: colonial depictions of land in, 8–9, 11–12; colonial depictions of Native people in, 11–12; Native political use of, 12; Western, Monkman's critique of history of, 121–22, 129. *See also specific genres and works*
visual culture, primacy of, 11–12, 60–61
vocational training, 42–43, 44
Vos, Maerten de, 25–26, 25*fig.*
voting rights, Canadian, 53, 55
voyage motif, 77

Walking with Our Sisters project, 95
Wall Street Journal, 117
War Department, US, 126
War of 1812, 33
Washington, George, 33, 34
Washita River, Battle of the, 137
Wayne, John, 132, 134, 136. See also *Searchers, The* (film)
Weber, Max, 7
Welch, James, 167n4
WELSA. *See* White Earth Land Settlement Act
Welsh, Christine, *Finding Dawn*, 21, 95, 107–16, 111*fig.*, 115*fig.*
West as America, The (exhibition), 117–20, 167n3
Western films: depictions of Native people in, 132–33, 168n20; family homes in, 134–35, 137–38; frontier myth in, 119, 131; gender in, 135–36; Native filmmakers' use of genre, 131, 168n20; origins of genre, 131, 136, 168n26. *See also specific films*
westward expansion: in Bierstadt's *Mount Corcoran*, 124–26; in historical landscape paintings, 21, 118–20, 122–24; in Monkman's *History Is Painted by the Victors*, 129–30; resistance to rethinking history of, 117–19; in US national identity, 33, 118–19, 122
Wet'suwet'en, 2–3, 17
Wexman, Virginia Wright, 134–35, 168n23
White Earth Anishinaabe Reservation, 64–65, 162n5, 163n7

White Earth Land Recovery Project, 157n6, 163n6
White Earth Land Settlement Act (WELSA) of 1985 (US), 20, 64, 162n6
white men: masculinity of, 128–30, 136; vs. Native men, imagery of, 128–30
white supremacy, 89
white women, in *The Searchers* (film), 135–37, 144
"Who Owns the Land?" (Erdrich and Dorris), 64–65
wife stealing, 142
Wildcat, Daniel, 15
wilderness, conquest of, 118, 122
Williams, Robert, Jr., 161n26
Williamson, Robert G., 141
Wilson, Maddy, 116
Wilson, Ramona, 111, 115, 116
Wister, Owen, 131
Wiyot, 157n3
Wolfe, Patrick, 34
women: association of nature with, 24, 27–29, 153; depictions of land as, 9–10, 24, 95, 100, 148; white, in *The Searchers* (film), 135–37, 144
women, Native: as allegorical figures, 19, 23; depictions of land as, 9–10, 24, 95, 100, 148; in matrilineal societies, 43, 52–53, 55; vs. Native men, imagery of, 128; politics of cultural works by, 13–15; role in dispossession, gaps in scholarship on, 13–14. *See also bodies; gender; specific activities and issues*
Women of All Red Nations, 92
Women's Memorial March, 93
world's fairs, 45, 160n18
World War II, 55
Wrestlers, The (Eakins), 129
"Writing Deeper Maps" (Johnson), 162n3
Wyandotte Nation, 157n3

Young, Mary Lynn, 164n1

Zuni Pueblo, 45–46, 46*fig.*, 160n19

Founded in 1893,
UNIVERSITY OF CALIFORNIA PRESS
publishes bold, progressive books and journals
on topics in the arts, humanities, social sciences,
and natural sciences—with a focus on social
justice issues—that inspire thought and action
among readers worldwide.

The UC PRESS FOUNDATION
raises funds to uphold the press's vital role
as an independent, nonprofit publisher, and
receives philanthropic support from a wide
range of individuals and institutions—and from
committed readers like you. To learn more, visit
ucpress.edu/supportus.

www.ingramcontent.com/pod-product-compliance
Lightning Source LLC
Chambersburg PA
CBHW020815230426
43666CB00007B/1018